Treating Sexual Distress

For Bob

Treating Sexual Distress

Integrative Systems Therapy

Jane DiVita Woody

SAGE Publications
International Educational and Professional Publisher
Newbury Park London New Delhi

For information address:

SAGE Publications, Inc.
2455 Teller Road
Newbury Park, California 91320

SAGE Publications Ltd.
6 Bonhill Street
London EC2A 4PU
United Kingdom

SAGE Publications India Pvt. Ltd.
M-32 Market
Greater Kailash I
New Delhi 110 048 India

Printed in the United States of America

Library of Congress Cataloging-in-Publication Data

Woody, Jane DiVita.
Treating sexual distress : integrative systems therapy / Jane DiVita Woody
p. cm.
Includes bibliographical references and index.
ISBN 0-8039-4199-4. — ISBN 0-8039-4200-1 (pbk.)
1. Sex therapy. 2. Marital psychotherapy. I. Title.
RC557.W66 1992
616.85'830651—dc20 92-4786

92 93 94 10 9 8 7 6 5 4 3 2 1

Sage Production Editor: Diane S. Foster

Contents

Foreword

Clinical experience tells us that a dysfunctional relationship is likely to be characterized by accompanying complaints of a sexual nature. However, the sequence and interaction are not always obvious, and we are left with the proverbial chicken or egg question. Which came first? Were the couple's nonsexual conflicts carried into the bedroom, with the resulting sexual problem now appearing as a sequela of the relationship difficulties? Would systems therapy, therefore, directed toward the overall relationship simultaneously resolve the sexual concerns? Was a specific sexual problem primary, with dysfunction in turn generalizing out into the nonsexual relationship? Would focus on the sexual problem with behavioral/cognitive sex therapy heal the relationship concerns as well? Or, did the sexual and nonsexual concerns develop interactively and as the two sides of the same coin, requiring a therapeutic approach that blends and balances an emphasis on both emotional and physical intimacy?

Only a naive or novice practitioner would believe that sexual distress could be treated without attention to the context of the relationship within which it occurs, or that one could treat a relationship without also attending to the sexual concerns present. In this book, Dr. Woody challenges our thinking about a dichotomy of treatment approaches and treatment focuses, getting us beyond the mutually exclusive concept of sex therapy for sexual distress and, as a totally separate process, systems (marital) therapy for relationship concerns. To do so, Dr. Woody takes on the difficult task of integrating the principles of sex therapy and the basics of systems theory/

therapy. With a rich supply of case examples, she then demonstrates the compatibility of these two approaches when combined and utilized creatively in the wholistic treatment of a relationship.

In the era of "super sex do-it-yourself manuals," it is refreshing that Dr. Woody recognizes the responsibility of the partners within the dyad to ultimately define what is "good enough" for them. The therapist is not in the position to set the sexual standards for the clients.

In the early chapters and in the setting, the stage for the introduction of the Integrated Systems Therapy Model, Dr. Woody emphasizes what she calls the sexuality/intimacy connection. In so doing, she has forewarned the reader that her integrated concept is not limited to a therapy which is directed solely at the reversal of an impersonal physical problem. Words like "intimacy," "love," and "commitment" are often omitted from books dealing specifically with genital sex, but not so here as Dr. Woody elucidates a therapy modality that goes beyond sexual mechanics. It is clear that her concepts include the enhancement of both emotional and physical fulfillment.

This book is a welcome addition to the professonal literature for all those who work with relationships. It is through the integrative lens that sexuality is brought into focus in the context of a dynamic system. With this view, Dr. Woody offers a guide for the development of effective interventions, being strongly systemic, but without diminishing the established value of traditional sex therapy strategies.

—ROBERT W. BIRCH, PH.D.

Preface

My hope is that students, trainees, and busy therapists will find this book to have immediate practical application to their professional development. The format offers overviews of several theories plus an integrative intervention model aimed at allowing clinicians to release their own creativity in the therapeutic process. For experienced sex therapists and marital/family therapists, the book can encourage them to take a closer look at the contributions of the other. While most professionals believe in and practice in an integrative or eclectic manner, little has been written about this when it comes to sexuality and relationship problems.

The importance of acquiring and maintaining a wholistic understanding of sexual functioning seems obvious, but it is dealt with here as the central assumption of the book. Sexuality and sexual functioning are not separate from personality, needs, and character, or from the quality of one's relationship with another whole person.

Most therapists, I believe, hold this same view; but for various reasons, the actual practice of "sex therapy" and "marital therapy" does not always reflect it. Given the vagaries of professional and theoretical development, perhaps this flaw was inevitable. The pioneers of both sex therapy and marital/family therapy wanted to distinguish their methods from psychoanalysis. Their works do, in fact, discuss various elements of the whole person, but they do not clearly articulate how these elements interact to produce sexual fulfillment vs. sexual frustration. From sex therapy, what actually captured the professional imagination were the new behavioral/

experiential tasks and techniques. Many of these are quite rich in tapping into the dynamics of whole persons and intimate relationships. Nonetheless, through the years, proponents and opponents alike amplified the importance of the techniques and at the same time simplified their content and impact.

Times change. The Berlin wall is gone, and professional turf battlelines are fading. Like Solomon, we know that it makes no sense to divide the client, giving one half to the sex therapist and the other to the marital therapist. I believe that effective sex therapy and marital therapy have always proceeded from a holistic understanding of sexuality and intimacy. But those who have written about these methods have not had much interest in articulating this point.

This book represents a step toward a unified conceptualization of sexual distress and its treatment. The intent is to remind us of knowledge and wisdom that we already likely possess. There is no attempt to provide an exhaustive analysis of any one theoretical model or tell colleagues exactly how to do therapy. Each of us internalizes, accesses, and translates knowledge idiosyncratically into conversations with clients. And much more than knowledge goes into this interactional process—both the therapist's and the client's personality, cultural identity, and moral vision as well. Hopefully, readers will be stimulated to use their current knowledge, expand it if necessary, and creatively integrate it to develop an enriched understanding of and innovative strategies for treating sexual distress.

Acknowledgments

My husband and children deserve mention first. The thanks that go to Robert Henley Woody are not simply for his support of my writing this book. Throughout our long relationship he has always assumed that I would meet and master a professional challenge even before it occurred to me to undertake it. To this project he has generously contributed his energy, academic expertise, editorial acumen, and a special kind of patience. Also appreciated were the interest in the topic and my work shown by my daughter, Jennifer Baughman. From my two sons, Bob and Matt, I discerned respect, although at this stage they do not prefer to think of Mom as a sex therapist.

Several colleagues and friends have offered helpful suggestions at various stages. Robert Birch, Dorothy Strauss, and Flossie Shelso provided detailed and thoughtful comments on the completed manuscript; and James Hansen and Sandra Cole offered support and encouragement for my initial prospectus for the book. Thanks are also due to Sunny Andrews, Director of the School of Social Work, and David Hinton, Dean of the College of Public Affairs and Community Service at the University of Nebraska at Omaha, for their enduring support of my research and writing efforts.

I feel much gratitude toward my clients for their unheralded contribution to the book. I have learned from them every step of the way as they courageously shared their vulnerabilities, trusted, and took great risks toward growth and change.

Final thanks go to my editor at Sage, Marquita Fleming, for the unflagging personal interest and enthusiasm she has shown for this project from the beginning to its completion.

Introduction

> "Everything to do with love is mystery; it is more than a day's work to investigate this science."
>
> MARIANNE MOORE, from *Marriage*

Sexuality and intimacy—to many, the words likely evoke sensations and images of pleasure, comfort, excitement, and closeness. They may also trigger tension, hesitance, or anxiety.

The so-called sexual revolution has come and gone, and the legacy of ambivalence and mixed societal messages about sex remains. For many reasons, achieving a satisfying intimate and sexual relationship is a greater challenge today than ever before. As society changes, each generation approaches relationships with new expectations for intimacy and sexual fulfillment. But today, people, married or single, who encounter barriers to these goals are likely to seek help for sexual distress and intimacy problems.

Sex Therapy, Marital Therapy, and the Promise of Integration

Experienced professionals recognize that sexual problems require a broad range of knowledge and therapeutic skill. Sex therapists have been regarded as the almost singular experts in this area. Yet sex therapy has continued to focus primarily on treating sexual dysfunction via a fairly circumscribed cognitive-behavioral method. At the same time, the field of marital and family therapy has tended, until very recently, to ignore sexuality. Compartmentalization of professional expertise continues in spite of the fact that clients' problems are not so tidily packaged. Some time ago, certain critics began to question the effectiveness of "standard" sex therapy for dealing with desire disorders and even other dysfunctions (Zilbergeld & Kilmann, 1984). But while sex therapists have quietly complained that the "easy cases" have disappeared (Kaplan, 1979) and that sex therapy alone is no match for the "complex" cases (Slowinski, 1984; Zilbergeld & Ellison, 1980; LoPiccolo & Stock, 1986), change has been slow in coming.

It is time to reexamine assumptions about treating sexual problems. Theoretical explanation and therapeutic strategy simply have not kept pace with the reality of client problems. A meaningless, insidious dichotomy has controlled clinical practice for two decades. It consists of two assumptions: (a) sexual dysfunction deserves treatment and is the province of sex therapy; and (b) marital or couple relationship dysfunction (sexual distress is rarely noted) deserves treatment and is the province of marital/family therapy. Both fields are the worse for maintaining these parallel tracks. This rigid conceptualization even appears in two recent so-called integrative efforts (Weeks & Hof, 1987; Nichols, 1988). Regarding the former work, both LoPiccolo (1989) and Schnarch (1989) note the limited degree of meaningful integration of sex therapy and marital therapy. And Nichols (1988) also maintains the distinction in referring to treatment of sexual dysfunction only in a few paragraphs that call for traditional sex therapy.

For a number of years my practice has consisted primarily of couples and individuals seeking therapy for sexual dysfunction. Initially I did "sex therapy." Other clients presented with sexual distress or disorders but had no dysfunction; so sex therapy was not quite applicable to their problems. Gradually I began incorporating other concepts, especially systems strategies, in working with both sexual and marital problems. I assumed that other clinicians too were beginning to take a more holistic perspective of sexuality and intimacy and use integrative methods in treatment. Until recently, little evidence of this, however, appeared in the literature; so I continued to formulate an integrative model of practice. This book represents the product of that effort.

Sexual distress represents a broader classification than sexual dysfunction. It can exist not only within a couple relationship but also for individuals not necessarily involved in relationships. Moreover sexuality is not merely a physiological function that somehow requires treatment apart from the person's overall personality or the couple's overall relationship. Sexuality and intimacy needs are connected, and therapists ought to be able to treat them holistically. While a few recent attempts in this direction have appeared (Scharff, 1982; Goldner, 1989; Kahn, 1989; Woody, 1989), much work remains to be done.

Efforts to integrate systems thinking and sex therapy reflect two general trends. First, several sex therapists have incorporated selected systems concepts into sex therapy primarily in an attempt to increase effectiveness with resistant clients or desire disorders. Their work typically does not elaborate on theoretical explanations and rationales for the systemic dimensions (Verhulst & Heiman, 1979; Zilbergeld & Ellison, 1980; Talmadge & Talmadge, 1986; Altof, 1989; Heiman, 1986; Heiman & Grafton-Becker, 1989; LoPiccolo & Stock, 1986; Rosen & Leiblum, 1989; LoPiccolo, 1991). The second trend is reflected in the work of family therapists. They have tended to apply a given systems model of treatment to sexual dysfunction, also with a primary interest in resistant clients and desire disorders. Their work typically does include a theoretical explanation and rationale for the proposed systemic treatment model (Fish, Fish, & Sprenkle, 1984; Berman & Hof, 1987; Weeks, 1987; Duncan & Parks, 1988; May & Bobele, 1988, Goldner, 1989; Kahn, 1989; Sanders, 1988; Sanders & Tomm, 1989). This body of literature reflects varying degrees of success in conceptualizing an integrative, systemic treatment approach applicable to the range of sexual distress. Chapter 4 includes brief reviews and evaluations of the major systemic applications to sexual dysfunction by both sex therapists and family therapists.

This book integrates material on several levels. The first set of assumptions aims to integrate certain facets of human behavior.

1. Sexuality is a pervasive dimension of personality; it permeates one's sense of self and needs for relatedness and relationships.
2. The needs for sexual expression and intimacy are deeply linked.
3. Intimacy is conceptualized as a broad construct that enables people to bond and function within the context of that bond across many domains of life; standards for both intimacy and sexuality emanate from the larger social context as well.
4. Sexuality is but one of several dimensions of intimacy.

The second set of assumptions supports an integrative therapy for sexual distress.

1. Sexual distress has a multicausal etiology encompassing both individual and systemic facets of functioning.
2. Sexuality and intimacy mutually influence and impact on each other, both in causation and in the process of bringing about therapeutic change to remedy problems.
3. A multitheoretical integrative approach is necessary for effectively treating sexual distress in a wholistic manner.

The Book and the Reader

This book is directed to professionals of various disciplines and levels of training, including graduate students. For the seasoned sex therapist, it offers an updated and expanded understanding of traditional sex therapy and the opportunity to hone clinical skills through conscious incorporation of systems principles and strategies. For the seasoned marital and family therapist, it brings sexuality to the forefront, provides a detailed review of sexual distress and sex-focused techniques, and offers a systemically integrated treatment format. For other mental health professionals and trainees with an interest in sexuality, it serves as a sound introduction to the nature and treatment of sexual distress, its historical precedents, and current theoretical advances toward an integrative therapy for intimacy and sexual problems. Readers of all levels will hopefully find that the detailed discussion of theoretical concepts stimulates new perceptions, increases appreciation of integrative treatment, expands awareness of the complexity of sexual distress, and releases their own creative energies in the therapeutic process.

The focus of the book is limited to the treatment of sexual distress as viewed within the context of intimacy. It will not cover the whole range of marital and couple problems that do not involve a sexual component (although such problems likely reflect dysfunction in other dimensions of intimacy broadly defined). This book does not aim to fit the strict classification of either sex therapy or couple/marital therapy, although it encompasses some elements of both. One reason is that it deals with sexual concerns other than dysfunction (the usual province of sex therapy), and thus expands "standard" or "traditional" sex therapy. Moreover the integrative therapy proposed is applicable to individuals as well as to couples.

A guiding principle is to offer a pragmatic model of treatment that addresses clinical realities. One assumption is that sexual distress is, broadly defined, a mental health problem in living. People react to sexual distress via emotional and mental turmoil, and that leads them to consult a "counselor" or "therapist." A second assumption is that most therapists work alone, not with co-therapists or teams; so interventions presented are suitable for the solo practitioner to implement. A third assumption, well grounded in reality, is that therapy should be as brief as possible because most clients want or can afford only short-term treatment. Finally, following the eclectic leanings of the majority of therapists, the model enthusiastically draws from selected theoretical concepts and strategies believed to enhance understanding of sexual distress and promote efficient and effective treatment.

People with sexual and intimacy problems seek help in various service settings and from diverse mental health professionals. Those clients who know that they are experiencing a sexual dysfunction may contact a sex therapist. But clients with other forms of sexual distress might see a marriage and family therapist, social worker, psychologist, psychiatrist, or mental health counselor. Sadly, some clients never articulate their sexual concerns or dilemmas because of the practitioner's lack of knowledge and skill.

This book is directed to clinicians and students with a special interest in and commitment to working with sexual concerns. It assumes that the professional has already obtained some specialized knowledge of sexuality through at least one of several avenues: (a) meeting certification standards of the American Association of Sex Educators, Counselors, and Therapists (AASECT); (b) membership in other professional organizations devoted to the sexuality specialization such as the Society for the Scientific Study of Sex (SSSS); or (c) though independent study and enrollment in specialized academic courses or training seminars and supervision of clinical work involving sexuality. It further assumes that the professional is familiar with major therapeutic modalities. Components from several of these make up the integrative model of treatment, and they are briefly summarized in later chapters. Finally, the book assumes that the professional audience holds high ethical standards to match the high degree of vulnerability that clients with sexual distress experience.

Ethical issues appear throughout and are addressed in detail in the final chapter.

Overview of the Contents

Part One of *Treating Sexual Distress: Integrative Systems Therapy* sets forth the theoretical base for Integrative Systems Therapy (IST), whereas Part Two covers the therapeutic process in terms of stages of treatment and consideration of critical therapeutic issues.

Chapter 1 argues for a wholistic view of sexuality and intimacy. It explores the evolution of this view; definitions of intimacy; standards for intimacy and sexual satisfaction; and paradoxes within intimacy, sexuality, and marriage that may play a role in sexual distress.

Chapter 2 discusses the various manifestations of sexual distress and the importance of diagnostic precision. Within a systemic framework, accurate diagnostic description captures the individual's experience of symptoms and has a place in IST as a valid first step in the total assessment process.

Chapter 3 reviews the pioneering contribution of sex therapy. Succinct summaries cover general sex therapy procedures and techniques, as well as therapeutic procedures for specific sexual dysfunctions. The discussion notes the systemic potential in traditional sex therapy strategies and the importance of the therapist's clinical competence in using these methods. The legacy of traditional sex therapy, capsulized as the cognitive-behavioral problem paradigm, is a major component of IST.

Chapter 4 explains four broad systemic facets that are relevant to sexual distress and the models from which they derive. These are the sociocultural environment, family structure, the problem-interactional sequence, and the individual family-of-origin interface. The discussion also reviews examples in the literature of systemic treatment for sexual problems. These four facets too are major components of IST.

Chapter 5 introduces the IST model. This includes a discussion of theoretical foundations for integration, general principles, application of the model's conceptual components to the assessment of a case, and a preview of the four stages of IST treatment.

Chapter 6 offers insight into the contributions of IST to the first stage of therapy, developing the therapeutic system. The discussion centers on six interrelated therapeutic processes—from assessing suitability for IST to consolidating professional credibility.

Chapter 7 delves into the tasks of the second stage of therapy, initial assessment and early intervention. It discusses how a systemic awareness and flexibility contribute to the use of formal assessment measures, problem definition, contracting, formulating an initial assessment, and implementing and evaluating early interventions.

Chapter 8 discusses the third stage of therapy, the process and results of refocusing made possible with an integrative systemic treatment model. Emphasis is on the creative elements of refocusing and designing "power interventions." Detailed case analyses illustrate these processes.

Chapter 9 explores elements of the final stage of IST therapy, maintaining progress and terminating. The client's changing reality calls for increasing client autonomy and tempering the therapeutic alliance. Giving and receiving credit, as well as evaluating the therapy, are also part of this stage.

Chapter 10 identifies several issues critical to psychotherapy for sexual distress. Topics discussed include the diversity of sexual attitudes and values, increasing objectivity through the IST model, ethical responsibilities of the therapist, and standards for specialized training in sexuality.

References

Altof, S. E. (1989). Psychogenic impotence: Treatment of men and couples. In S. R. Leiblum & R. C. Rosen (Eds.), *Principles and practice of sex therapy* (pp. 237-265). New York: Guilford Press.

Berman, E. M., & Hof, L. (1987). The sexual genogram—Assessing family of origin factors in the treatment of sexual dysfunction. In G. R. Weeks & L. Hof (Eds.), *Integrating sex and marital therapy* (pp. 37-56). New York: Brunner/Mazel.

Duncan, B. L., & Parks, M. B. (1988). Integrating individual and systems approaches: Strategic-behavioral therapy. *Journal of Marital and Family Therapy, 14,*(2), 151-161.

Fish, L. S., Fish, R. C., & Sprenkle, D. H. (1984). Treating inhibited sexual desire: A marital therapy approach. *American Journal of Family Therapy, 12,*(3), 3-12.

Goldner, V. (1989). Sex, power, and gender: The politics of passion. In D. Kantor & B. F. Okun (Eds.), *Intimate environments: Sex, intimacy, and gender in families* (pp. 28-53). New York: Guilford Press.

Heiman, J. (1986). Treating sexually distressed marital relationships. In N. S. Jacobson & A. S. Gurman (Eds.), *Clinical handbook of marital therapy* (pp. 361-384). New York: Guilford Press.

Heiman, J. R., & Grafton-Becker, V. (1989). Orgasmic disorders in women. In S. R. Leiblum & R. C. Rosen (Eds.), *Principles and practice of sex therapy* (pp. 51-88). New York: Guilford Press.

Kahn, M. D. (1989). Through a glass brightly: Treating sexual intimacy as a restoration of the whole person. In D. Kantor & B. F. Okun (Eds.), *Intimate environments: Sex, intimacy, and gender in families* (pp. 54-73). New York: Guilford Press.

Kaplan, H. S. (1979). *Disorders of sexual desire and other new concepts and techniques in sex therapy.* New York: Brunner/Mazel.

LoPiccolo, J. (1989). Review of G. R. Weeks & L. Hof (Eds.). Integrating sex and marital therapy. *Journal of Marital and Family Therapy, 15*,(4), 439-441.

LoPiccolo, J. (1991, May 4). *Post-modern sex therapy.* Paper presented at the annual meeting of the American Association of Sex Educators, Counselors, and Therapists, St. Louis, MO.

LoPiccolo, J., & Stock, W. (1986). Treatment of sexual dysfunction. *Journal of Consulting and Clinical Psychology, 54*,(2), 158-167.

May, J. L., & Bobele, M. (1988). Sexual dysfunction and the unemployed male professional. *Journal of Sex & Marital Therapy, 14*,(4), 253-262.

Nichols, W. C. (1988). *Marital therapy: An integrative approach.* New York: Gardner Press.

Rosen, R., & Leiblum, S. R. (1989). Assessment and treatment of desire disorders. In S. R. Leiblum & R. Rosen (Eds.), *Principles and practice of sex therapy* (pp. 19-47). New York: Guilford Press.

Sanders, G. (1988). Of cybernetics and sexuality. *Family Therapy Networker, 12,* 38-41, 79-84.

Sanders, G., & Tomm, K. (1989). A cybernetic-systemic approach to problems in sexual functioning. In D. Kantor & B. F. Okun (Eds.), *Intimate environments: Sex, intimacy, and gender in families* (pp. 346-380). New York: Guilford Press.

Scharff, D. E. (1982). *The sexual relationship: An object relations view of sex and the family.* New York: Routledge, Chapman & Hall.

Slowinski, J. (1984). Reflections on sex therapy: An interview with Harold I. Lief and Arnold Lazarus. *Journal of Sex Education and Therapy, 10,* 13-21.

Schnarch, D. (1989). Review of G. R. Hof & L. Weeks (Eds.) Integrating Sex and Marital Therapy. *Journal of Sex & Marital Therapy, 15*,(1), 78-80.

Talmadge, L. D., & Talmadge, W. C. (1986). Relational sexuality: An understanding of low sexual desire. *Journal of Sex & Marital Therapy, 12*,(1), 3-21.

Verhulst, J., & Heiman, J. (1979). An interactional approach to sexual dysfunction. *American Journal of Family Therapy, 7,* 19-36.

Weeks, G. R. (1987). Systematic treatment of inhibited sexual desire in G. R. Weeks & L. Hof (Eds.), *Integrating sex and marital therapy* (pp. 183-201). New York: Brunner/Mazel.

Weeks, G. R., & Hof, L. (Eds.). (1987). *Integrating sex and marital therapy.* New York: Brunner/Mazel.

Woody, J. D. (1989). The reality of an integrative sex therapy. *Journal of Sex & Marital Therapy, 15*,(1), 62-73.

Zilbergeld, B. (1978). *Male sexuality.* Boston: Little, Brown.

Zilbergeld, B., & Ellison, C. R. (1980). Desire discrepancies and arousal problems in sex therapy. In S. R. Leiblum & R. C. Rosen (Eds.), *Principles and practice of sex therapy* (pp. 66-101). New York: Guilford Press.

Zilbergeld, B., & Kilmann, P. R. (1984). The scope and effectiveness of sex therapy. *Psychotherapy,* 1,(3), 319-326.

Part One

Theoretical Components and Integration

1

The Sexuality / Intimacy Connection

> This painful love dissect to the last shred:
> abjure it, it will not be solved in bed;
>
> CONRAD AIKEN, from "The Lovers"

During the past 20 years, the fields of sex therapy and marital therapy took separate paths. The dominant view was that a couple's problem was primarily either a sexual dysfunction or a marital problem, and that the therapist should treat one or the other, or first one and then the other (Kaplan, 1974; Sager, 1974). This view has persisted even in initial attempts to integrate marital therapy and sex therapy (Weeks & Hof, 1987). Yet clinicians readily recognize that this dichotomy is an oversimplification that is neither meaningful nor useful in practice.

The separation of marital therapy and sex therapy suggests that sexuality is narrowly a physiological function, and all other aspects of a couple's relationship involve whole persons and personalities. The net result is the separation of sex and intimacy, which may be a convenience for professionals, but it does not reflect the typical client's expectations of love. People today pair up with the hope of satisfying both sexual and emotional needs. This does not mean that couples readily achieve that goal, nor does it mean that theorists agree on how intimacy and sexuality are related or what degree of each is necessary for a satisfying relationship. Nonetheless, clinicians need a holistic understanding of sexuality and intimacy to match their clients' approach to love and the complexity of their problems.

The following case illustrates the connection between intimacy and sexuality and the need for a flexible approach to treatment:

> Ann and Adam, both 35, were referred to a sex therapist by a pastoral counselor. Their marriage was in crisis as a result of Adam's second affair in the past 6 months. Adam blamed Ann, his wife of 10 years, for these affairs, claiming that following the birth of their only child 2 years ago, Ann had gained weight and become overinvolved in her mothering role to the extent that she was not attractive to him.
>
> Both acknowledged, however, that their sexual relationship (even during courtship) had never been very intense, frequent, or satisfying. Ann indicated that she had long ago stopped initiating sex because Adam was unresponsive to her attempts and uninterested in her pleasure. From the beginning, they had poured their energies into achieving business and financial success. Through the years they experienced quick, perfunctory intercourse, perhaps once a month. Ann said she received no pleasure from intercourse and did not think that she ever had an orgasm. Even these contacts had disappeared during the past 2 years following Adam's heart attack and bypass surgery and the birth of their son.
>
> Adam indicated that he was not giving up the affair and was not interested in therapy for the marriage or for improving their sexual relationship. His view was that Ann needed to discover her sexuality on her own. In the meantime, he intended to continue the affair as he attempted to sort things out. He also insisted that they continue to live together and that Ann keep this whole matter private to protect their social, familial, and business status. Ann, whose only goals were to capture Adam's love and keep the marriage, wanted to work on their overall marital and sexual relationship. Although numerous options were presented to the couple to begin resolving the crisis, Adam dismissed all of them, and Ann agreed to his demands. Each was willing to enter individual therapy to help deal with the continuing crisis.

To categorize this couple's problem as either a marital problem or sexual dysfunction is simply not useful—even as a starting point. The case history certainly suggests the presence of possible sexual dysfunctions; but also suggested are long-term unacknowledged sexual complaints and intimacy problems, which include the recent difficulties in coping with life-threatening illness and the transition to parenthood.

To treat intimacy and sexuality problems in a holistic manner does not require the therapist to take a moral position that the present relationship must automatically be or remain the focus of treatment.

When a couple seeks treatment, the therapist attempts to treat the relationship while also staying aware of each partner as an individual. Clients seek therapy with their relationships in varying stages of deterioration.

The ethical therapist elicits each partner's goals for the relationship and self, helps them strengthen the relationship when that is their goal and it is backed up by commitment, but also remains attuned to each individual's concerns about destructive or oppressive aspects of the relationship. Philosophically, then, the therapist respects and values intimate commitments and marriage, but likewise respects and values each individual's right to make decisions about these. Obviously, where ambivalence and hopelessness are present, therapy should offer new experiences and information that can help clients to understand the relationship, resolve doubts, and make logical and wise decisions.

This chapter elaborates on a holistic view of sexuality and intimacy in light of the therapeutic endeavor. It discusses the evolution of this view within a societal context. It explores definitions of intimacy and their origins. It points to the need for flexible standards in defining "good enough" intimacy and sexual satisfaction. It identifies numerous paradoxes within intimacy, sexuality, and marriage that may play a role in sexual distress. The overall purpose is to suggest a realistic professional stance and ethic on these issues that can promote effective treatment for the range of clients' sexual distress.

Sexuality, Intimacy, and Societal Values

A holistic perspective sees sexuality and intimacy as interrelated needs and functions of an individual's total personality. People typically want both needs fulfilled in the context of an intimate, committed relationship. This was not always the case in Western industrialized societies. Moreover, it does not mean that today the two needs are equally pursued or met in every sexual or intimate encounter. There may be situations, relationships, and/or stages in the life cycle where a person has a singular rather than the dual focus. There may be many trials and errors. And for some people, attaining a sexually satisfying as well as intimate relationship with the same partner is not even a goal. Still, most clients seeking help with relationship/marital and sexual concerns typically expect both emotional and sexual satisfaction in the context of that committed relationship. Today this is also a goal for many gay and lesbian couples, who are increasingly speaking vows of love and commitment in ceremonies before family and friends (Markowitz, 1991).

Taking an opposite position, Gagnon (1987) argues that the Western view is relatively recent in history and is only one of many cultural and individual arrangements for intimacy and sexual needs. He believes that therapists who advocate this cultural arrangement may contribute to inauthentic expressions of intimacy, hinder erotic experience, and erode individual boundaries. These concerns, though expressed recently, reflect the liberal sexual attitudes of the 1960s and 1970s, which, to a degree, endorsed casual sex. Yet, even during that period, love, commitment, and marriage, with all its expectations, never went out of style.

It is true that the linking of intimacy and sexuality within a love or committed relationship is a relatively recent development. The Victorian era clearly did not subscribe to this value. Sex was regarded as a base animal instinct (perhaps necessary for men and the lower class) that did not quite fit with the purer motives of love that marriage embodied. Nor was intimacy as defined today an ideal in marriage. Certainly, some gradual changes took place in the early 20th century toward greater integration of sexuality into married life. But it was the 1960s that brought blatant changes in sexual values.

The "sexual revolution" turned sexuality from a private experience to a public medium for making a political statement. The goodness and pleasure of sex became symbols of freedom from the oppression of the "traditional establishment." Part of the statement was to assert the right to enjoy sex apart from marriage and commitment. Although this was the most blatant message of that era about sexuality, others were also evolving.

The liberalized attitudes enabled many persons to appreciate the goodness of sexual pleasure and to integrate this into love and marital relationships. For these people, the culture's definition of love expanded. Sexual pleasure was unabashedly accepted for both men and women. Another development was also occurring that would further expand the definition of love. This was the value placed on the "humanistic encounter." At its best this generally meant the honest expression of self, especially deep feelings, in a context of equality and mutuality with another person. In addition to sexuality, people began to want this kind of emotional exchange as well in their love relationships. The humanistic encounter was the basis for what theorists today label *intimacy.*

During the 1960s, sexuality and intimacy were often used as symbols of rebellion against the establishment, but these human dimensions subsequently became woven into the fabric of the larger culture in a different way. The product is a mainstream value wherein marriage or a committed relationship is expected to satisfy a range of needs, especially sexuality and intimacy.

The ethics of the 1990s for intimate relationships are quite complex. Because of diverse sociocultural changes and problems, a conservative tenor has been growing (Kelly, 1990; Leiblum & Rosen, 1989). Both marriage and monogamy are highlighted as a means for individual fulfillment. But this now has expanded to encompass a broader need for personal and economic security in the face of economic uncertainty and such social problems as AIDS (acquired immunodeficiency syndrome). Today's ethics, however, do not and cannot represent a simple return to so-called "traditional" values. The new ethics must coexist with a mixed bag of societal values. It is no wonder that both relationship "conservatives" and "liberals" feel besieged by the various societal values.

People can get caught in the middle of society's mixed messages about sex and intimacy. Under these circumstances, it is not easy to find and maintain a relationship that will satisfy all needs. These difficulties are central to the problems brought to therapy. The therapist's role is to listen and remain attuned to the client's values and expectations for the relationship and goals in seeking help.

The case of Ann and Adam cited earlier illustrates these points. Adam was into a period of "sexual liberation" that did not include his wife. The couple had never been able to incorporate either satisfying sex or intimacy into their marriage, but other benefits such as financial and social success had compensated for the lack. Ann hoped to work with Adam to put both qualities into their relationship, but Adam at that point was satisfied to have his sexual needs alone met. In fact, he had little capacity for intimacy—either the need to give or receive—in the marriage or affair relationships. Nonetheless, he wished to maintain the marriage as a social, business, and familial convenience. His compulsions changed from financial power and success to self-focused sexual gratification. Individual treatment with three different therapists had little impact on Adam's way of being in relationships.

The therapist must be skilled to deal with the complexity of social life. Contrary to Gagnon's (1987) position, the therapist's role is not to advocate either liberal or conservative sexual attitudes. That dichotomy simply does not do justice to current values. But there is another therapeutic stance that poses new risks. That is for therapists to assume that blending intimacy and sexuality in committed relationships is an easy task or that we know a recipe for the mix that will suit the tastes of all clients.

Definitions

It is relatively easy to find definitions of intimacy, but more difficult to sort out their theoretical underpinnings. Clarification of meanings, however, is necessary for eventually developing therapeutic methods to help clients with this dimension of life. Several theoretical threads run through the fabric of intimacy. And early on some theorists proposed integrative conceptualizations. The following discussion touches on humanistic, psychodynamic, empirical, and object relations facets within definitions of intimacy.

There is a good bit of humanistic and phenomenological theory in discussions of intimacy. The common element in many broad definitions is an intense connection between whole persons. For example, intimacy in a relationship refers to "joining of innermost feelings and qualities, an emotional closeness that is deep (as opposed to superficial) and is mutual or reciprocal" (Combrinck-Graham & Kerns, 1989, p. 74). Whitaker (1989) characterizes intimacy as the "psychological interpenetration of two persons" (p. 112). Bograd (1989) refers to "closeness, familiarity, thorough knowledge of another, and access to another's most private personal details" (p. 165). Before these rather broad definitions found their way into the literature, several serious efforts explored the theoretical bases for intimacy in dyadic relationships.

L'Abate and associates (L'Abate & L'Abate, 1979; L'Abate, Sloan, Wagner, & Malone, 1980) offer an integration of humanistic and systemic elements. In the context of the human resources of being, doing, and having, intimacy fits in the category of being, with its philosophical base in existentialism. Intimacy encompasses "the ability to live and be with oneself—to meditate, think, feel, experience, relax, rest, and reflect." It includes feelings "of self-esteem, self-worth, and contentment" as based on existence not achievement. Another existential element of being is "the continual resolution of the individual identity as the self-originating creator of meaning." Being "requires a non-dominating relation to one's environment" (L'Abate et. al., 1980, pp. 238-239). Being is essential to "authentic caring and sharing." For purposes of therapy, the essence of dyadic intimacy is thus encapsulated as "sharing of hurt and fears of being hurt" (L'Abate & L'Abate, 1979, p. 176). The emphasis in this account of intimacy is on the here and now, on the existential challenge to "be" in life, and on the impact this challenge has when played out in dyadic relationships. This explanation carries strong reminders of the humanistic mood of the 1960s.

Feldman (1979) also posits an integrative view of intimacy that encompasses psychodynamic, behavioral, and systemic assumptions. The emphasis is on unconscious process to account for ambivalence about intimacy. Five types of intimacy anxiety are: fear of merger, fear of exposure, fear of attack, fear of abandonment, and fear of one's own destructive impulses. As unconscious anxiety appears, it gives way to interpersonal conflict, which takes on a systemic life of its own. The feedback process then continues to reinforce both the anxiety and the conflict. Such an integrative framework opens the door for combining various intervention strategies. The goal is to establish a new relationship equilibrium in which both partners could participate in genuine intimacy in a way that would promote individual growth as well as development of the marital system.

There is an empirical approach to intimacy that has focused on operationalizing and measuring intimacy (Schaefer & Olson, 1981; Tolstedt & Stokes, 1983). Waring and Reddon (1983) epitomize this approach. They see intimacy as a quality involving both partners' personalities affecting many aspects of the total relationship. Their scale for measuring intimacy in marriage views it as a composite of eight dimensions: (a) conflict resolution, (b) affection, (c) cohesion, (d) sexuality, (e) identity, (f) compatibility, (g) autonomy, and (h) expressiveness. This broadened definition operationalizes intimacy as a far-reaching dimension involving the interaction of the partners' personalities and affecting the total relationship.

In fact, the eight dimensions cited by Waring and Reddon (1983) suggest that many of the complaints that couples bring to therapy are actually intimacy problems. *Conflict*, arguments, and failure to resolve these are common marital complaints, regardless of the content of the conflict. Problems in *affection* may be overtly stated or may underlie other difficulties as partners report a lack of affection, feelings of being unloved or unappreciated, or differences in affectional needs. *Cohesion* problems center on the lack of a couple identity or sense of being a team and demonstrating this appropriately. The dimension of *sexuality* can encompass the gamut from sexual complaints to sexual dysfunctions and disorders. *Identity* problems affect couples as difficulties in having an integrated sense of self and in sharing this with the trust of finding support and acceptance. This factor often underlies the inability to make a commitment to a partner. *Compatibility* problems exist when partners sharply disagree on life's meaning, goals, values, and the day-to-day acting on these. *Autonomy* becomes an issue when mates do not experience a reasonable sense of independence, individuality, and power in the relationship. Finally, *expressiveness* encompasses a whole range of communication difficulties, from a lack of communication on one or many life issues to failures in listening or hearing messages to inability to solve problems and make decisions.

It is notable that all of the above dimensions have been placed under the rubric of "intimacy." Intimacy in this way becomes a global construct for what it takes for two people to find satisfaction through living together in a committed relationship. By necessity, it points to both an intensive and extensive connection as the partners share the many aspects of their lives and personalities with each other.

The most recent theoretical emphasis in explaining intimacy draws on object relations theories. These explanations add depth and clarity because they offer insight into the specific linkage between sexuality and intimacy. Object relations thinking locates the origin of the capacity for achieving satisfying sexual and intimate relations in the individual's earliest caretaking experience. There is also a systemic element, however, as reflected in the interaction in both the original caretaking relationship as well as in subsequent adult relationships.

The reason that intimacy is difficult to achieve is not simply because of its intensity or its touching so many aspects of a couple's life. It is elusive because each person either exposes or defends a core sense of self throughout all the interactions. Object relations theories account for the development of self and explain the deep connection between sexuality and intimacy.

The individual's first nurturing relationship is highly physical. It encompasses feeding, holding, touching, and gazing. But these contacts with the caregiver also bring emotional comfort as well to the child. The pattern and expectation is thus set for adult intimate relationships. In a typical scenario the expectation is that physical (sexual) needs will be met in such a way to bring emotional security (Kahn, 1989; Scharff, 1982).

The capacity for achieving a satisfying intimate and sexual relationship in adult life derives from the early experience with the primary caretaker. A "good enough" nurturing experience is necessary for the emergence of the person's "true self." This achievement allows the person to experience and enjoy with a partner sensual and sexual satisfaction as well as feelings of caring and being cared for, loving while giving love, and tolerating and forgiving. Deprivation in that first relationship leads to a "false self," which, in adult life, experiences sexual/emotional encounters with fears of loss of self, or of abandonment, or of annihilation. These unconscious fears trigger a range of defensive responses that block the satisfaction of sexual/intimacy needs (Kahn, 1989; Scharff, 1982).

It is not only early nurturing, however, that plays a part. There is learning in the family context throughout childhood and adult experience as well that contribute to the quality of one's intimate and sexual capacity. The sexual relationship between parents and the child's sexuality mutually affect each other. This overall family systemic context can encourage either sexualization of the child, satisfactory sexual development, or repression of the child's emerging sexuality.

The object relations account of the sexuality/intimacy connection gives needed depth to the broad definitions of intimacy. It explains why people are so vulnerable in sexual relationships. When the individual's development has been adequate, sex can be both pleasurable and emotionally soothing. When development has been impaired, a sexual encounter may threaten a replay of early conscious or unconscious feelings of deprivation or abandonment. And when the self moves into a defensive stance, often both the sexual and emotional systems shut down. Rather than feeling complete, the individual may feel a sense of personal dissolution (Kahn, 1989; Scharff, 1982).

Each partner's response to the other's needs and capacity for intimacy then sets the stage for a systemic patterning of the relationship. The capacity to attain satisfaction of intimacy and sexual needs may best be understood as a continuum. At one end, the individual seeks and enjoys a satisfying intimate and sexual relationship, whereas at the other end, the self may be so impaired that this goal may not even exist or is not achieved. Thus in an intimate relationship the pattern that evolves could encompass a range of sexual/intimacy disturbances.

The reason for clarifying the theoretical assumptions in the definitions of intimacy lies in the pragmatics of therapy. Deeper level understandings are crucial, but the array of explanations should lend a degree of skepticism about wholesale adoption of a singular explanation for intimacy problems and sexual distress. Failures in self and identity development stemming from the earliest nurturing experience may be operating in the most severe symptoms, or perhaps even in most problems to some degree. Other problems, however, may have more recent and powerful contributors; and all may benefit from an integrative systemic perspective rather than a single theoretical bias.

How Much Is Enough?

Exactly what constitutes satisfying sexuality and intimacy? And how much is enough? First, sexual satisfaction in a relationship typically refers to arousing, pleasurable, and a mutual erotic exchange that leads to orgasmic release, as each individual desires. Since the 1960s, societal values and beliefs have largely endorsed this same general standard of sexual expression and fulfillment for both women and men. But this is a broad description subject to many qualifiers. It cannot be applied in a rigid manner as a fixed indicator of "healthy sexuality." There must be some flexibility for partners to define overall satisfying sex for their unique situation. For example, definitions would likely change over the life cycle or stages of a relationship. Or the definition might differ during a period of illness, stress, or family crisis. The therapeutic task is to help the individual or couple with sexual distress specify the level of satisfying sex that they hope to attain through treatment.

The same flexibility also applies to intimacy. A philosophy of "more is always better" is an oversimplification. Conceptualizing this dimension as falling on a continuum best meshes with the reality of clinical work. Intimacy cuts across many aspects of a couple's life, with a key ingredient being a deep level of mutual disclosure, with the expectation of a partner's understanding and acceptance. Couples will desire and be able to achieve varying degrees of this quality. In therapeutic work, there is no singular standard that is applicable to all individuals or couples.

Until recently intimacy was hardly a conscious expectation for marriage or long-term committed relationships. Rigid gender roles meant that men and women often spent more time with persons of their own sex than they did with spouses. But as society's values have changed regarding the purposes and expectations of marriage, intimacy has become a priority for many, but not all couples.

As sexual satisfaction and intimacy within couple relationships have become widespread expectations, therapists need to be sensitive to what is actually known about these dimensions and their connection to overall relationship satisfaction or "health." We would do well not to set for clients "peak" standards for either. Rather, the sexuality-intimacy component of a relationship needs only to be "good enough" for each partner to define it as satisfactory.

Research has generally supported that intimacy is strongly related to marital satisfaction (Harper & Elliot, 1988; Tolstedt & Stokes, 1983). But satisfaction is not measured simply by the amount of intimacy present. Harper and Elliot (1988) found that marital satisfaction among couples related to the discrepancy between the amount of intimacy perceived and the amount desired. They also noted that there seems to be a critical point where intimacy needs become satiated. When this happens, satisfaction can decrease, and intimacy loses its power to promote growth in the marriage.

People know when intimacy is not what they want it to be in their lives, and many bring the concern to therapy. But clients themselves must have a say in what is "good enough" intimacy for them. Obviously, the ideal would vary from couple to couple as well as between partners. Therapists who arbitrarily, consciously or unconsciously, set standards for clients at either the low or high end of the continuum are likely struggling with their own unresolved issues with sexuality and intimacy.

The Paradoxes of Sexuality, Intimacy, and Marriage

Numerous paradoxes abound within the experience of sexuality, intimacy, and marriage and complicate the quest for meaning and fulfillment in relationships. Paradoxes emerge because sexuality powerfully affects both the individual and society. Contradiction is an inevitable result. The inherent paradoxes complicate the therapeutic task but should also inspire a degree of humility as we intrude in this very private and powerful dimension of people's lives. The following are simply a few of the many contradictions people attempt to live with and resolve.

1. *Marriage, Yes—Divorce, Yes.* Marriage is a much desired goal and state—in spite of its known track record for disappointing many who pursue it. Today, more so than in the past, people marry with high expectations for personal happiness. Yet, inevitably, a part of their consciousness is aware of the high probabilities of failure.

2. *Fidelity—Some, Maybe.* The high value placed on marriage and monogamy must somehow coexist with the widespread attitude that a certain amount of casual, uncommitted sex is acceptable, especially if viewed as a precursor or trial process for an ultimate marital bond. Does this latter attitude inevitably remove the mystery and specialness of sex? It allows some people to experience sexual activity in a routine, matter-of-fact manner, although at some point they may want to invest sex with more meaning. At the other extreme, a person may imbue one relationship or every sexual act with the demand for an almost magical specialness. Operating at the extremes of investing sex with either little meaning or a sacred specialness may cause problems for some people.

3. *Gender Programming—My Way, My Way.* It is paradoxical that society invests the heterosexual love bond with so much value in view of the different programming for intimacy and sexual needs received by men and women. Different expectations and relationship styles result from the different conscious and unconscious learning acquired by the sexes through the family and society. In general, women seem to value verbal and emotional communication as an avenue to intimacy, whereas men often value the sexual experience as the major

avenue of connectedness and affirmation. Although there is much generalizing and criticizing of gender programming, problems may be due primarily to extreme forms of this programming. Some differentness on these dimensions may, in fact, give heterosexual relationships a degree of tension that keeps them dynamic and that serves as a crucible for emotional growth for both partners. Same-sex relationships, in which partners often hold similar attitudes toward intimacy and sexuality, are not necessarily problem free in these areas.

4. *Excitement and Comfort—Maybe.* What are the chances of maintaining over time high levels of both intimacy and sexual satisfaction with the same person? Intimacy involves a deep closeness, security, and familiarity that arises from sharing of selves across many domains of life. On the other hand, achieving sexual satisfaction depends on a high degree of excitement in the rather narrowly focused context of sensual and genital pleasure. If the hallmark of intimacy is a high degree of emotional comfort whereas that of sexual fulfillment is a high degree of sensual tension, some persons may experience these as reciprocally inhibiting qualities. Achieving a synergistic mix in which each enhances the other is not a simple process.

5. *Romance or Sex—Whose Fantasy?* The contradiction between the romantic and physical dimensions in sexual satisfaction is real for many persons. Again, this paradox may stem from gender programming. Many women seem to value a romantic ambiance as a precursor to sex—this might mean emotional closeness, cuddling, or a preferred scenario for environment, dress, or seduction rituals. Men, on the other hand, may value the high degree of arousal that comes from direct physical and sensual overtures. Sexual experience may, in fact, be enhanced if partners can flexibly incorporate both qualities into their sexual lives. Achieving this added richness will likely demand breaking out of powerful gender stereotypes.

6. *Regression-Maturity.* Another paradox involves the place of regression in so-called mature love. In mature love, partners commit themselves to care for and value each other as whole persons, as opposed to using the partner as a fantasied object for purely self-focused emotional or sexual fulfillment. Yet psychodynamic theories suggest that mature love should also be able to accommodate the

temporary infantile regression in sexual experience that allows a sense of symbiotic merger with the partner.

7. *Self-Centered Mutuality.* Mutuality is an ideal for mature love and sexual expression. It is a quality in which both partners desire and experience the sex act as pleasurable and satisfying and thus each values the partner's pleasure as much as one's own. This ideal has emerged primarily since the "sexual revolution" and has come to mean for women (as it always has for men) the specific pleasure of orgasm. Yet within the context of mutuality, the nature of orgasm may require (at least for a few moments) the individual to intensely or "selfishly" focus on and pursue one's own genital sensations and pleasure. This quality also relates to infantile regression mentioned above.

Many of these paradoxes clearly reflect the interaction of sociocultural attitudes with individual psychological and familial influences. In general, the nature of the interaction has changed as societal sexual attitudes have become more liberal. Sexual problems, however, have not disappeared; they merely take different forms. The paradoxes powerfully affect people's lives, and this fact makes it even more important that professionals have a broad understanding of sexual distress. A multitheoretical approach that encompasses sociocultural and family systems influences, as well as individual development and personality, is needed. Moreover, paradox in treatment strategy may be a key ingredient for resolving the paradoxes involved in clients' sexual distress.

Conclusion

Intimacy encompasses not a narrow but a broad range of couple interactions. Thus intimacy problems may include the following: unresolved conflicts (about any content); complaints about affection; lack of cohesion; sexual complaints, dysfunctions, or disorders; identity problems (these affect trust, sharing of self, and making a commitment); incompatibility of values and goals and ways of implementing these; lack of a sense of personal autonomy in the relationship; and problems in expressiveness (these encompass serious deficits in communication skills necessary to maintain an intimate relationship).

As these various dimensions suggest, intimacy problems affect the core elements involved in the deep sharing of self across several aspects of living. The categories mentioned above clearly encompass many of the relationship problems that clients bring to therapy. But intimacy disorders may also be involved in such individual symptoms as depression, anxiety, phobias, eating disorders, substance abuse, and so forth. It is the therapist's theoretical orientation that determines whether intimacy factors are assessed for such "individual" symptoms.

One of the major dimensions of intimacy is sexuality. When it goes awry, sexual distress is the result. The various manifestations of sexual distress are a main focus of this book. Acknowledging the deep connection between sexuality and intimacy does not mean that individual personality is always the primary factor in relationship problems or that treatment must focus on deep-level contributors. On the contrary, a multitheoretical approach is best. But because intimacy involves the pervasive sharing of self, it is necessary to account for the nature of self and the developmental connection between sexuality and intimacy. At the same time, it is necessary to go beyond the mutual influence of personality and intimate relationships to examine the role of social learning as well as other systemic factors in sexual distress.

Over the next three chapters, the components that contribute to the multitheoretical approach, referred to herein as integrative systems therapy (IST), are discussed. Chapter 2 elaborates on the various manifestations of sexual distress and advocates for precision in diagnostic description. Chapter 3 reviews the legacy of traditional sex therapy to establish the role of social learning in sexual/intimacy dysfunctions and the continuing importance of sex therapy treatment strategies. Chapter 4 presents four additional views of sexual distress and treatment strategies afforded by systemic concepts, including both object relations and intergenerational concepts as falling within the realm of systemic thinking.

References

Bograd, M. (1989). Passions of therapy: Hidden sexual dimensions. In D. Kantor & B. F. Okun (Eds.), *Intimate environments: Sex, intimacy, and gender in families* (pp. 163-195). New York: Guilford Press.

Combrinck-Graham, L., & Kerns. L. (1989). Intimacy in families with young children. In D. Kantor & B. F. Okun (Eds.), *Intimate environments: Sex, intimacy, and gender in families* (pp. 74-92). New York: Guilford Press.

Feldman, L. B. (1979). Marital conflict and marital intimacy: An integrative psychodynamic-behavioral-systemic model. *Family Process, 18*, 69-78.

Gagnon, J. (1987, March 13). *A sociologic perspective*. Paper presented at the annual meeting of the Society for Sex Therapy and Research, New Orleans, LA.

Harper, J. M., & Elliot, M. L. (1988). Can there be too much of a good thing? The relationship between desired level of intimacy and marital adjustment. *American Journal of Family Therapy, 16*(4), 351-360.

Kahn, M. D. (1989). Through a glass brightly: Treating sexual intimacy as a restoration of the whole person. In D. Kantor & B. F. Okun (Eds.), *Intimate environments: Sex, intimacy, and gender in families* (pp. 54-73). New York: Guilford Press.

Kaplan, H. S. (1974). *The new sex therapy*. New York: Brunner/Mazel.

Kelly, G. (1990). *Sexuality today: The human perspective* (2nd ed.). Guilford, CT: Dushkin.

L'Abate, L., & L'Abate. (1979). The paradoxes of intimacy. *Family Therapy, 6*(3), 175-184.

L'Abate, L., Sloan, S., Wagner, V., & Malone, K. (1980). The differentiation of resources. *Family Therapy, 7*(3), 237-246.

Leiblum, S., & Rosen, R. C. (1989). Introduction: Sex therapy in the age of AIDS. In S. R. Leiblum & R. C. Rosen (Eds.), *Principles and practice of sex therapy* (pp. 1-16). New York: Guilford Press.

Markowitz, L. M. (1991). Homosexuality: Are we still in the dark? *Family Therapy Networker, 15*(1), 26-35.

Sager, C. J. (1974). Sexual dysfunctions and marital discord. In H. S. Kaplan (Ed.), *The new sex therapy* (pp. 501-518). New York: Brunner/Mazel.

Schaefer, M. T., & Olson, D. H. (1981). Assessing intimacy: The PAIR inventory. *Journal of Marital and Family Therapy, 7*, 47-60.

Scharff, D. E. (1982). *The sexual relationship: An object relations view of sex and the family*. New York: Routledge, Chapman & Hall.

Tolstedt, B. E., & Stokes, J. P. (1983). Relation of verbal, affective, and physical intimacy to marital satisfaction. *Journal of Counseling Psychology, 30*(4), 573-580.

Waring, E. M., & Reddon, J. R. (1983). The measurement of intimacy in marriage: The Waring Intimacy Questionnaire. *Journal of Clinical Psychology, 39*(1), 53-57.

Weeks, G. R., & Hof, L. (1987). *Integrating sex and marital therapy*. New York: Brunner/Mazel.

Whitaker, C. (1989). Thoughts about sex, love and intimacy. In D. Kantor & B. F. Okun (Eds.), *Intimate environments: Sex, intimacy, and gender in families* (pp. 108-128). New York: Guilford Press.

2

The Many Faces of Sexual Distress: Diagnostic Descriptors

> To love is good; love being difficult. For one human being to love another; that is perhaps the most difficult of all our tasks . . .
>
> RAINER MARIA RILKE, from *Letters to a Young Poet* (translation by M. D. Herter Norton)

The term *sexual distress* encompasses several types of sexual problems. These may manifest as rather minor difficulties or as severe conditions that significantly impair individual or relationship functioning, or both. When it comes to sexual problems, considerable specialization exists among mental health professionals. Some clinicians work with sexual dysfunctions; others treat sexual abuse—perhaps working only with victims. The treatment of sex offenders and clients with paraphilias is an area that has recently begun to capture the interest of a small professional audience. Typically, the different specialists do not delve into the others' professional turf and consequently do not communicate with each other.

This type of separation has come about as a result of the evolution of sexual studies. The early work on sexuality focused on sex education and sexual dysfunctions, whereas latter day developments have centered on sexual victimization and societal sexual problems. Regardless of origin, such separation can result in an unnecessarily narrow focus and limited understanding of sexuality. One of the goals of this book is to bridge the gap between artificial professional specializations.

Definitions and Classifications

What is sexual distress according to the broad definition proposed here? First, it is a symptom or complaint that an individual experiences and voices. The complainant may describe effects that apply only to himself or herself, such as self-esteem, emotions, behaviors, or cognitions. But the person (or both partners) may also describe the sexual distress in terms of a relationship disturbance.

Second, sexual distress consists of concern, dissatisfaction, or anxiety about the effects on either the individual or the relationship or both. It may include any of the following: (a) a sexual dysfunction; (b) complaints about one's sexual experiences or lack thereof; (c) concerns about one's relationship(s) (e.g., type, frequency, quality, behaviors, fantasies, roles); (d) obsessive-compulsive patterns in sexual experiences or relationships; (e) conflicts between values and sexual behavior; (f) worry about sexual/body image and attractiveness; (g) concern about object choice in sexual fantasy and behavior; (h) gender identity disturbance; and (i) concern about sexual orientation (affectional preference).

Sexual distress obviously has numerous manifestations. One problem that is not covered here is incest. An eclectic, systemic treatment for this problem is advisable and has been presented (Trepper & Barrett, 1989), but this topic cannot be covered within the format of this book.

There is much to gain from understanding the full array of sexual distress and seeing the common thread as its connection to intimacy. This requires first a clear delineation of the various complaints or problems. This chapter begins with a description of common sexual complaints and continues with a review of the DSM-III-R (American Psychiatric Association, 1987) classifications of sexual dysfunctions and other sexual disorders (e.g., paraphilias, gender identity disorder, and atypical sexual disorder).

The latter two categories, sexual dysfunctions and sexual disorders, by virtue of being in the DSM III-R (1987), come under the rubric of "mental disorders," and this label may raise some philosophical issues. Valid questions center on the validity of the term "mental disorders," on the usefulness of classifications for treatment planning, and on the misuse of classifications to label and thereby dehumanize clients. Most therapists find a way to resolve beliefs about the distinctions between or the lack of distinctions between "problems in living" and so-called "mental disorders." The pragmatics of clinical work allow most professionals to see both the uses and potential abuses of diagnostic descriptors.

In the definition of sexual distress above, the client or couple acknowledges or owns the complaint and the problems connected to it. Considering the symptom for the moment only from the perspective of the person experiencing it, the diagnostic classifications afford a fairly precise description of the symptom. These typically include the type, frequency, and duration of the sexual behavior but also encompass physical, emotional, and cognitive dimensions as well.

Consider the basic need to distinguish one sexual symptom from another, for example, determining whether a man is experiencing premature ejaculation versus hypoactive sexual desire versus exhibitionism, or to specify with some certainty that he is experiencing several symptoms. The diagnostic classifications are critical to this part of the assessment process.

Arriving at an accurate description of this one piece of information—a symptom in terms of the individual's precise experience—is entirely different from other issues. It does not explain how that piece is affected by or affects the person's sense of self, an intimate relationship, or another social system. It does not specify whether the symptomatic person sincerely owns the sexual symptom as the source of the distress. And it does not convey what kind of treatment to use. The diagnostic description is simply a starting point in assessing the full nature of the problem and developing a treatment plan unique to each client's or couple's sexual distress. So in the example above, determining that the man is experiencing premature ejaculation is simply basic to proceeding to hypothesize its connection to his personality, his capacity for intimacy, his relationship with his wife, or to any number of factors.

"SEXUAL ADDICTION" AS AN EXAMPLE OF DIAGNOSTIC CONFUSION

Diagnostic precision as a starting point is especially important given the popularity of global classifications such as "sexual addiction" (Carnes, 1983) or "co-dependence" (Bradshaw, 1988; Whitfield, 1987) that are currently being used to cover a variety of sexual disturbances. Professionals have a responsibility to evaluate the expansion of addiction concepts to cover a variety of human problems.

The concept of "sexual addiction" has triggered numerous criticisms and an ongoing controversy. A central concern is that the concept ignores or negates the broad knowledge base that defines professionalism in favor of a simplistic lay understanding. In fact, behavioral science would allow us to accept the "sexual addiction" diagnosis as valid for some persons, but would also demand examination of the limitations of this label.

Many of the criticisms focus on the lack of attention to biological and psychological factors (Renshaw, 1989). First noted is the distinction between addiction and compulsion (Coleman, 1986; Comfort, 1989; Klein, 1989), namely, the physiological withdrawal response associated with the physiological dependence of addiction. Second, compulsion is a psychological element that can be present in addictive but also in nonaddictive problem behaviors. Third, the concept of sexual addiction locates the problem within the individual as a disease of the will. Finally, proponents seem willing to label as sexual addiction a variety of sexual behaviors without careful attention to whether these behaviors can have a healthy manifestation as well as a destructive one. For example, the implication is that behaviors such as masturbation, use of pornography, casual or uncommitted sex, extramarital affairs, incest, and various paraphilias are all equally dangerous to individuals and explainable in terms of addiction.

In contrast, many behavioral scientists prefer to understand human behavior according to its diverse manifestations and causal factors. They look to comprehensive and interactive biosociopsychological concepts such as human development, personality, learning, and social systems (which distinguish private consensual sex from sexual offenses). Thus a person's problematic sexual behavior could reflect poor problem-solving skills, poor impulse control, manic-depressive illness, or sociopathic, narcissistic, or obsessive-compulsive personality disorders, and so on (Klein, 1989; Levine & Troiden, 1988; Renshaw, 1989).

In the same vein, criticism centers on the singular treatment approach for all sexual addictions regardless of severity, namely, a 12-step group modality. This treatment bias essentially rules out the need for a comprehensive assessment. Factors such as personality, learned arousal patterns, the problem-interactional pattern, life stressors, and couple and family structure and themes are inconsequential compared to the principles of the standard treatment method. Critics argue that the 12-step method derived from the addiction movement is antisexual, removes power from clients, and glosses over the actual range of issues that may be complicating their sexual lives. The very few who do not have the ability to control sexual urges "don't just need help saying 'no' one day at a time. They need assistance in restructuring their character" (Klein, 1989, p. 4).

Consider how a different concept, the capacity for intimacy, as derived from object relations theory, allows for distinctions with regard to sexual behaviors. People vary in their sense of wholeness and integration of self and in the capacity to experience intimacy that includes sexual and emotional gratification. A person who compulsively pursues a sexual behavior or type of relationship to bolster an impaired self will likely continue to experience increasing levels of shame, alienation, and perhaps disturbance in a valued relationship. This could be the result, regardless of whether the behavior falls within the range of "normal", "pathological," or criminal. On the other hand, some behaviors may have "normal" manifestations; thus, another individual may choose to masturbate, use pornography, or have an uncommitted sexual encounter without the same motivation as in the above example and without the effect of self-denigration, anxiety, or hurting a valued relationship.

Whether the proponents of the sexual addiction construct intend it or not, it is used as a global diagnosis, it oversimplifies problems as diseases of the will, and it plays into an antisexual political atmosphere that separates sexuality from a person's humanity. A positive sign is that dialogue is taking place around the controversy, and efforts toward integration are emerging—for example, the incorporation of some systemic thinking with addiction concepts (Carnes, 1991; Earle & Crow, 1989). Peele (1989) proposes that the vision of behavioral science can enable us to attain a complex rather than simple understanding of addiction. This vision draws on various dimensions of human nature—the scientific, psychological, and moral. It argues for understanding human beings in society, for using knowledge and experience to learn healthful behaviors, for understanding the critical impact of parental-child interaction, for insisting on standards of decency, and for affirming that people can manage the complexity of life and its problems.

The final point here is that instead of latching onto a global label that blurs important diagnostic distinctions, professionals have a responsibility to strive for precise descriptions of sexual disorders and dysfunction. It is unfortunate that the diagnosis of "sexual addiction" often marks the end point in the assessment process. But the same abuse can occur with DSM-III-R descriptors as well. It is imperative in assessment to go beyond this largely medical classification system to encompass an understanding of sexual problems that derives from psychological, behavioral, and systems theories.

Common Sexual Complaints

Clients often bring complaints about their sex lives that do not constitute a sexual dysfunction or disorder but cause distress nonetheless. Professionals in all mental health disciplines are apt to encounter clients with "sexual problems in living." The complaint may be the reason for seeking therapy, or it may surface as part of other marital/couple problems or as part of an individual's overall life problems. Common concerns center on (a) frequency of sexual activity, (b) types of sexual activity, (c) initiating or refusing sex, (d) arguments over sex, and (e) attraction to others and sexual affairs. Such complaints may simply reflect the normal challenges in the development of an individual's sexual identity or intimate relationship, or they may mirror more serious problems. The following discussion centers primarily on the complaints in the context of a relationship.

Having differences over the frequency of sex is to be expected as two people attempt to live together in a committed relationship. Each person uniquely experiences self and other, the different stages of the relationship, and life itself. So desire for and interest in sex are not likely to mesh at all times. How partners resolve the differences, however, is critical. Ideally, both partners compromise somewhat and continue to enjoy a sexual and intimate relationship that makes compromise worthwhile. Other solutions find mates angry and resentful; one may feel deprived, whereas the other feels misunderstood or rejected. Without meaningful resolution, the negative emotions can lead to reactions such as withdrawal, nagging, coercion, resentful compliance, mechanical involvement, or withholding of sex, affection, or both.

Partners may also differ about the type, conditions, or quality of sexual activity in which they engage. One may prefer (and may or may not suggest) variations in acts, locations, or patterns, for example, more kissing, body caressing, talking, or oral-genital sex; or having the lights on or using a certain method of contraception; or prefaced by a certain atmosphere, mood, or intimate intensity. Without a meaningful resolution of expected differences, negative emotions and actions can reduce sexual satisfaction and intimacy. Such complaints emerge in therapy incidentally or as the primary problem. For example, a young woman was in counseling to help her cope with the stress of having given birth to a handicapped child. Within three sessions, she complained about the sexual relationship with her husband. He had little interest in sex, and it proceeded in a hurried, mechanized manner, bringing her no pleasure. She had tried unsuccessfully to make her husband jealous, was having sexual fantasies about a family friend, and was thinking about having an affair with him.

Complaints about initiating and refusing sex are common. Outside of therapy, most partners rarely discuss and resolve their difficulties in this area. Instead, painful emotions are denied or find a voice in accusations; and hurtful actions such as retaliation in kind, nagging, labeling, or withdrawal perpetuate the problem. A common pattern is that one partner complains that the other rarely initiates sex, while the other laments that he or she never gets the chance to initiate or that refusal is not possible without negative consequences.

Some couples regularly quarrel over sex. Arguments can be about any type of dissatisfaction, but they result from symmetrical communication, each giving "tit for tat" as they vent emotions and take action. Such quarrels may erupt and prevent a couple from engaging in sex, or they may routinely take place after the sexual activity. Hostilities may escalate and carry over to the total relationship, leading to additional arguments, withdrawal, hopelessness, and an increasing tension and estrangement pattern that is broken only by the couple's engaging in sex or instigating a new argument, thereby continuing the pattern.

Discovered or disclosed sexual affairs within a marriage or committed relationship typically create a crisis. Yet secret sexual attractions to others and undetected affairs are also troubling for some clients. Obviously, there are various types of affairs, from the one-time situational encounter to compulsive promiscuity. A comprehensive assessment is necessary to examine the meaning of the affair, if disclosed, for each partner; the strength of the overall relationship; decision-making and coping processes; and each partner's individual personality structure. The presence of affairs, either discovered or secret, is extremely common in clinical work.

All of the above sexual complaints may manifest, on one end of a continuum, as part of the expected vicissitudes of committed intimate relationships, or at the other end as severe dysfunction in the couple system. At the so-called normal end of the continuum, the differences result in a manageable degree of relationship tension, which the partners tolerate and resolve so as to continue to have a pleasurable sexual and intimate relationship. At the dysfunctional end, although each partner functions sexually, overall pleasure is so compromised that a stable but unsatisfactory self or couple interaction structure evolves. Examples of the latter might be partners who have no sexual contact or those who say: "We quarrel about sex, but we quarrel about everything," or "We quarrel about sex, but otherwise we get along great." The sexual complaints discussed above can obviously lead to or exist along with full-blown sexual dysfunctions.

The case of Ann and Adam, described earlier, suggests the presence of sexual dissatisfactions on the part of both partners early in the relationship. These remained largely unacknowledged and unresolved, with both partners distancing from each other sexually, losing desire, and substituting other activities and patterns for sexual and intimate fulfillment. The pattern remained stable for 10 years until change—the birth of a child and life-threatening illness—triggered new but ineffective coping responses that produced the marital crisis.

Individuals who are not involved in more or less stable relationships may also have sexual complaints that are neither dysfunctions nor disorders. These may relate to normative crises or transitions (e.g., young adulthood, loss of an intimate relationship through breaking up or divorcing, etc.). On the other hand, they may represent more chronic problems with intimacy due to the interaction of personality and family of origin factors. The complaint may be of no sexual life, no sexual relationships, and no intimate relationships, perhaps not even masturbation as a form of sexual expression, although the client may desire a sexual dimension in his or her life. Individuals may also complain about their preferred sexual fantasies or behaviors and question the place of these in their lives.

Such sexual complaints are often central to a primary symptom of depression. For example, one young man was troubled by his frequent masturbation, but felt it was all he had because of his inability to get dates or establish intimate relationships with girls. Another man's experience in a sexual relationship was limited to having had sexual intercourse once; his sexual complaint was but one dimension of depression characterized by isolation, low self-esteem, and severe lack of social skills. As always, it is important to distinguish sexual complaints from symptoms that constitute a sexual dysfunction or disorder.

The Sexual Dysfunctions

As sex therapy evolved during the 1970s, many professionals became familiar for the first time with the sexual dysfunctions. Clinicians trained in the 1980s, however, may lack this familiarity as professional attention has turned more toward treating sexual problems such as abuse and incest. Ongoing efforts have produced refinement in the diagnosis and classification of sexual dysfunctions. Today's clinician needs more than a passing familiarity with the sexual dysfunctions and other sexual disorders that come under the rubric of sexual distress; hence this section and the next review the newest definitions.

As indicated above a diagnostic classification system based on individual functioning is relevant to an integrative systemic approach to sexual problems. The definitions describe, in physiological and/or cognitive-emotional terms what an individual with the symptom experiences. This is no different from the need to distinguish between anorexia and bulimia. Having a precise understanding of the symptom experienced by an individual is not inconsistent with a systemic approach to the problem. The classifications of sexual disorders describe; they do not posit causes and effects. The multitheoretical approach, however, does deal with causes and effects.

The classification of sexual dysfunctions in the current DSM-III-R (1987) represents the distillation of some 20 years of progress in the study of sexuality. Masters and Johnson's (1970) research on sexual physiology resulted in a four-stage description of the sexual response cycle. This evolved to the triphasic model posited by Kaplan (1979). The three phases—desire, arousal, and orgasm—were incorporated into the previous DSM III (American Psychiatric Association, 1980) with the new development being that desire disorders were included in the classification of sexual dysfunctions. A further refinement is that the current DSM-III-R (1987) now includes the individual's subjective evaluation in the definition of arousal disorders. That is, arousal disorders are characterized by either a lack of physiological response or the individual's subjective sense of the lack of pleasure and excitement. Understanding the distinctions made in the classifications is critical to the assessment and treatment of sexual problems.

In general, the sexual dysfunctions are defined as "inhibitions in the appetitive or psychophysiological changes" characteristic of the sexual response cycle. Dysfunctions typically occur in sex with a partner but may apply to masturbation. Further distinctions are psychogenic or both biogenic and psychogenic, lifelong or acquired, and generalized or situational. The classifications are not used if the sexual dysfunction has a known organic or biogenic cause or if it "occurs during the course of another Axis I disorder" (American Psychiatric Association, 1987, p. 293). All of the definitions are preceded by the terms "persistent or recurrent," but the clinician subjectively makes this judgment. In this and the following section on sexual disorders, succinct definitions are listed without discussion or example. This format should be sufficient to familiarize the reader with the range of sexual disorders and to document the need for diagnostic precision. Subsequent chapters presenting the framework for integrative systems therapy contain extensive discussion and case examples that demonstrate the importance of diagnostic classification in the overall treatment process.

The sexual desire disorders are (a) *hypoactive sexual desire,* characterized by "deficient or absent sexual fantasies and desire for sexual activity" and (b) *sexual aversion disorder,* defined as "extreme aversion to, and avoidance of all or almost all, genital sexual contact with a partner" (p. 293).

There are two sexual arousal dysfunctions: (a) *Female sexual arousal disorder* is characterized by either "partial or complete failure to attain or maintain the lubrication-swelling response" or "lack of a subjective sense of sexual excitement and pleasure;" and (b) *male erectile disorder* is characterized by either "partial or complete failure . . . to attain or maintain erection until completion of the sexual activity" or "lack of a subjective sense of sexual excitement and pleasure . . . during sexual activity" (p. 294).

There are three orgasm disorders: (a) *Inhibited female orgasm* refers to "delay in or absence of orgasm in a female following a normal sexual excitement phase during sexual activity that the clinician judges to be adequate in focus, intensity, and duration" (the inability to attain orgasm during coitus without manual clitoral stimulation in most situations represents a normal variation in female sexual response). (b) *Inhibited male orgasm* refers to "delay in, or absence of, orgasm in a male following a normal excitement phase during sexual activity that the clinician, taking into account the person's age, judges to be adequate in focus, intensity, and duration . . . , usually restricted to an inability to reach orgasm in the vagina, with orgasm possible with other types of stimulation, such as masturbation." (c) *Premature ejaculation* refers to "ejaculation with minimal sexual stimulation or before, upon, or shortly after penetration and before the person wishes it," with the clinician taking "into account factors that affect duration of the excitement phase, such as age, novelty of the sexual partner or situation, and frequency of sexual activity" (pp. 294-295).

A fourth category deals with sexual pain disorders: (a) *Dyspareunia* refers to "genital pain in either a male or a female before, during, or after sexual intercourse . . . not caused by lack of lubrication or by vaginismus." (b) *Vaginismus* refers to "involuntary spasm of the musculature of the outer third of the vagina that interferes with coitus . . . not caused exclusively by a physical disorder" (p. 295).

A final nonspecific category of sexual dysfunctions (not due to organic factors) offers several examples: lack of erotic sensation or even numbness in the presence of physiological orgasm, premature female orgasm, and pain in the genitals while masturbating.

The major classifications for the sexual dysfunctions represent an advance over such global terms as frigidity and impotence, which were widely used in the past. The origins of these words imply a denigrating label of the whole person, rather than describe a specific sexual dysfunction. It is especially unfortunate that the pejorative term "impotence" continues to be used by the medical profession in the formal names for clinics established to treat men with sexual dysfunctions.

In contrast, the DSM-III-R (American Psychiatric Association, 1987) classifications specify not only the missing physiological concomitants of the sexual response cycle but also subjectively defined elements as well. The judgment of the clinician, however, based on a comprehensive assessment, carries considerable weight in defining the meaning of "persistent and recurrent" and other terms. Finally, the specificity achieved now makes it imperative for the therapist to assess carefully whether more than one dysfunction is present. For example, does a client's erectile disorder exist along with hypoactive desire and/or aversion disorder? If so, did these two latter conditions predate or follow the erectile disorder? Such distinctions in diagnosis are critical.

Other Sexual Disorders

It is important to have an accurate grasp of other sexual disorders that may figure into sexual distress. As popularized global terms such as *sexual addiction* and *co-dependency* pervade the professional consciousness, it is time to review the carefully defined classifications of disorders involving paraphilias (previously called deviations or variations), gender identity, and atypical sexual behaviors. These diagnostic categories permit diagnostic specificity, which contributes to a comprehensive assessment and a meaningful treatment plan.

Once again, the literature suggests that treatment for sexual deviations is a separate entity from sex therapy for sexual dysfunction and from marital therapy for relationship problems. It is as if the client with paraphilic behavior never marries; or, if he does, neither he nor his wife ever experiences sexual distress related to his behavior.

Why these treatment models have evolved as separate entities is an interesting question. It may be that sex therapy as a specialty actually promulgated the myth of sexual dysfunction as a normative, circumscribed middle-class problem for which clients would voluntarily seek treatment. At the same time, during the 1960s and 1970s, there was a tendency to depathologize the victimless sexual variations as nonproblems. Those persons who did harm others or entail criminal offenses because of paraphilic behavior were typically regarded as involuntary, unmotivated, often untreatable, clients. They were certainly not "desirable" clients in the same way that couples with sexual dysfunctions were.

None of this arbitrary separation into distinct types of sexual disturbances/treatments speaks to the clinical reality that practitioners see. Only a holistic multitheoretical understanding of intimacy and sexuality can provide a conceptual framework for working with the various manifestations of sexual distress that couples and individuals actually present. The case of Brent illustrates this point.

> Twenty-eight years old, married, and the father of a 2-year-old child, Brent entered therapy when his wife discovered his ongoing affair that had started early in their 4-year marriage and he subsequently learned of her recent affair. Brent's history revealed his own sexual abuse by a male relative and the recent uncovering of incest by another person in his family of origin. Brent's own current sexual disorders included exhibitionism and making obscene phone calls. In addition, while exhibiting, he experienced fantasies of control and rape, and he routinely coerced his wife into sexual intercourse. Brent acknowledged a lack of intimacy with both his affair partner and his wife and overall dissatisfaction with himself and with his marriage, which he hoped to preserve and improve. Although his wife was orgasmic and he enjoyed this quality in her, they rarely had sex that included her sexual satisfaction. Both had impaired capacities for intimacy that created a stable but highly unsatisfactory relationship pattern, a pattern that guaranteed continued sexual frustration and failures in intimacy for both.

In this case the therapist needs a diagnostic understanding not only of sexual complaints (the affairs), marital distress, intimacy failures, sexual offenses, but also of paraphilias.

The paraphilias "are characterized by arousal in response to sexual objects or situations that are not part of normative arousal-activity patterns and that in varying degrees may interfere with the capacity for reciprocal, affectional sexual activity" (American Psychiatric Association, 1987, p. 279). For the diagnosis to apply, the person must have, over a period of at least 6 months, either acted on the urges or be markedly distressed by them. The severity of a specific paraphilia is assessed as: (a) mild, if the person is considerably distressed but has not acted on the urges; (b) moderate, if the person has acted on the paraphilic urge occasionally; and (c) severe, if the person has acted on the urges repeatedly. Clinical significance would also include the degree to which the paraphilic imagery or fantasy is necessary for sexual arousal, whether there has been harm to self or others, amount of subjective distress, and social or occupational problems directly related to the paraphilia. Differential diagnosis is critical, and multiple diagnoses may apply. It has been recently noted that persons "with a Paraphilia commonly suffer from several varieties" (p. 288).

This section reviews the classifications of the paraphilias in order to enable clinicians to use these in developing a comprehensive assessment. Persons presenting for individual, couple, family, and sex therapy may engage in paraphilic behavior; and the DSM-III-R definitions allow greater precision than such global constructs as sexual addiction (Carnes, 1983). As mentioned above, this construct actually blurs distinctions and, moreover, calls for a singular, 12-step recovery approach for all degrees of dysfunction. The more precise diagnosis afforded by the DSM III-R definitions and criteria constitutes a piece of a comprehensive assessment, which should explain how the paraphilia fits into the major problems for which the client is seeking help. From this assessment the clinician can then develop a treatment plan tailored to the client's unique situation.

It is important to remember that a critical element in the definition of the paraphilias is that the person is distressed by the behavior. The person owns or acknowledges the distress—either because he is intrinsically troubled by the behavior or its impact on his partner, marriage, and family, or because he is charged with a criminal offense. In the latter case, the person is sufficiently distressed by the paraphilic behavior to enter treatment voluntarily or involuntarily.

The more common paraphilias seen in clinical practice are defined below. One should remember that part of each definition (but not repeated below) is *"recurrent and intense sexual urges and sexually arousing fantasies"* involving the specific paraphilia. This dimension must be present for the diagnosis to apply, unless otherwise explained.

1. *Exhibitionism:* "the exposure of one's genitals to an unsuspecting stranger."
2. *Fetishism:* "the use of nonliving objects by themselves (e.g., female undergarments)." The person may at times "use the nonliving object with a partner" (p. 283).
3. *Frotteurism:* "touching and rubbing against a nonconsenting person." The behavior usually occurs in crowded public places, and it is the touching not the coercion that is sexually exciting. (p. 284)
4. *Pedophilia:* "sexual activity with a prepubescent child or children (generally age 13 or younger)." The diagnosis is made only if "the person is at least 16 years old and at least 5 years older than the child or children." Excluded would be an adolescent involved with a 12- or 13-year old in an ongoing sexual relationship. Differential diagnosis would distinguish pedophilia from isolated sexual acts precipitated by life stressors. Further specifications would be if the behavior is limited to incest, involves the same or opposite sex or both, and is exclusive (attracted only to children) or nonexclusive (p. 285).

5. *Sexual Masochism:* "the act (real not simulated) of being humiliated, beaten, bound, or otherwise made to suffer" (p. 287).
6. *Sexual Sadism:* "acts (real not simulated) in which the psychological or physical suffering (including humiliation) of the victim is sexually exciting to the person." The diagnosis may include the person who commits rape or other sexual assault if the victim's suffering is experienced as sexually arousing. However, other rapists who are sexually aroused by coercion of a nonconsenting partner but are not aroused by the victim's suffering should not be given this diagnosis (pp. 287-288).
7. *Transvestic Fetishism:* "in a heterosexual male, recurrent intense sexual urges and sexually arousing fantasies involving cross-dressing." This does not include female impersonation or cross-dressing done, not for sexual excitement, but for the relief of tension of gender discomfort (as in gender identity disorder, nontranssexual type), and does not include cross-dressing for masquerade or dramatic effect occasionally engaged in by some homosexual males (p. 289).
8. *Voyeurism:* "the act of observing an unsuspecting person who is naked, in the process of disrobing, or engaging in sexual activity" (p. 290).

A gender identity disturbance may also occasionally be part of a client's sexual problems. Such disturbances affect both children and adults.

In the case of children, the most relevant diagnosis is that of *gender disorder of childhood*. This disturbance is characterized by intense and persistent distress in a child who has not yet reached puberty about "his or her assigned sex and the desire to be, or insistence that he or she is, of the other sex" (p. 71). There is repudiation of one's anatomic characteristics or preoccupation with stereotypical activities and dress of the opposite sex. *Transsexualism* is the classification that applies to a person who has reached puberty and experiences a "a persistent discomfort and sense of inappropriateness about one's assigned sex"; these feelings must have persisted for at least 2 years. There is preoccupation with "getting rid of one's primary and secondary sex characteristics and acquiring the sex characteristics of the other sex. Because of discomfort with clothes of the assigned sex, the person may dress in clothes of the opposite sex. It is important to understand distinctions between childhood and adult gender disorders and differentiating these from transvestic fetishism.

In adulthood, clients may present with a gender disturbance that is not typically full-blown transsexualism. Rather, it may meet criteria for *"gender identity disturbance of adolescence or adulthood, nontranssexual type."* This involves discomfort about one's assigned sex, cross-dressing in actuality or fantasy (but not for sexual excitement), and no preoccupation with changing one's sex. It is important to distinguish this disorder from transvestic fetishism, where cross-dressing is connected to sexual fantasy and arousal. Some persons, however, may have characteristics of both disorders. Another distinction is that of "adults with transient, stress-related cross-dressing behavior," which falls under the classification of *"gender disorder not otherwise specified"* (American Psychiatric Association, 1987, pp. 77-78). Two cases discussed in Chapter 7 ("Harry" and "Roger") highlight these diagnostic distinctions.

One final category of sexual disorders is a global one: *sexual disorder not otherwise specified.* This nonspecific classification contains as an example "distress about a pattern of repeated sexual conquests or other forms of nonparaphilic sexual addiction, involving a succession of people who exist only as things to be used" (American Psychiatric Association, 1987, p. 296) Here the term *sexual addiction* is differentiated from the paraphilias and centers on the use of people as objects. Carnes (1983), on the other hand, uses sexual addiction to cover an array of sexual behaviors, including paraphilias, to emphasize their compulsive quality. Another example in this nonspecific category refers to "persistent and marked distress about one's sexual orientation" (p. 296). Although this may be the remnant of the previous classification of "ego-dystonic homosexuality," the new example is general enough to encompass distress about any sexual orientation—heterosexual, bisexual, or homosexual. In fact, Nichols (1989) has noted that sexual identity issues can be quite complex and has posited three types that therapists may encounter: the "frightened homosexual," the "heterosexual bisexual," and the "gay bisexual" (Nichols, 1989).

To summarize, it is important to strive for diagnostic accuracy in identifying whether sexual disorders figure into a client's, a couple's, or even a family's sexual distress. Accurate diagnostic description for all of the presenting complaints will enhance the development of a comprehensive assessment and individualized treatment plan.

Conclusion

Sexual distress is not a singular or simple entity. It may manifest as sexual complaints, sexual dysfunction, other sexual disorders, or combinations of these. In addition to the importance of arriving at accurate diagnostic description of symptoms as experienced by an individual, much will be gained from further viewing these problems as connected to the dimension of intimacy. This view allows for tapping into the complexity that often underlies the most difficult cases. It has already been noted that the educational-behavioral methods of traditional sex therapy do not seem to be effective with the more complex cases such as desire disorders (Slowinski, 1984).

A multitheoretical approach that encompasses social learning, individual development and personality, and key systems concepts should be applicable to the simplest of sexual complaints as well as to the most complicated sexual and intimacy dysfunctions. The remainder of the book explicates the components, rationale, and method for this type of systemic integration.

References

American Psychiatric Association. (1980). *Diagnostic and statistical manual of mental disorders, third edition (DSM-III).* Washington, DC: Author.

American Psychiatric Association. (1987). *Diagnostic and statistical manual of mental disorders, third edition revised (DSM-III-R).* Washington, DC: Author.

Bradshaw, J. (1988). *Healing the shame that binds you.* Deerfield Beach, FL: Health Communications.

Carnes, P. (1983). *Out of the shadows: Understanding sexual addiction.* Minneapolis, MN: Comp Care Publications.

Carnes, P. (1991, May 3). *Implications of sex addiction for sex therapists.* Paper presented at the annual meeting of the American Association of Sex Educators, Counselors, and Therapists Annual Conference, St. Louis, MO.

Coleman, E. (1986). Sexual compulsion vs. sexual addiction. *SIECUS Report,* July.

Comfort, A. (1989). Feedback: "It is damaging to confuse addiction and compulsion." *Contemporary Sexuality, 21*(11), 8.

Earle, R., & Crow, G. (1989). *Lonely all the time: Recognizing, understanding, and overcoming sex addiction, for addicts and co-dependents.* New York: Pocket Books.

Kaplan, H. S. (1979). *Disorders of sexual desire and other new concepts and techniques in sex therapy.* New York: Brunner/Mazel.

Klein, M. (1989). Why there's no such thing as sexual addiction—and why it matters. *Ohio AAMFT News, 7,* 3, 4. (Reprinted from *The California Therapist,* December, 1989)

Levine, M. P., & Troiden, R. R. (1988). The myth of sexual compulsivity. *Journal of Sex Research, 25*(3), 347-363.

Masters, W. H., & Johnson, V. E. (1970). *Human sexual inadequacy*. Boston: Little, Brown.

Nichols, M. (1989). Sex therapy with lesbians, gay men, and bisexuals. In S. R. Leiblum & R. C. Rosen (Eds.), *Principles and practice of sex therapy* (pp. 269-297). New York: Guilford Press.

Peele, S. (1989). *The diseasing of America: How the addiction industry captured our soul.* Lexington, MA: Lexington Books.

Renshaw, D. (1989). Flaws in analogy to alcohol addiction. *Contemporary Sexuality*, October, 3-5.

Slowinski, J. (1984). Reflections on sex therapy: An interview with Harold I. Lief and Arnold Lazarus. *Journal of Sex Education and Therapy, 10*, 13-21.

Trepper, T. S., & Barrett, M. J. (1989). Systemic treatment of incest: *A therapeutic handbook*. New York: Brunner/Mazel.

Whitfield, C. L. (1987). *Healing the child within*. Deerfield Beach, FL: Health Communications.

3

The Legacy of Sex Therapy

> Married men ought never to attempt or hurry their initial enterprise if they do not find themselves ready for it. If a man discovers himself to be agitated and on edge, it is better to give up outright any attempt at marital commerce and await a further occasion when he is less upset. . . .
>
> MONTAIGNE, from *Autobiography*

The legacy of sex therapy is considerable and rich. It is itself a highly eclectic therapeutic approach, and much of what I call "standard" or "traditional" sex therapy has a place in integrative systems therapy (IST) proposed in this book. The difference, however, is that the goal, rationale, and method for implementing the strategies may not be the same as they are in traditional sex therapy.

Standard or traditional sex therapy refers to the approach that evolved from Masters and Johnson's seminal work (1970) along with elaborations and refinements of the basic method. Cognitive, behavioral, and experiential elements were present in the original method, but these were not labeled as such, because Masters and Johnson highlighted pragmatic rather than theoretical concepts. Subsequently, behaviorists who practiced sex therapy developed new behavioral and cognitive techniques specifically to expand behavioral repertoires, eliminate sexual phobias, and restructure irrational cognitions and stereotypes (LoPiccolo & LoPiccolo, 1978; McCarthy, 1989). Practitioners who endorsed humanistic theory devised additional experiential tasks to evoke emotion and increase awareness as a way of enhancing new sexual learning (Hartman & Fithian, 1972). Kaplan (1974, 1979) added a psychodynamic dimension, but this was reserved for the most difficult cases that were unresponsive to the basic methods. Finally, practitioners with a feminist bent highlighted the sexist factors in the definition and treatment of women's sexual dysfunctions; and their version of sex therapy aimed specifically to help women counteract these (Barbach, 1975, 1980).

A few strategies within sex therapy were controversial from the beginning and were largely disavowed by the majority of practitioners dedicated to unequivocal ethical standards of professional practice. For example, Masters and Johnson (1970) initially used sex surrogates in the treatment of male clients without partners. They abandoned this practice in the face of legal and ethical problems. Most sex therapists with concern for professional standards and credibility never used or endorsed the option of sex surrogates. Similarly, certain interventions advocated primarily by humanistic/encounter practitioners were also largely rejected—for example, sexual contact between therapist and client, teaching sexual techniques through demonstration or contact, and so forth.

Early on, ethics, standards, and credibility became major concerns. A symposium held in 1977 addressed these issues and published its proceedings (Masters, Johnson, & Kolodny, 1977). These same issues have also been addressed in an ongoing manner through the certification process and code of ethics developed by the American Association for Sex Educators, Counselors, and Therapists (AASECT, 1980). Moreover, during the 1980's sex therapists have become even more sensitive to ethical and legal issues as these became paramount in the whole field of psychotherapy (Haas & Malouf, 1989; R. Woody, 1988).

Throughout the years, students and trainees have repeatedly requested a single source that briefly identifies and describes the major sex therapy interventions. This chapter aims to meet that need, but a more important goal is to demonstrate the eclectic richness of sex therapy and why it has a place in IST. This vantage point will, however, also suggest the limitations of traditional sex therapy for understanding sexual distress within the context of intimacy.

Basic Principles

What was new about sex therapy was the direct treatment of sexual dysfunction as a problem in its own right that deserved to be remedied. Another innovation was locating the causes of dysfunction in anxiety about sexual performance experienced in current sexual encounters. This was called spectator anxiety to refer the emotional response associated with self-consciousness and self-observation during sex due to concern about failure. This was not a deep-seated intrapsychic anxiety but was thought to be fueled by societal sexual myths and learned sexual inhibitions.

The elements of Masters and Johnson's (1970) approach that have remained integral to sex therapy are (a) treatment of the dyad; (b) viewing the sexual dysfunction as the problem to treat and remedy; (c) assessing sexual attitudes and specific sexual behaviors; (d) providing accurate information about sexuality and eliminating myths and sex-negative attitudes; and (e) assigning clients behavioral/experiential tasks to be done at home. The latter included prohibiting sexual intercourse, sensate focus consisting of various stages and types of sensual pleasuring, and other tasks for specific dysfunctions.

Nearly a decade later, LoPiccolo and LoPiccolo (1978) summarized seven basic principles of sex therapy that reflect the original foundation:

1. Mutual responsibility emphasizes the view of sexual dysfunction as a shared disorder in which both partners must participate in the solution.
2. Information and education are provided by the therapist through discussion, recommended readings, films, and so on, to overcome clients' ignorance of sexual response and function.
3. Attitude change is indicated when clients hold negative attitudes toward sex or sexual pleasure.
4. Eliminating performance anxiety is essential, because many clients endorse sociocultural myths and stereotypes that emphasize the end goal of erection, orgasm, and ejaculation as opposed to mutual sensual and sexual enjoyment.
5. Increasing communication about and effectiveness of sexual technique is encouraged through home assignments, as well as through therapy discussions and advice about communication skills.

6. Changing destructive life styles and sex roles is actively encouraged by the therapist to enable clients to reserve quality time for their sexual relationship or change lifestyle behaviors that are destructive to their sexuality.
7. Prescribing changes in behavior involves the therapist's assigning a planned series of at-home experiences, with the exact prescription depending on the specific sexual dysfunction.

The major procedures and techniques associated with sex therapy merit careful review. These may seem relatively straightforward, but they are only part of a larger therapeutic process. Competent therapists do not employ the procedures and tasks in a "cookbook" manner. Broad and accurate knowledge of human sexuality is necessary as is keen awareness of one's own personal sexual attitudes and issues and of how these might impact on clinical work. Clients' sexual lives deserve to be treated respectfully and with expertise. In this arena, clearly "a little knowledge is a dangerous thing."

Through the years clients have reported situations with prior therapists who dealt with their sexual concerns in a crass or incompetent manner, while assuming they were using sex therapy techniques appropriately. The majority of mental health professionals do not receive formal academic training or supervised clinical experience in the treatment of sexual dysfunctions. A small percentage may obtain this special expertise, but most acquire, through their own independent study and effort, only a passing familiarity with sex therapy. Clinicians have an ethical responsibility to assess their overall competence to deal with sexual problems and to acquire, as needed, further training in his area.

Before proceeding, another caveat is in order. The following discussion of procedures is organized, for didactic purposes, in a concise format emphasizing the goals and details of sex therapy interventions. This format cannot capture the actual process of therapy—the way one makes clinical decisions as to if and when to use a given technique and how to implement it. For this dimension, the therapist's broad clinical expertise is assumed. Although the description of interventions appears in summary or outline fashion, this must not convey that sex therapy is a simplistic process.

General Sex Therapy Procedures and Techniques

The tradition of a comprehensive assessment of sexual dysfunction began with Masters and Johnson (1970), and continues today, though with modifications. It encompasses the evaluation of both medical and sociopsychological factors.

ASSESSMENT

Medical and Physical Factors

Diagnosis of individual medical or physical factors is much more extensive today than in the past. One must assess the symptomatic individual's overall physical and mental health as well as the potential organic effects from the use of alcohol, tobacco, and illegal or prescription drugs. Summaries of the effects of various drugs and illnesses on sexual function are available in several sources (Kaplan, 1983; Woods, 1984); the most up-to-date source is an index of all medications (Drug Interactions and Side Effects Index, 1991). Numerous technological advances now permit diagnosis of organic contributors to sexual dysfunction—primarily erectile disorder. As a result of these diagnostic refinements, current estimates suggest that 50% of erectile disorders in men of all age groups may involve organic conditions (Kaplan, 1983; Tiefer & Melman, 1989).

"High tech" physiological assessment procedures are now fairly accessible because urologists have established facilities in most urban areas to treat "impotence" problems. The measurement of nocturnal penile tumescence (NPT) is available at such centers or through facilities for treating sleep disorders, or patients may use the stamp-ring or Snap Gauge tests at home (Dacomed, Minneapolis, MN). These methods measure penile circumference during spontaneous nocturnal erections, but this measurement does not consistently correlate with erections sufficiently rigid for intercourse. Another instrument, the Rigiscan (Dacomed, Minneapolis, MN) measures both tumescence and rigidity. It is a computer-driven portable device that a patient may use at home. Other physiological measures gauge penile arterial blood flow. Obtaining this measure is accomplished through a blood pressure reading but also with direct injection of papaverine into the penile shaft that produces a "pharmaceutical erection," which allows study of the ability of the corpus cavernosal arteries to dilate. Papaverine has also been used for treatment of some organic-based erectile dysfunctions. It is commercially available to physicians for clinic use and for prescribing home self-injection for patients; however, it is not approved by the FDA for the treatment of this dysfunction (Tiefer & Melman, 1989).

Other medical procedures include endocrine tests, cavernosography (an X-ray technique to measure dynamic changes of erection), and glucose tolerance testing (for precise detection of diabetic conditions).

For women, a general physical and a gynecological/urological examination are typically recommended. The latter is especially critical for dyspareunia and vaginismus in order to rule out organic factors. When making a medical referral, the clinician should carefully select the physician and specify referral questions. Physicians vary in their interest, knowledge, and comfort regarding sexual problems; and their ability to conduct a thorough exam involving the genitalia can be compromised by these factors.

In terms of the legacy of sex therapy, the careful attention to ruling out organic contributors to sexual dysfunction was central. The rationale was that standard sex therapy was the appropriate treatment if there was no demonstrated organic basis for the dysfunction.

As sex therapy has evolved over 2 decades, the understanding of individual "physical" or "physiological" contributors has become more sophisticated. Kaplan (1974) posited the concept of an individual's psychosomatic vulnerability to sexual dysfunction, in which it was viewed as similar to other psychosomatic conditions (such as ulcerative colitis, asthma, etc.). More recently, Heiman and Grafton-Becker (1989) have suggested that subclinical levels of mood disorders may figure in the etiology of desire disorders. This means that it is important to screen for chronic low-level depression and its indicators such as low self-esteem. Providing further support for the role of undiagnosed physiological factors, others have suggested that unknown organic factors may be involved in cases of lifelong and global premature ejaculation (Strassberg, Mahoney, & Schaugaard, 1988).

The fact is that both biological and psychogenic factors are likely interwoven and interactive in the sexual problems of some clients and that flexibility in treatment method is critical. Lief (1989) reported on a man who had experienced over 10 years of hypoactive sexual desire, but had also been in psychotherapy off and on for some 31 years for obsessive concern about the past lovers of any of his female partners. In his most recent treatment, endocrine tests revealed a pituitary tumor. Once this was surgically removed, the man's sexual desire returned. The obsessiveness remained, and his history suggested many psychogenic factors as contributing to this. When further therapy brought no relief, the drug Prozac was prescribed, and the obsessiveness disappeared.

The point is that some cases may very well require medical treatment instead of or concurrent with therapy, and IST certainly allows for these options. Today sex therapy is recommended as a critical component when medical or surgical treatment is used for sexual dysfunction with a known organic etiology. For example, Schover and vonEschenbach (1985) assert that sex therapy may be essential in assisting a couple to adapt to a surgically implanted prosthesis. The same guideline would apply in the use of the new penile injections to treat erectile dysfunction. Unfortunately, many medical programs for the treatment of male sexual dysfunctions do not provide sex therapy or any type of counseling. Similarly, many therapists maintain an exclusively psychogenic focus in spite of its not remedying the client's sexual distress.

Sociopsychological Factors

The sociopsychological assessment is an extensive process that encompasses the social, emotional, psychological, and behavioral facets of the client's or couple's life. This includes a history of the sexual problem; a complete or abbreviated sex, relationship, and marital history of each partner; as well as assessment of current individual, interpersonal, and situational issues for each. As part of this process, some therapists routinely administer personality tests and marital or relationship inventories. One point merits special attention here, and that is the importance of exploring in each individual's history for sexual abuse and assault—either as a perpetrator or a victim. This information, along with other family sexual secrets, often emerges through use of the sexual genogram (discussed in Chapter 5).

In traditional sex therapy, the most critical focus in the sociopsychological assessment centered on analysis of client beliefs about sexuality and actual sexual behaviors. Once organic factors were ruled out, the early forms of sex therapy assumed a fairly singular and linear cause of dysfunction. That is, the client's acceptance of negative sexual attitudes and myths structured sexual encounters toward a mechanical, driven pursuit of the end goal of intercourse and orgasm. This atmosphere, fraught with anxiety, was inimical to natural sexual functioning; hence sexual dysfunction resulted.

As sex therapy has evolved, the psychological assessment has expanded to encompass beliefs and attitudes, not only about sex, but about self, including self-worth, self-image, success, competency and coping, and gender-based roles in relationships (Ellis, 1980; Kaplan, 1979; Lazarus, 1989; McCarthy, 1989). Interventions based on a broad cognitive analysis may then aim to change attitudes and behaviors, other than strictly sexual ones, believed to contribute to the sexual dysfunction.

Sex therapy, as it is practiced today, is noted for detailed assessment of the client's specific sexual dysfunction. This includes its onset; manifestations; frequency; behaviors, cognitions, attitudes, and emotions during problematic sexual encounters; interest in and desire for sex; fantasies; and solutions attempted or prior treatment. In addition to the clinical interview, sexual inventories and scales are often used to obtain an objective assessment of these factors. (See Chapter 8 for a discussion of sexual inventories and of the Sexual Interaction System Scale developed specifically for the IST treatment for sexual distress.)

During this assessment process, the therapist must be not only highly knowledgeable about the human sexual response but also competent to elicit intimate details in an ethical and respectful manner. Such details are necessary for an accurate diagnosis of which dysfunction(s) are present, but a diagnostic descriptor is only a first step in the assessment process. Out of full assessment data, the therapist develops causal and treatment hypotheses, a clear understanding of client and therapeutic goals, and a contract for working on these.

The following outline (Table 3.1), adapted from LoPiccolo and Heiman (1978, pp. 104-112), suggests the major content areas that a comprehensive assessment should cover. Such an outline can serve as a framework for obtaining information in the give-and-take atmosphere of the therapeutic interview. Rather than proceeding as an inquisitor, the therapist can simply bring up the major topics and

TABLE 3.1 Outline for Problem and Sociopsychological Assessment

HISTORICAL INFORMATION

I. Background and Early Childhood

   A. Family Background
      Details of birth, parents' marriage(s), occupations, siblings, quality of parental, parental-child, and family relationships.
   B. Religious Influences
      Denomination(s), parental involvement, church and parochial school attendance.
   C. Attitudes Toward Sex in the Home
      Asking sex questions, parental and parental-child shows of affection, sex education provided.
   D. Emerging Sexuality
      Sexual awareness, experimentation, upsetting experiences.

II. Puberty and Adolescence
   A. Sexual Education
      Problems, need for information, sexual learning, menstruation, dreams, fantasies, nocturnal emissions, parental messages about sex.
   B. Dating Behavior
      Attractions, age, extent, petting, other sexual contacts.
   C. Coital Experiences
      Premarital, sexual, emotional, and cognitive responses, contraception, problems.
   D. Other Experiences
      Pornography, masturbation, same-sex activity, sexual molestation.
   E. Premarital Experiences
      Sexual or love relationships, engagements, prior marriages, quality of these relationships.

CURRENT INFORMATION

I. Current Attitudes and Beliefs
   A. Positive, negative, neutral regarding various sexual facets of sexuality—body, behaviors, fantasies. Partner's perceptions, roles of men and women and role of sex in marriage.
   B. Current Behavior
      (Pursued as relevant to the sexual problem). Noncoital activity, homosexuality, affairs, communication, overall relationship, life-style.
   C. Nature of the Sexual Problem
      Description, length of time, ideas of cause, impact on partner, solutions attempted.
   D. Additional details needed relevant to the specific dysfunction.
   E. Anything else the client thinks may bear on the sexual problem.

allow the client to present information at a comfortable pace and depth. Added inquiries along the way can produce needed missing details.

This type of outline suggests the importance sex therapy places on a comprehensive assessment of sexual history and current attitudes and experiences in the context of the sexual problem and the role of sexuality in the client's life. An important goal is to understand how attitudes, values, and experiences might have produced negative learnings such as ignorance, myths, and painful emotions in association with sex. This cognitive-behavioral focus continues to characterize sex therapy today.

GENERAL TREATMENT PROCEDURES

Sex therapists routinely acknowledge that the dyad is the preferred unit of treatment. But an accompanying assumption is that sex therapy requires a couple with a sufficiently strong bond and without major relationship problems, and individuals without psychopathology. The reasoning is that these criteria are necessary for partners to carry out their conjoint sensual and sexual tasks (Masters & Johnson, 1970). Kaplan (1974, 1979) specifically recommends marital therapy, not sex therapy, for couples with relationship problems severe enough to prevent cooperative effort towards remedying the sexual dysfunction. With this legacy, most standard sex therapy procedures assume a cooperative, committed dyad; therefore, the interventions directly focus on helping partners to learn to experience a positive, pleasurable, non-demand sensual/sexual relationship. This experiential process should also enrich the couple's overall relationship, strengthen their sense of being a team, and increase their mutual respect and attraction.

This point is highly relevant to the following discussion of techniques. The techniques are described as they were developed for relatively stable couples who could carry out the required cooperative tasks. The fact is, however, is that many individual and couple clients do not meet the high standards of emotional and relationship health suggestive of their readiness for traditional sex therapy. And the IST model of treatment advocated in this book will not maintain these distinctions. But before proceeding to the IST model, the reader needs an understanding of the major techniques of traditional sex therapy.

A number of procedures are generic in the sense that they are appropriate to any sexual dissatisfaction or dysfunction. That is, the therapist may incorporate these in varying degrees prior to or concurrent with techniques designed to alleviate specific dysfunctions. These generic strategies are discussed first.

Providing Sexual Information and Education

The new knowledge of human sexuality and the sexual response came out of the pioneering work of Masters and Johnson (1966, 1970). Their four-stage cycle, based on physiological research, consists of excitement, plateau, orgasm, and resolution. They hypothesize that these stages naturally occur unless inhibited by factors such as performance anxiety or internalized religious, cultural, and parental negative injunctions and stereotypes about sexuality.

As clients began to present with lack of desire for sex, therapists were stymied as to how this complaint would fit into the sexual response cycle. Kaplan modified the sexual response cycle to a triphasic model consisting of desire, arousal, and orgasm (Kaplan, 1979). Subsequently, additional refinements were added. Descriptions of sexual dysfunction now allow for the person's subjective evaluation of a given phase of the sexual response, not simply physiological reactions of the body. Another refinement is the view that the various stages of sexual response are more or less independent (Zilbergeld and Ellison, 1980). For example, a person could have no desire for sex, but engage in it, and perhaps even experience orgasm, without a subjective sense or even much physiological evidence of arousal. These refinements have expanded understanding of the human sexual response.

Having accurate knowledge about the sexual response is critical to the provision of sexual information and education. The therapist assesses sexual ignorance, misinformation, myths and stereotypes, and other client cognitions. Offering new information and promoting positive sexual attitudes are essential in moving the client to experience sensual enjoyment. These new attitudes or outlooks replace the client's performance demands on self and partner for the end goal of intercourse and orgasm. In treatment, the therapist challenges commonly held myths such as good women are uninterested in sex; women should appear sexy but not be sexual; simultaneous orgasm through intercourse is the "normal" way to enjoy sex; and males are always ready for sex and are responsible for the female's orgasm.

There is no precise formula for the provision of information and education. According to Annon (1976), information and education alone may resolve many sexual problems. The PLISSIT model (an acronym) identifies four levels of increasing complexity for treating problems. At the simplest level, *P*ERMISSION regarding sexual concerns or inhibitions may suffice to resolve a client's problem. Next *LI*MITED INFORMATION specific to the problem may lead to solution. *S*PECIFIC *S*UGGESTIONS encompassing one or several at-home sensual or intimacy exercises may be effective for sexual dissatisfactions or some dysfunctions. The last level, *I*NTENSIVE *T*HERAPY, generally refers to comprehensive sex therapy consisting of full assessment and a series of carefully planned interventions carried out in a brief therapy format.

An informal but directly educative style appears to be the norm. For example, Masters and Johnson (1970) held "roundtable" discussions with clients. And early group methods for treating dysfunctions typically included minilectures, assigned readings, group discussions, communication exercises, and films used for assessing and restructuring attitudes (Cole, 1983). In therapy sessions, the most effective method for providing information and education will likely be one that is uniquely tailored to the client It is respectful and sensitively attuned to his or her readiness and learning style. It considers the quality of the therapeutic relationship. And it incorporates the therapist's unique style of communicating.

The strong informational and educational component of sex therapy has remained. In fact, this component is central in the numerous self-help books authored by well-known sex therapists (e.g., Barbach, 1975, 1980; Heiman & LoPiccolo, 1976, 1988; Kaplan, 1989; McCarthy & McCarthy, 1984, 1988, 1989; Zilbergeld, 1978). The assumption is that information and education may enable some readers, without professional therapy, to remedy their own sexual dysfunctions and dissatisfactions. These sources also commonly contain directions for carrying out the same at-home exercises typically assigned during sex therapy. Professionals unfamiliar with the sex therapy literature will find ideas in the self-help materials for providing information and education to clients and for assigning the at-home tasks. For example, the therapist may give a photocopy or paraphrase of a book's description of a given task; the printed word can serve to reinforce and augment verbal instructions.

Cognitive Restructuring

Cognitive restructuring is an extension of the information/education strategy, but it directly focuses on the goal of attitude change. It involves challenges to the client's deeply ingrained automatic thought patterns that are irrational, self-defeating, or destructive to sexuality and sexual goals. These latter could encompass the myths cited above that remain in spite of information and education. They may also extend to other cognitions about the nature of the problem or of sexual contact or sexual experience; views of the self or partner as sexual beings; the meaning of the marriage or relationship; and expectations and evaluations of self and partner during the sexual act.

The exact method and timing for implementing cognitive restructuring is a critical question left to the clinician's judgment. The general process probably begins even in the first session, and it is reinforced as well in the instructions and content of many of the at-home tasks. But more direct cognitive-restructuring procedures may be necessary, such as analysis and rebuttal of beliefs on the basis of irrationality or faulty logic. The range of cognitive methods would be applicable here (Dobson, 1988; Goldfried & Davison, 1976; Lazarus, 1989). Also Kaplan (1974, 1979) suggests the use of psychodynamic methods to break through defenses that support self-defeating cognitions. In terms of timing, McCarthy (1989) notes that a common therapist error is to emphasize cognitive change prior to clients' doing behavioral assignments. Integration of the cognitive restructuring with other elements of sex therapy is likely to be most effective.

At-Home Behavioral/Experiential Assignments

Sensual or sexual homework is what many lay persons and professionals think of as constituting sex therapy. Although that is an oversimplification, tasks are integral to and reinforcing of the information/educational and cognitive restructuring components. The therapist uses tasks in a planful manner based on assessment of the client's situation and on what has been accomplished in the therapy sessions. Then the clients' reports of their experience in doing the assignments provide data for ongoing assessment and critical material to work with therapeutically.

The detailed instructions that accompany an assigned task are essential to maximize its potential success. They also embody information and new attitudes and values about sex that the therapist has likely introduced during clinical interviews and discussions. The content, instructions, and manner of presenting a task will determine its effectiveness; printed as well as verbal directions may be appropriate for many clients. For thorough discussions of the tasks and instructions to clients, the reader is referred to Masters and Johnson (1970), Kaplan (1974, 1979), Heiman and LoPiccolo (1988), and Zilbergeld (1978).

The following section briefly describes tasks that are often part of the treatment plan for any of the sexual dysfunctions or dissatisfactions. A subsequent section reviews tasks to remedy specific dysfunctions. Therapist judgment is always the key factor in assigning any task. There must be clarity about the its purpose in the treatment plan and belief in the client's readiness to carry it out so as to achieve that purpose.

Sensate focus, developed by Masters and Johnson (1970), consists of a series of pleasuring exercises. The first level calls for partners to take turns pleasuring each other via gently caressing or massaging the whole body, but omitting the breasts and genitals (and maintaining a moratorium on intercourse). The couple is instructed to focus only on sensation either through giving or receiving; the experience is not to be sexual. It is to be done under certain ideal conditions: the partners are feeling good about each other; they will plan it so as to have time, energy, and privacy; and communication during the experience will consist only of positive suggestions to the partner that will enhance pleasure.

The next level of sensate focus repeats the above process, but permits breast and genital caressing (only for the purpose of sensual, not sexual experience). Further levels encompass focused genital touching, various stages of sensually focused intercourse, and restraint of orgasm. Additional discussion of sensate focus in the section on tasks for arousal disorders shows the step-wise progression of the pleasuring exercises. Masters and Johnson (1970) emphasize that the therapist never prescribes orgasm.

Although sensate focus became the sine qua non of standard sex therapy, more recent positions question routine prescription of this task. It may not be suited to certain dysfunctions or to a client's unique personal characteristics, history, or life situation (Heiman, 1986; Leiblum, Pervin & Campbell, 1989; J. Woody, 1989). Sensate focus may be antitherapeutic for the person experiencing hypoactive sexual desire or sexual aversion. For example, as one client reported in response to the assignment: "The cure is worse than the disease."

Prohibiting sexual intercourse is a directive that is routinely given as part of the sensate focus task, but it is a powerful intervention in and of itself. It is the behavioral correlate of the cognitive challenge to the myth that intercourse and orgasm are the essence of sexual fulfillment. It relieves both partners from the cognitive expectation of sexual performance and the anxiety attendant to that and the spectator anxiety stemming from prior failures. In conjunction with sensate focus, prohibiting intercourse frees partners to experience and relearn sensual pleasure both as giver and receiver. But this directive may create other benefits based on other theoretical assumptions. For example, it can immediately interrupt the conditioning process whereby sexual encounters are associated with physical pain or highly negative emotional and cognitive responses. And it may have other far-reaching effects based on a systemic understanding of sexual dysfunction; these are discussed in later chapters.

Although prohibiting sexual intercourse can be a powerful behavioral intervention, it may not be routinely necessary or appropriate; one must recall that Masters and Johnson (1970) devised it for a 2-week intensive, in-residence treatment format. Experience with outpatient formats, which are typical of the actual practice of sex therapy, suggest that this, as with any intervention, should be tailored to the overall assessment of the client's situation and problem.

Guiding partner's touch takes partners beyond the first two levels of sensate focus. In this stage, the partners take turns in placing their own hand on the partner's hand so as to give nonverbal guidance in genital caressing. This serves to educate the partner about the kind of sensual touch one enjoys.

Sharing information about masturbation is a task that encourages a couple to share and demonstrate for the partner one's own effective masturbation techniques. It is a way of giving permission for partners to give and receive pleasure. It attacks the myth that partners should automatically know what pleases the other. It increases the ability to communicate honestly about sex and the kind of activity that is pleasurable.

The partner-guided genital exam is suggested by Masters and Johnson (1970) as a task to assure that each partner is thoroughly familiar with the other's genitalia. This task can enable partners to break through inhibitions about looking at or having an interest in sex organs. They often learn of parts of which they were unaware or of names for them or of their response to touch. It can permit them to become aware of attitudes or emotional responses that figure into the problem.

Experiencing explicit erotic literature and films is a way for the client to remove inhibitions and increase awareness of the variety of sexual behaviors, some of which they may want to add to their own repertoire. This task is aligned with the humanistic-experiential approach to sex therapy. Recently sex therapists have acknowledged the potential antitherapeutic impact of this task for some clients and urge caution in assigning it (Heiman, 1986).

Presensate focus tasks encompass a variety of assignments judged to be necessary prior to assigning the direct pleasuring exercises. They are designed to accomplish several purposes, for example, to foster intimacy without the anxiety some clients might anticipate with the sensate focus or to help clients change life style patterns that devalue togetherness and the sexual relationship (Annon, 1976). These might include planning and going on "dates," spending time together communicating, or sharing affection, attention, and appreciation without any sexual overtones. For some dysfunctions, especially sexual desire problems, it may be necessary to prohibit any sexual behavior in order to foster the goals of presensate focus tasks.

The mirror exercise requires the client, in a private, at-home situation, to stand alone nude in front of a full-length mirror and visually and kinesthetically explore all parts of the body, including genitals, and to verbally express or note attitudes about each body part. The client then brings back to the therapy session these written or remembered responses for review. The aim is to resolve physical and sexual self-esteem problems that are likely contributors to the sexual problem (Hartman & Fithian, 1972; Heiman & LoPiccolo, 1988).

The conjoint medical examination is a procedure conducted by a physician-sex therapist in which the treating doctor can give and receive information as the gynecological and urological examinations are done in the presence of the spouse. It may be particularly valuable for a couple in which the wife experiences vaginismus or dyspareunia. Its use, however, is obviously restricted if the sex therapist is not also a physician or if a physician-sex therapist is not available as a referral resource.

Communicating about sexual needs, wishes, and sensations may encompass various aspects of sexually-focused communication. It can be as simple as asking the couple to discuss and decide when or if they will have sex, to share their sexual attitudes, to ask for a particular type of sex or sensual stimulation or behavioral accompaniment, or to learn effective ways of initiating and refusing sex. The goal is to encourage open and effective communication about sexuality and thus remove it from the realms of taboo and mind-reading (Masters & Johnson, 1970; LoPiccolo, 1978). Many of the tasks described above obviously are intended to promote more honest and comfortable communication about sex.

The tasks described thus far could be useful for any of the sexual dysfunctions or sexual complaints. The therapist, however, selects and assigns a task on the basis of an assessment of the client's unique situation and a judgment that the task will accomplish a therapeutic goal that is part of the overall treatment plan. For example, the suggestion to read erotic literature may be appropriate only at certain stages of therapy or for clients who indicate this could enhance sensuality.

Procedures for Specific Dysfunctions

Each of the different sexual dysfunctions has unique factors. The understanding of these led to development of specific procedures that seemed to work best with a given dysfunction. The following reviews what sex therapy offers for treating specific dysfunctions.

DESIRE DISORDERS

Desire disorders include *hypoactive sexual desire* and *sexual aversion*. The early sex therapy literature did not recognize or address these problems until Kaplan (1979), and most subsequent experts have noted the limitations of traditional sex therapy for desire dysfunctions. The more recent trend in treatment is to emphasize in-office psychotherapeutic methods and also to adapt the homework tasks for each clinical situation. The following discussion highlights several adaptations, but devising behavioral tasks is limited only by the therapist's theoretical, clinical, and creative capacities.

In vivo desensitization is a procedure useful in treating sexual aversion; it consists of the assignment of low-level intimacy tasks that are developed with the client. Kaplan (1979) uses this technique for both behavioral and psychodynamic goals. The initial goal is to eliminate the client's phobic avoidance of sexual situations, contacts, and acts. Such tasks might include having the couple simply lie close together while clothed, exchange brief touches or casual kisses, or have the phobic client stroke herself or himself in the presence of the partner. The client is to stop the task only in the face of intolerable negative feelings. When the client reports reactions to the task, the therapist moves into a pychotherapeutic mode to deal with resistances. Once phobic avoidance subsides, the client may be able to benefit from other standard sex therapy tasks.

With hypoactive sexual desire, the goal is to change the tendency to inhibit erotic impulses. Psychotherapy is the main mode for addressing this problem, but assigned tasks may aid in evoking material for psychodynamic analysis. Kaplan (1979) acknowledges, however, that only a small percentage of clients with this problem will respond positively to sensual tasks. Yet, if careful assessment indicates their use, the therapist may assign sensate focus and then nondemand coitus (i.e., slow, rhythmical, sensual movement with no thrusting for orgasm). The client's psychic responses to the tasks then become the focus of such psychodynamic methods as support, encouragement, interpretation, and confrontation. Apfelbaum (1989) recommends having the couple do a detailed, written report of their responses to the tasks; he also uses a 50-item Script Lines Checklist for this same purpose of generating material for use in psychotherapy.

As noted earlier, the current literature continues to point to the limitations of standard sex therapy with desire disorders. Behavioral tasks which do not require sensual or sexual contact may accomplish diverse therapeutic goals (Zilbergeld & Ellison, 1980; J. Woody, 1989). A few will be cited shortly, and later chapters will further explore their theoretical rationales.

Proscribing all sexual contact between partners (or for an individual) is often an effective initial intervention. This is especially true if the low desire partner continues to engage in sex at the partner's requests or demands, perhaps out of guilt or other motives. Such encounters often produce various negative outcomes for both—anger, resentment, numbness, boredom, disgust, depression, etc. Couples often readily agree, sometimes with relief, to stop this damaging, aversive practice.

The sexual log or diary is a form of cognitive-behavioral self-monitoring of various aspects of one's sexuality. The therapist gives the client a form that contains columns indicating: date; day of menstrual cycle (for women); sexual interest or response (genital sensation, image, fantasy); situation evoking these; emotions experienced; cognitions about these (thoughts, evaluations, attributions); and actions taken. As with any type of cognitive-behavioral monitoring, this assignment can serve many purposes. For example, it can provide needed base-line data, efficiently reveal detailed sexual data about the client for assessment and treatment, give the client permission to focus on suppressed internal and external sexual cues, increase awareness of all aspects of one's sexuality, and encourage insight into the relationship between sexual stimuli, emotions, cognitions, and behavior. In addition, it can serve as a low-level in vivo desensitization procedure. Finally, operating paradoxically, the sexual log may enable some clients to increase sexual activity precisely because it does not ask for this.

Fantasy training may take several forms. One assignment asks the client to create a sexual fantasy. That is, the client is to think about and write up a sexual scenario or fantasy that would seem enjoyable or ideal. This too can serve many of the functions cited for the sexual log. For example, female clients with desire problems often create romantic fantasies that are devoid of physical or sensual elements. A related task suggests that the client consciously take fantasy breaks for several minutes during the day to daydream about or have a sexual fantasy.

The mirror exercise described above may be appropriate for the client with a desire problem. It can increase awareness of body image and sensation and accompanying affects. It also encourages labeling of these processes and working through of associated negative evaluations and emotions that may contribute to low desire or sexual aversion.

Experts acknowledge desire problems to be the most difficult of the dysfunctions to treat. Their complexity has actually served as the impetus to expand standard sex therapy. Typically, the few efforts by sex therapists to incorporate systemic thinking in sex therapy have focused on this dysfunction (LoPiccolo & Friedman, 1986; Rosen & Leiblum, 1989; Zilbergeld & Ellison, 1980). The need for innovations in treating desire disorders has led to the multitheoretical approach to sexual and intimacy problems espoused in this book.

AROUSAL DISORDERS

Arousal disorders received much of the attention in early sex therapy, with homework tasks being a major component. These are now termed female sexual arousal disorder and male erectile disorder. Masters and Johnson (1970) developed in considerable detail the stepwise progression to use in assigning tasks for arousal disorders. These appear in the following brief list in the typical order of assignment. Although the procedure is essentially the same for either male erectile disorder or female arousal disorder, additional comments clarify if a given step applies only to one. As with all homework tasks, clients report back to the therapist their experience so that this feedback becomes the basis for in-session clinical work and decisions about assigning the next step. Only tasks not previously described are explained. The series of tasks include the following:

1. Proscribing sexual intercourse for the couple.
2. Sensate Focus I.
3. Sensate Focus II.
4. Teasing technique. Partner stimulates genitals but is to stop as this becomes arousing and then starts again after arousal subsides. For the male, this permits learning that erections come and go and thus removes anxiety about a flaccid penis.
5. Sensate Focus III. Taking turns as the giver and receiver, partners may, if they wish, manually stimulate each other to orgasm.
6. Intravaginal containment. Female in astride position and in control, inserts penis, but does not move; focus is to be only on sensation.
7. Coital teasing technique. As in the prior teasing technique, the female moves gently and then stops when sensations become arousing.
8. Nondemand female movement. Slow, rhythmical movement only, with neither partner moving with rapid thrusting for orgasm.
9. Male slow sensual thrusting (for erectile dysfunction) in which he is in control of movement.
10. Simultaneous pelvic pleasuring. Both partners may move to enhance and enjoy pleasurable sensations.

11. Restraint from ejaculation (for male erectile disorder).
12. Vigorous intercourse if the couple wishes.

The overall goals of this procedure are to slow down dramatically the couple's sexual encounter, to permit only sensual experience, and to remove concerns about coital orgasm. The therapist never tells the couple to go on to or try for coital orgasm, even in the last stage. The effectiveness of the whole procedure is likely due to its multitheoretical richness; that is, it can potentially tap into and modify many of the psychological, cognitive, behavioral, and dyadic contributors to arousal dysfunctions. The experiential tasks are only part of standard sex therapy, but this form of treatment may not prove effective for arousal disorders that are both lifelong and generalized.

Kaplan (1974) added other dimensions of these exercises. Distracting obsessional thoughts is a suggestion that the client counter obsessive thoughts during the pleasuring sessions with favorite sexual fantasies. For example, a male client would be asked to become aware of an exciting fantasy that he has had; then if he begins to obsess about his wife's opinion of him or whether she is getting tired, he is to shift consciously to the fantasy; because sexual fantasies are often quite vivid and enjoyable, they can take the place of obsessive thinking. Permission to be selfish is a behavioral directive for one partner (with the other partner's knowledge) during pleasuring to be selfish, disregard the other's needs, and focus on one's own gratification; this is a refinement of the principle of "taking turns" devised by Masters and Johnson (1970).

In addition to the couple sensual pleasuring steps listed above, other experiential tasks could benefit a given client's situation. For example, presensate focus, the mirror exercise, the sexual log, fantasy training, and especially for females, self-exploration and self-stimulation (the latter is explained next).

ORGASMIC DYSFUNCTIONS

It is in the treatment of orgasmic dysfunctions (especially inhibited female orgasm and premature ejaculation) that traditional sex therapy is assumed to be quite effective. Kaplan (1989) most recently asserts that 95% of premature ejaculators "attain satisfactory control . . . within an average of fourteen sessions of sex therapy" (pp. 59-60). Others are less optimistic on treatment for this disorder, as they now suspect that unknown organic factors are likely involved in lifelong and global premature ejaculation (Strassberg et al., 1988). This supposition may also apply to some women whose orgasm dysfunction is unresponsive to treatment; but there is much less research on neurophysiological bases of orgasm in women than for men (Heiman & Grafton-Becker, 1989).

Premature Ejaculation

The behavioral/experiential tasks for premature ejaculation (PE) are quite straightforward, and a precise step-wise progression is essential. Since Masters and Johnson (1970), others have added to or refined the basic stages of the "squeeze technique" and given more emphasis to cognitive factors (Kaplan, 1974, 1989; LoPiccolo & LoPiccolo, 1978; McCarthy, 1989; Perelman, 1980). Rather than the squeeze technique, Semans' (1956) original "stop-start" method is now preferred. Once the couple begins the stop-start procedure (described below), the general instruction is for them to do a given stage three to four times or even daily over the course of one week. This suggested schedule should, however, be reasonably adapted to the age and situation of the client. Clients report back to the therapist, and as they successfully accomplish each stage, they are permitted to proceed to the next. The stages of the stop-start procedure are

1. Prohibiting intercourse until the assigned exercise permits it.
2. Private masturbation is suggested as the first stage for the man to gain awareness of the premonitory sensation (PS) that signals ejaculatory inevitability (EI). He is to concentrate only on the pleasurable sensations and on enjoying these. When he becomes aware of PS, and well before the point of EI, he is to stop stimulation and let the erection partially subside. At that point he begins stimulation again. He is to use this stop-start method four times and then ejaculate. He is told to expect times when he does not stop early enough during this learning process, and if that occurs, to simply enjoy the orgasm, and do the exercise again on the next scheduled day.
3. Sensate Focus (optional).
4. Providing female partner with manual or oral orgasm, if desired, in a context other than the male's stop-start exercises (optional).
5. Stop-start procedure with partner.

a. The partner provides manual stimulation with the male signaling when to stop; both are told that he should be selfish and focus only on his own sensation and pleasure. As above and in the following stages, the stop-start series proceeds four times and ends with the male's ejaculation. The couple proceeds to the next stage as the male experiences control in the previous one and as directed by the therapist.
b. Manual stimulation by partner with use of lubricant.
c. Oral stimulation by partner (if compatible with couple's values).
d. Vaginal containment ("quiet vagina"). Female in on top position guides intromission for the purpose of vaginal containment and later for gentle movement guided by her partner. Again, stop-start takes place four times.
e. Intercourse positions other than the male on top and different kinds of thrusting. This may consist of several stages. Stop-start applies.
f. Male on top position with slow, non-demand thrusting. Stop-start applies.
g. Incorporating a slow-down approach, but not stopping, in thrusting.
h. As needed, the couple can continue to use the slow-down approach in their preferred intercourse positions as a regular and positive element in sex.

Inhibited Female Orgasm

The behavioral tasks used in the current treatment of inhibited female orgasm nearly always center on sensual self-exploration and self-stimulation, which is generally labeled masturbation training or directed masturbation (LoPiccolo & Lobitz, 1978). Other experiential tasks to increase all aspects of self-awareness also often accompany directed masturbation. The guiding principle is to begin with tasks that have a low sensual/sexual focus on the assumption that the woman will be able to do these without experiencing the kind of anxiety that inhibits her orgasm. This gradual exposure to increasingly sensual/sexual experiences enables her to relax and learn about and enjoy her body. The following list contains a progression of major tasks that sex therapists often employ to promote conditions in which a woman may learn to experience orgasm. The self-help books on this topic are especially rich in detailed descriptions and instructions which are useful to the clinician (Barbach, 1975, 1980; Heiman & LoPiccolo, 1988). Tasks described previously are listed but not explained.

1. Reviewing one's sex education, sex history, and sex attitudes, etc.
2. Doing the mirror exercise.
3. Kegel exercises. The woman consciously practices contracting and relaxing the vaginal (pubococcygeal) muscles in order to increase acceptance and awareness of and potential for genital sensation.
4. Keeping a sexual log.
5. Doing the hand mirror exercise. She examines her genitals thoroughly with a magnifying hand mirror to become familiar with and accepting of all parts of the genitalia.
6. Fantasy training.
7. Bodily self-exploration (as in Sensate Focus I).
8. Bodily self-exploration including genitals and breasts (Sensate Focus II).
9. Focused genital touching for discovering pleasurable types of stimulation.
10. Use of fantasy to increase sensual focus and distract intruding thoughts (or perhaps to trigger orgasm).
11. Role-playing orgasm in order to elicit and confront unconscious emotions that may be inhibiting the orgasmic response.
12. Focused genital stimulation to intensify arousal and pleasure.
13. Use of vibrator for sensual genital stimulation.

When the woman attains orgasm through self-stimulation and if she chooses to involve her partner, the subsequent experiential tasks typically begin with the sensate focus exercises and others described in detail above in the section on general tasks and those for arousal disorders (e.g., Sensate Focus I, II, teasing technique, partner guided genital exam, guiding partners touch, sharing information about masturbation, Sensate Focus III, etc.). The woman may wish to have an orgasm through self-stimulation with her partner present and/or to have the partner stimulate her. At some point she may wish to try the slow, nondemand coital movements to maximize her experience of pleasurable vaginal sensations. Since many women do not readily experience coital orgasm, this may nor may not interest her. It is important that these choices remain with the woman.

One final point merits emphasis. The above are the steps as developed within traditional sex therapy. But this does not mean that sex therapists prescribe them in an automatic way. The clinician always judges whether the typical progression is advisable for a given client. For women who are strongly opposed to masturbation, it is necessary to devise other strategies. Perhaps before any behavioral/experiential tasks are assigned, other therapeutic goals must be accomplished. Or it may be appropriate to start with sensate focus with her partner.

Inhibited Male Orgasm

Inhibited male orgasm is, according to the DSM-III-R (American Psychiatric Association, 1987), the failure to reach orgasm, "usually restricted to an inability to reach orgasm in the vagina" (p. 295). Masters and Johnson (1970) differentiated "ejaculatory incompetence" as the *inability* to ejaculate from retarded ejaculation as *difficulty* in ejaculating. They reported it to be relatively rare, and others have agreed (Apfelbaum, 1980, 1989; LoPiccolo & Stock, 1986). However, Birch (1991) believes that retarded ejaculation, not restricted to vaginal intercourse, is not so rare. It is necessary to keep in mind, however, that the sexual dysfunction diagnosis does not apply if the dysfunction is attributable entirely to organic factors (e.g., the effects of drugs) or to a mental disorder. Treatment would certainly differ if organic causes were assessed to be primary.

There is considerable disagreement about its nature, etiology, and tasks used in the treatment of inhibited male orgasm. The controversy as discussed below applies to inability to reach orgasm in the partner's vagina.

Masters and Johnson (1970) and Kaplan (1974) recommend the following progression of stages, with Kaplan's added steps noted, as assigned tasks:

1. Prohibition of intercourse and orgasm initially.
2. Sensate focus exercises with female partner.
3. Male is to manipulate female to orgasm, both to meet her sexual needs and to experience and benefit from his own arousal at her pleasure.

4. Male is given permission to ejaculate but only in the manner in which he knows he will be able to do this, e.g., masturbation in private or with partner present (Kaplan, 1974).
5. Female partner is to manually stimulate penis demandingly, asking male for input as to what is most stimulating.
6. Her manual stimulation should be with penis in close proximity to her vagina (Kaplan, 1974).
7. At the point of ejaculatory inevitability from manual stimulation, she is to move to rapid intromission in female on top position and demanding pelvic thrusting.
8. If he does not ejaculate, they stop intercourse and return to manual stimulation.
9. The goal is for him to ejaculate in proximity or partially into the vagina in order to break his mental block against this act.

Apfelbaum (1980, 1984, 1989) strongly rejects this experiential approach. He views this male dysfunction as similar to inhibited female orgasm and accuses Masters and Johnson and Kaplan of sexism in their forceful and demanding approach, which only serves to increase performance demands for the male. He asserts that it is a mistake to assume that erection means arousal since automatic erections are common to men with this disorder. The male also typically accepts the beliefs that his behavior means that he is ungiving, that he should enjoy his partner's touch, and that he should have coital orgasm. As a result of these beliefs, he often develops a compulsion to please his partner and becomes a "sexual workhorse."

Apfelbaum (1980, 1984, 1989) recommends an "ego-analytic" strategy of encouraging the client to express suppressed feelings (his lack of arousal and negative feelings of distance, hostility, and of being used by his partner). This strategy can validate his own unaccepted experience and relieve him of performance demands. Sensate pleasuring sessions are used primarily to elicit feelings, faulty beliefs, and obsessions to process in therapy.

It is unfortunate, as Apfelbaum himself acknowledges, that most of his work with this dysfunction has involved not couples but the use of female body-work therapists. "This method is a revision of Masters and Johnson's surrogate partner program in which . . . paraprofessional staff members . . . function both as co-therapists in the therapy sessions and as body-work therapists in sessions [private] comparable to those in which couples carry out their assignments"

(Apfelbaum, 1989, p. 192). He does not comment on ethical/legal issues but does note that this approach is not used by other sex therapists. It is quite surprising to see this method presented in a professional text (Leiblum & Rosen, 1989) without the authors' or editors' mentioning the ethical and legal questions and risks associated with it.

In summary, Apfelbaum's (1980, 1984, 1989) view of inhibited male orgasm implies but does not acknowledge its likely etiological complexity that could encompass individual organic, developmental, learning, and intimacy factors as well as a couple's relationship dynamics and patterns. These factors merit exploration whether the problem appears within heterosexual or gay relationships or with masturbation.

PAIN DISORDERS

The last category of sexual dysfunctions, pain disorders, includes vaginismus and dyspareunia, with the latter mostly limited to females. Males rarely have pain as a complaint for which they seek therapy; more often it is due to organic etiology and requires medical treatment.

Vaginismus

For vaginismus, the sex therapy components of information and education, cognitive-restructuring, and psychodynamic analysis are important. And the comprehensive assessment serves as the basis for developing a therapeutic plan. Regarding behavioral tasks, many of the presensate focus and other tasks listed in the general section above could be appropriate. One important assignment is the conjoint gynecological examination in which the partner is present for the woman's gynecological examination so that they both receive information and education from the examining physician about the female genitalia and the involuntary vaginal spasm. Other general tasks might include Kegel exercises, fantasy training, and sensate focus.

The main set of at-home experiences for treatment of vaginismus is unique to this disorder. The goal is to enable the woman to learn gradually to insert objects of increasing size into the vagina comfortably and without experiencing the spasm. Since Masters and Johnson's (1970) and Kaplan's (1974) early work with this method, more recent sex therapists have modified it to give greater control and responsibility to the woman (Leiblum et al., 1989). Medical dilators (Hegar) and flexible silicone (Mylex), unbreakable Pyrex tubes of graduated sizes, or her own fingers serve for this process. Training in relaxation and perhaps systematic desensitization may be necessary before the client is ready for the at-home assignments. There is no prescribed amount of time that this process should take, but, as always in sex therapy, the client reports back to the therapist on reactions to and results of doing the tasks. This feedback provides important content for therapeutic sessions and for devising subsequent interventions and tasks.

Under her own control and in private, the woman starts, while maintaining a relaxed state, inserting the smallest dilator, tube, or her little finger. The use of a lubricant as well as focus on sexual arousal can facilitate the process. She proceeds with objects of increasing size until she can comfortably insert several fingers or the dilator the size of a penis. She may then proceed to repeat this same process with her partner present, although an alternate approach has him present from the beginning with her as she uses the dilators. When the woman is ready for the next stage, she has the partner touch the vaginal area and next proceed with inserting the objects of gradually increasing size, with intromission to follow only after these prior experiences are successful. Again, these exercises are done only with the woman's permission, readiness, and stated sense of being in control.

Dyspareunia

Dyspareunia, or painful intercourse, may result from numerous organic conditions; so a thorough physical and gynecological/urological examination is essential, before undertaking sex therapy, to rule out organic causes of the pain. In practical terms, treatment issues center on women because genital pain experienced by men typically has an organic cause. Because psychogenic dyspareunia likely has multiple causation, a broad-based therapeutic approach is indicated. Neither Masters and Johnson (1970) nor Kaplan (1974, 1979) mentioned sex therapy for this disorder in their early works. LoPiccolo and LoPiccolo (1978) noted that affective responses such as fears, guilt, and shame may lead to the psychosomatic pain reaction, although it may also be a learned response of anticipated anxiety due to a prior sexual event with actual discomfort. The only recommendation was for information and education, especially regarding the importance of lubrication.

Subsequent therapists, especially Lazarus (1980, 1989), employ a broad-based, eclectic therapeutic model, with emphasis on comprehensive assessment and on the use of basic cognitive-behavioral strategies. These might address not only specific sexual concerns but also general adjustment factors such as fears; obsessive-compulsive patterns; and self-esteem, coping, and interpersonal problems. On the basis of the comprehensive assessment, the therapist judges whether and when to assign any sensual/sexual tasks such as those described above. There is no set pattern or series of experiential tasks that is routinely recommended for this disorder. Since avoidance of sex is likely occurring in order for the woman to avoid physical and emotional pain, a possible first directive might be prohibiting intercourse.

Conclusion

In reviewing major principles and procedures, this chapter has attempted to capture the rich legacy of sex therapy. Information and education, attitude change through cognitive-restructuring, and psychodynamic intervention are typically integrated with selective use of at-home behavioral/experiential tasks. Some of these latter procedures are applicable to any dysfunction, whereas others address specific disorders.

The therapist's knowledge of sexuality and overall clinical competence are essential to carry out the comprehensive assessment necessary for treatment decisions. The succinct summaries of the various tasks or their progression appear in outline format for didactic purposes. These lists or stages do not direct the course of therapy; they are but one ingredient. It is the therapist who must make clinical judgments as to the appropriate use of behavioral assignments. Typically, only one task or one stage is assigned until the client feedback suggests, and the therapist judges, readiness to move to the next.

The procedures of traditional sex therapy have an important place in the IST treatment model for sexual distress. The overall goal of sex therapy is to promote new sexual learning through interventions that directly impact on thinking, feeling, sensing, imaging, and behaving. The most essential theoretical ingredients in traditional sex therapy derive from cognitive-behavioral theory. In later sections the contribution of sex therapy is termed the cognitive-behavioral dimension. The cognitive-behavioral dimension is one of five major components that comprise the IST model.

References

American Association of Sex Educators, Counselors, and Therapists. (1980). *Code of ethics*. Washington, DC: Author.

American Psychiatric Association. (1987). *Diagnostic and statistical manual, third edition revised (DSM-III-R)*. (1987). Washington, DC: Author.

Annon, J. S. (1976). *The behavioral treatment of sexual problems, revised edition, Vol. I: Brief therapy*. New York: Harper & Row.

Apfelbaum, B. (1980). The diagnosis and treatment of retarded ejaculation. In S. R. Leiblum & L. A. Pervin (Eds.), *Principles and practice of sex therapy* (pp. 263-296). New York: Guilford Press.

Apfelbaum, B. (1984). The ego-analytic approach to individual body-work sex therapy: Five case examples. *Journal of Sex Research, 20*,(1), 44-70.

Apfelbaum, B. (1989). Retarded ejaculation: A much-misunderstood syndrome. In S. R. Leiblum & R. C. Rosen (Eds.), *Principles and practice of sex therapy* (pp. 168-206). New York: Guilford Press.

Barbach, L. (1975). *For yourself: The fulfillment of female sexuality*. New York: Doubleday.

Barbach, L. (1980). *Women discover orgasm*. New York: Free Press.

Birch, R. (1991). Personal communication.

Cole, C. (1983). Sexual disorders and the family therapist. In J. D. Woody & R. H. Woody (Eds.), *Sexual issues in family therapy* (pp. 49-61). Rockville, MD: Aspen Systems.

Dobson, K. S. (1988). *Handbook of cognitive-behavioral therapies*. New York: Guilford Press.

Drug interactions and side effects index. (1991). Oradell, NY: Medical Economics Co. Inc.

Ellis, A. (1980). Treatment of erectile dysfunction. In S. R. Leiblum & L. A. Pervin (Eds.). *Principles and practice of sex therapy* (pp. 235-261). New York: Guilford Press.

Goldfried, M. R. & Davison, G. C. (1976). *Clinical behavior therapy*. New York: Holt, Rinehart and Winston.

Haas, L. J., & Malouf, J. L. (1989). *Keeping up the good work: A practitioners' guide to mental health ethics*. Sarasota, FL: Professional Resource Exchange.

Hartman, W. E., & Fithian, M. A. (1972). *Treatment of sexual dysfunction*. Long Beach, CA: California Center for Medical and Sexual Studies.

Heiman, J. (1986). Treating sexually distressed marital relationships. In N. S. Jacobson & A. S. Gurman (Eds.), *Clinical handbook of marital therapy* (pp. 361-384). New York: Guilford Press.

Heiman, J. R., & Grafton-Becker, V. (1989). Orgasmic disorders in women. In S. R. Leiblum & R. C. Rosen (Eds.), *Principles and practice of sex therapy* (pp. 51-88). New York: Guilford Press.

Heiman, J. R., & LoPiccolo, J. (1988). *Becoming orgasmic: A sexual growth program for women*. New York: Prentice Hall.

Heiman, J. R., LoPiccolo, L., & LoPiccolo, J. (1976). *Becoming orgasmic: A sexual growth program for women*. Englewood Cliffs, NJ: Prentice-Hall.
Kaplan, H. S. (1974). *The new sex therapy*. New York: Brunner/Mazel.
Kaplan, H. S. (1979). *Disorders of sexual desire and other new concepts and techniques in sex therapy*. New York: Brunner/Mazel.
Kaplan, H. S. (1983). *The evaluation of sexual disorders*. New York: Brunner/Mazel.
Kaplan, H. S. (1987). *Sexual aversion, sexual phobias, and panic disorder*. New York: Brunner/Mazel.
Kaplan, H. S. (1989). *PE: How to overcome premature ejaculation*. New York: Brunner/Mazel.
Lazarus, A. A. (1980). Psychological treatment of dyspareunia. In S. R. Leiblum & L. A. Pervin (Eds.), *Principles and practice of sex therapy* (pp. 147-166). New York: Guilford Press.
Lazarus, A. A. (1989). Dyspareunia: A multimodal psychotherapeutic perspective. In S. R. Leiblum & R. C. Rosen (Eds.), *Principles and practice of sex therapy* (pp. 89-111). New York: Guilford Press.
Leiblum, S. R., Pervin, L. A., & Campbell, E. H. (1989). The treatment of vaginismus: Success and failure. In S. R. Leiblum & R. C. Rosen (Eds.), *Principles and practice of sex therapy* (pp. 113-138). New York: Guilford Press.
Leiblum, S. R., & Rosen, R. C. (Eds.). (1989). *Principles and practice of sex therapy*. New York: Guilford Press.
Lief, H. (1989, October 27). *Putting more family therapy into sex therapy and vice versa*. Paper presented at the annual meeting of the American Association for Marital and Family Therapy, San Francisco, CA.
LoPiccolo, J. (1978). Direct treatment of sexual disfunction. In J. LoPiccolo & L. LoPiccolo (Eds.). *Handbook of sex therapy* (pp. 1-18), New York: Plenum Press.
LoPiccolo, J., & Friedman, J. (1986). Sex therapy: An integrative model. In S. Lynn & J. Garske (Eds.), *Contemporary psychotherapies: Models and methods*. New York: Bobbs-Merrill.
LoPiccolo, L., & Heiman, J. (1978). Sexual assessment and history interview. In J. LoPiccolo & L. LoPiccolo (Eds.), *Handbook of sex therapy* (pp. 103-112). New York: Plenum Press.
LoPiccolo, J., & Lobitz, W. C. (1978). The role of masturbation in the treatment of orgasmic dysfunction. In J. LoPiccolo & L. LoPiccolo (Eds.), *Handbook of sex therapy* (pp. 187-194). New York: Plenum Press.
LoPiccolo, J., & LoPiccolo, L. (Eds.). (1978). *Handbook of sex therapy*. New York: Plenum Press.
LoPiccolo, J. & Stock, W. (1986). Treatment of sexual dysfunction. *Journal of Consulting and Clinical Psychology, 54*,(2), 158-167.
Masters, W. H., & Johnson, V. E. (1966). *Human sexual response*. New York: Little, Brown.
Masters, W. H., & Johnson, V. E. (1970). *Human sexual inadequacy*. New York: Little, Brown.
Masters, W. H., Johnson, V. E., & Kolodny, R. C. (1977). *Ethical issues in sex therapy and research*. New York: Little, Brown.
McCarthy, B. (1989). Cognitive-behavioral strategies and techniques in the treatment of early ejaculation. In S. R. Leiblum & R. C. Rosen (Eds.), *Principles and practice of sex therapy* (pp. 141-167). New York: Guilford Press.

McCarthy, B., & McCarthy, E. (1984). *Sexual awareness: Enhancing sexual pleasure.* New York: Carrol and Graf.

McCarthy, B., & McCarthy, E. (1988). *Male sexual awareness: Increasing sexual pleasure.* New York: Carrol and Graf.

McCarthy, B., & McCarthy, E. (1989). *Female sexual awareness: Achieving sexual fulfillment.* New York: Carrol and Graf.

Perelman, M. (1980). Treatment of premature ejaculation. In S. R. Leiblum & L. A. Pervin (Eds.). *Principles and practice of sex therapy* (pp. 199-233). New York: Guilford Press.

Rosen, R. C., & Leiblum, S. R. (1989). Assessment and treatment of desire disorders. In S. R. Leiblum & R. C. Rosen (Eds.), *Principles and practice of sex therapy* (pp. 19-47). New York: Guilford Press.

Schover, L. R., & vonEschenbach, A. C. (1985). Sex therapy and the penile prosthesis: A synthesis. *Journal of Sex & Marital Therapy, 11*, 57-66.

Semans, J. (1956). Premature ejaculation. *Southern Medical Journal, 48*, 352-358.

Strassberg, D. S., Mahoney, J. M., & Schaugaard, M. (1988, April). *Ejaculatory latency among premature ejaculators.* Paper presented at the annual meeting of the American Association of Sex Educators, Counselors and Therapists, San Francisco, CA.

Tiefer, L., & Melman, A. (1989). Comprehensive evaluation of erectile dysfunction and medical treatments. In S. R. Leiblum & R. C. Rosen (Eds.), *Principles and practice of sex therapy* (pp. 207-236). New York: Guilford Press.

Woods, N. F. (Ed.). (1984). *Human sexuality in health and illness* (3rd ed). St. Louis: C. V. Mosby.

Woody, J. D. (1989). The reality of an integrative sex therapy. *Journal of Sex & Marital Therapy, 1*(1), 62-73.

Woody, R. H. (1988). *Protecting your mental health practice: How to minimize legal and financial risk.* San Francisco: Jossey Bass.

Zilbergeld, B. (1978). *Male sexuality.* Boston: Little, Brown.

Zilbergeld, B., & Ellison, C. R. (1980). Desire discrepancies and arousal problems in sex therapy. In S. R. Leiblum & R. C. Rosen (Eds.), *Principles and practice of sex therapy* (pp. 66-101). New York: Guilford Press.

4

New Views with Systemic Lenses

> This we know, all things are connected, like the blood which unites one family. All things are connected. Whatever befalls the earth, befalls the sons of the earth. Man did not weave the web of life; he is merely a strand in it. Whatever he does to the web, he does to himself.
>
> CHIEF SEATTLE of the Dwamish Tribe

As Chapter 3 reveals, sex therapy directs professional attention to remedying the immediate sexual dysfunction. Treatment attacks the problem with: the provision of accurate anatomical and physiological information; the fostering of positive attitudes to replace stereotypes about sexual pleasure; and the authoritative permission to experience new sensual/sexual encounters in a relaxed, intimate atmosphere in which the natural sexual response can emerge. This method reflects the physiological bias of Masters and Johnson's research (1966, 1970). In their view, satisfying sex naturally occurs unless inhibited by ignorance, myths, and negative stereotypes that produce dreary, driven, mechanical, and unsensual encounters, the breeding ground of sexual dissatisfactions and dysfunctions.

Traditional sex therapy no doubt represents a significant advance in the treatment of sexual dysfunction. Yet clinical experience and closer analysis of the research have led to questions about early claims of its effectiveness (Slowinski, 1984; Zilbergeld & Kilmann, 1984). It is time to expand on this valuable method to increase understanding of the complexity of sexual and intimacy problems.

In the past few decades, a so-called "systems revolution" has led to innovations in treating families. In general, the systems view centers on "facts and events in the context of wholes, forming integrated sets with their own properties and relationships" (Laszlo, 1972, p. 19). Beyond this general focus, however, systems thinking has spawned diverse forms of family therapy. Each model typically emphasizes one or a few facets of systems. For example, some stress structure; others, process; and still others, the family in a temporal perspective. It is as if each model markets its own specially designed camera lens, with its unique focus and shutter time and accompanying directions for use. By design, each lens (or therapy model) can render only a certain perspective of a problem. To get a different perspective, one must change to a different lens.

Systems thinking is beginning to affect sex therapy, but in a piecemeal fashion. The few applications that are in the literature typically address either certain clinical impasses such as client resistance or the hard-to-treat desire disorders. Thus far, few efforts attempt serious integration of systems therapies and traditional sex therapy; the common pattern is to apply first one and then the other approach. And none has considered the utility of systemic treatment for the entire range of sexual distress.

What can the major systemic models of therapy contribute to the treatment of these problems? This chapter answers that question. First, it identifies and explains four broad systemic facets that are relevant to sexual distress and the models they derive from. These are the sociocultural environment, family structure, family communication/interaction sequence, and the individual/family-of-origin interface. Major concepts and techniques associated with the four systemic facets are highlighted since these are components of integrative systems therapy, which will be detailed in Chapter 5. The discussion of the four systemic facets below also notes the few examples in the current literature that apply the concepts specifically to sexual dysfunction.

Theoretical Foundations

General systems theory and cybernetics serve as the overarching theoretical foundation for systemic therapies. General systems theory refers to all "self-regulating systems, of which the cybernetic or feedback model is one type" (Nichols, 1984, p. 128).

General systems theory as developed by Bertalanffy (1968) is broad. It emphasizes human activity and creativity and the interrelation of all parts of a social system, including the temporal element and change. Also prominent are the concepts of open systems and organization, with the latter encompassing wholeness, growth, and differentiation. Because systems are viewed as open, attention can be given to the system's environment, with which it exchanges energy and information. Other properties are feedback (positive and negative) and equifinality, which refers to the fact that a similar result may emerge from different beginnings and similar beginnings may eventuate in diverse results (Nichols, 1984).

Cybernetics refers to the control or regulatory function of systems by means of feedback loops. Family therapists emphasize "circular causality by way of the feedback loop" (Nichols, 1984, p. 128). This means that problems are perpetuated because each person's behavior is part of a circular pattern, and the sequence is not easily interrupted. Although cybernetics is related to information theory and communications theory, cybernetics emphasizes the control function, whereas the latter two theories stress messages and their meanings.

Family-Societal Interface

Social context appears minimally in Masters and Johnson's (1970) sex therapy in the form of cultural attitudes, values, myths, and misinformation. Their approach implies, however, that the impact of these is direct and linear: individuals soak up this negative societal legacy and translate it into a sexual atmosphere that inhibits the natural sexual response, with the result being sexual dysfunction. Traditional sex therapy also assesses life situation or life events as possible contributors to dysfunction. These are certainly valid contextual factors to consider, but systems thinking permits an interactional, rather than linear, explanation of their impact.

Two facets of the sociocultural environment are especially relevant to sexual distress. These are gender-based structures and themes; and family linkage to societal structures such as economic, educational, and social welfare institutions.

GENDER-BASED STRUCTURES AND THEMES

Deeply-embedded in the social context, gender-based structures and themes can create an ambiance that is constrictive, if not damaging, to sexual and intimate relationships. These pervade language and history and continue to define society as basically patriarchal, though in process of change on this dimension. Society still tends to endorse rigid gender-roles. Women are primarily responsible for child rearing, for emotional expressiveness, for nurturing and attending to all family members' emotional needs, and for carrying out these functions in addition to job and career responsibilities. This role is complementary to the male prerogative and responsibility of focusing on career and identity and playing a more peripheral role in the family.

This schema contributes to a power differential between men and women, which, in itself, may give rise to other problems such as family violence and abuse. Feminists have noted the absence of the societal context in the major models of family therapy (Taggart, 1985). Without awareness of social context, therapy often looks simply toward internal family dynamics as the sole source of family problems. In the following case vignette gender issues figure overtly and strongly in the couple's intimacy problems.

> Elena, 30, and Everett, 43, sought counseling after 2½ years of marriage, her first and his second. Elena reported loss of respect for and alienation from her husband. A former teacher and professed feminist, she had not worked since marriage and the ensuing birth of two children. Elena's complaint was that Everett controls everything. He assumes he will always drive her car when they go out together; she has no checkbook except one for the money she brought to the marriage; she has one credit card which Everett finally gave her after many complaints. Because she has the children all day, she wants him to help in the evenings, but feels that he does not want to share this responsibility. She complained that he collapses in front of the television when he gets home and is emotionally unavailable. She said she wants some power, some equal control in the relationship, and respect. Everett's complaint was that Elena is not affectionate and there is practically no sex (when there is she refuses to do any thing sensual or pleasing for him). She has no empathy for his experience at work: he is a commodities trader, makes a lot of money, but worries about debt. He knew of her feminist stance before marriage, but felt that he could live with it. Cultural values also figured in their problems, because Elena is a strict Catholic and had not faced the decision of effective birth control or reconciled many of

her own traditional values with her feminist views. The couple had also experienced two job-related moves in 2½ years.

The fallout from gender-based issues does not always appear in so obvious a manner in couple's problems. But they may be a factor nonetheless. Powerful gender structures and themes are so pervasive within the culture that they impact in an almost automatic, unconscious way. They do, in fact, become internalized as facets of an individual's sexual self and identity. Both clients and therapists can easily bypass them as givens. They serve to create different realities for men and women. It is critical to assess how they may figure in the schisms between partners.

Along with psychoanalytic and systemic concepts, gender-based structure is a critical concept in Goldner's (1989) recent integrative perspective of sexually disordered relationships. This approach is discussed in detail in the final section of this chapter in the section on individual/family-of-origin interface.

FAMILY LINKAGE TO SOCIAL INSTITUTIONS

Families and individuals vary greatly in the kind of linkage they have with societal institutions such as the economy, education, social welfare, and community. Some are very much connected to these elements as members of the dominant middle class culture, whereas others have only marginal connections because of belonging to various minorities. Either status can affect the search for intimacy. Without economic security to meet basic needs, a person may experience additional difficulties in developing and maintaining an intimate relationship. Such conditions may be chronic or arise under acute circumstances. The whole institution of marriage and moving through the stages of the family life cycle connects to other societal linkages. For example, institutional racism is cited as a factor in the problem that black couples have in establishing stable and satisfying marital/couple relationships. Acute loss of linkage to societal support structures may dramatically affect women who divorce and deprive them of social status and economic power.

Linkage to societal institutions is, in fact, an unacknowledged factor in the history of sex therapy. From its inception with Masters and Johnson's (1970) 2-week residential treatment program, sex therapy has remained primarily accessible to clients from upper socioeconomic levels. Class and income may very well have been involved in the high success rates claimed by sex therapy.

Mutuality of function between families and society is basic to sociological thinking. Social systems exchange energy, resources, and information with the larger environment to achieve mutually beneficial goals. The family both supports and derives sustenance from social, economic, and political institutions.

The family must maintain its linkage to societal structures as it evolves throughout the life cycle stages in the context of ever-present societal change as well. Problems are common during periods of family transition as internal family dynamics change and tasks relevant to the larger society also change. The following case vignette suggests this linkage to societal factors as these partners attempt to meet the various tasks of the stage of early parenthood.

> Carla, a 30-year old woman, pregnant with her second child, was experiencing no desire for or interest in sex, and was aversive to her husband's touching her. She saw sex as a burdensome obligation. Successful in a stressful management position, she earned more money than her husband. They planned, as with the first child, that she would continue working, with the use of childcare services, after the new baby arrived. The couple had recently purchased a home, which, along with their toddler and jobs, demanded much time. She also felt that she worked harder than her husband, both at her job and at home. Since the marriage and becoming a mother, Carla had become religious and active in a church. She worried obsessively about being a good mother and the heavy responsibilities of parenthood in view of the many dangers facing children, such as society's drug problem. Although she had been rather sexually active as a teen and young adult, she now looked on those experiences with guilt and regret.

What is present in this case is the couple's linkage to the social context, including gender issues and parenthood; but the impact is not linear. Each person, couple, and family experiences the social context in its unique way. It was not simply the giant steps into matrimony, parenthood, and career and economic success that robbed Carla of her sexuality. Societal demands and potential rewards are intertwined with cognitive, behavioral, and interactional processes.

The relevance of social context should be a part of assessment. As a starting point, the eco-map (Figure 4.1) is a basic assessment tool that graphically illustrates a family's connection to all societal support structures:

> The eco-map is a paper-and pencil simulation which maps in a dynamic way the ecological system whose boundaries encompass the person or family in the life space. Included within these boundaries are the major systems, together with all their relationships, that affect and are affected by the subject. The eco-map pictures the family in its life situation; it identifies and characterizes the significant nurturant or conflict-laden connections between the family and the world. It demonstrates the flow of family energy to external systems. (Hartman & Laird, 1983, p. 159)

The format and construction of the eco-map are shown in Figure 4.1 (p. 84).

Although some family therapists have claimed use of an ecosystemic model, they have been criticized as "content with purely ritual salutes to the larger social context" (Taggart, 1985, p. 123). Many family therapists, no doubt, do consider societal linkages and context, but the major family therapy theories essentially ignore this dimension. So the task remains for the therapist to interweave understanding of the societal dimension into a comprehensive assessment and treatment strategy. Understanding its importance can foster interventions that speak to all aspects of the client's reality. Another case vignette suggests how linkage to societal structures may permeate intimacy problems.

> Fred and Frannie, both 30, an Afro-American couple, complained of conflicts in many areas and of problems in affection, intimacy, and sex. Fred had earned steady promotions in a large corporation, which gave them a comfortable middle class lifestyle, but Fred was aiming for higher social status. He insisted on enrolling their daughter and son in an exclusive private school and supervised all their clothing purchases and social activities to ensure their acceptance. He did not trust Frannie's taste on these matters, disapproved of her style of dress, and doubted her commitment to his goals for the family. Frannie saw him as hypocritical because, for himself, he freely floated between his middle class lifestyle and occasional social activities with male friends of a lower-class racial subculture. She resented his controlling all aspects of their life and his constant criticizing of her "lack of ambition and her family background."

Although this discussion shows how various dimensions of the social environment figure into intimacy problems, no major family

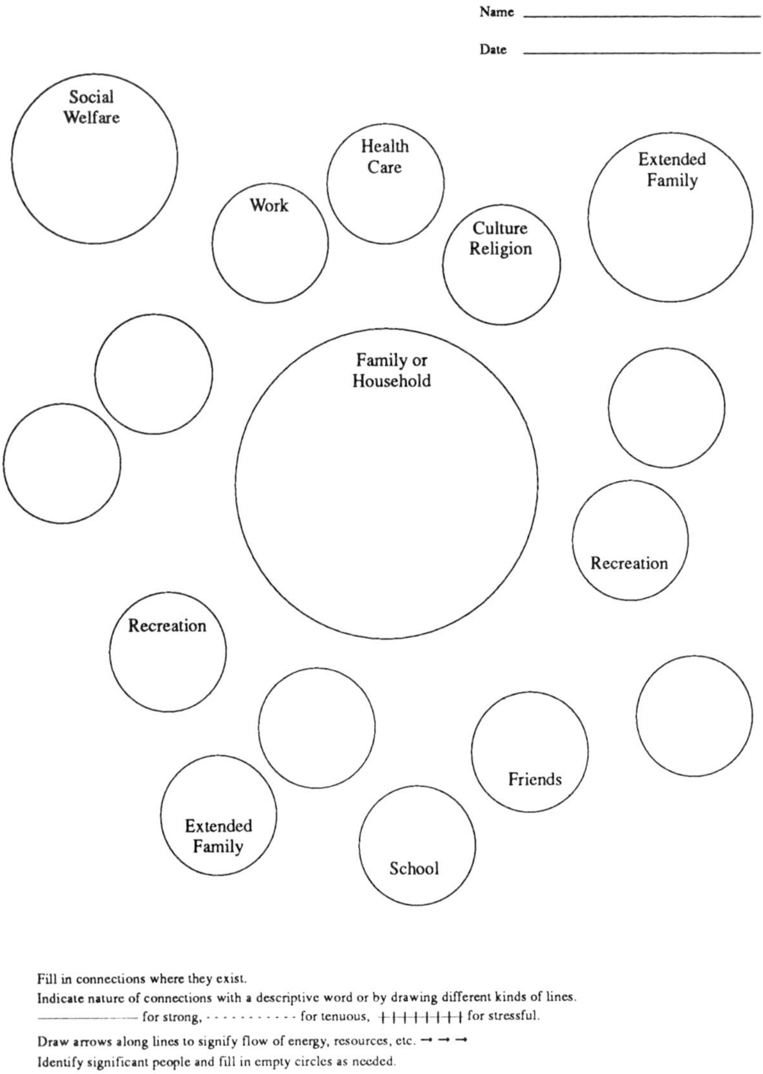

Figure 4.1. Sample Eco-Map

Reprinted by permission from Hartman, A., & Laird, J. (1983). *Family-centered social work practice.* New York: The Free Press, p. 160.

therapy model uses societal context as a point for intervention. It certainly plays a significant part in feminist therapy, which locates the source of problems in the human fallout from a patriarchal society. The social environment is also relevant in the generic problem solving model associated with social work, since intervention can aim at environmental as well as individual contributors to problems. Structural and strategic family therapy models prefer to separate the social content from process in clients' problems, and merely assert a stance of neutrality on content issues. But this denies the reality of clients' lives: the actual complications of social living and the moral dimensions of relationships, such as fairness. The challenge is to deal with content and process holistically, as they are experienced.

Family Structure

A social system's structure refers to the underlying organization that is reflected in its transactions. Transactions are predictable precisely because a covert set of rules evolves for governing various interactional sequences. Once established, such rules are not readily changed.

Certain structural features are necessary in all families, such as hierarchy and differentiation, but each family manifests these features in its own idiosyncratic manner. One can discern the structure only through having certain conceptual tools for analysis and through observation of family interaction over time.

Several key concepts deriving from structural family therapy (Minuchin, 1974) are useful. Subsystem refers to an individual or combination of individuals that performs various functions, for example, the spousal, parental, and sibling subsystems. Also important, however, are covert groupings such as alliances and coalitions; for example, a coalition of overinvolved parent and child may obviously affect a couple's sexual and intimate relationship. Boundaries refer to the rules that govern the amount and type of contact between family members and with outsiders. The two extremes on the continuum for boundaries are enmeshment and disengagement. Enmeshment describes overinvolvement between family members while disengagement describes a family pattern of isolation, indifference, and autonomous functioning. Either extreme can have a negative effect on the growth and autonomy of individuals.

Families must make structural adaptations, while maintaining necessary stability, as they move through the life-cycle stages. Those that do not make timely modifications will experience increased stress, and perhaps serious problems if they rigidly maintain the status quo. Structural family therapy aims to restructure the dysfunctional sets that restrict the family's abilities to cope with stress.

The single example in the literature of structural family therapy for a sexual dysfunction suggests the potential contributions of this model, but it does not reflect a high degree of integration with sex therapy. In treating a desire disorder, Fish, Fish, and Sprenkle (1984) focus on the couple's overall relationship. They emphasize the role that inhibited desire "plays in the maintenance of a couple's interactional style" (p. 6). In the case example they present, the assessment was that the woman's lack of desire "maintained territorial boundaries, defined power and control issues, and monitored intimacy level by regulating distance" (p. 8). Initial treatment goals aimed to strengthen each partner's individual boundaries. Other later interventions consisted of sensate focus (seen as an enactment by the authors), prohibitions on sex from time to time, communication training, problem solving aimed at the partner's divergent views of marriage, a contract for no violence and no coercing sex by the male partner, and other more general relationship contracts.

All of these later interventions derive from sex therapy or behavioral marital therapy, but are not identified as such. Given the range of interventions, it is unfortunate that the authors, without documentation, attribute the success of the case solely to one model: "A structural family therapy approach with its emphasis on the symptom as a system-maintained and system-maintaining phenomenon, made it possible to achieve a successful outcome" (Fish et al., 1984, p. 11).

Family structure is an important component in the integrative systems therapy model to be presented in Chapter 5. Attention to the couple subsystem, especially the sexual/intimate dimension, in relation to other subsystems, should be part of the initial assessment. Does this subsystem receive sufficient priority compared to the couple's executive and parental functions? The concept of boundaries is useful to determine the rules for their intimate/sexual contact, and not only for the overall relationship or major interactional pattern. Some couples are appropriately bonded in terms of parenting and earning a living, but disengaged in their intimate/sexual relationship. The enmeshment-disengagement continuum may also illuminate boundaries for actual sexual encounters: are boundaries flexible, allowing for varying degrees of physical closeness and access to each other's bodies or rigid at the extreme of either enmeshment or disengagement? For example, a young male client openly ruled out kissing, touching his partner's body, and pleasuring her; a quick, occasional act of intercourse constituted their sex life for years. The boundaries for their intimate contact had evolved and were rigidly drawn, with both partners playing their parts in maintaining them.

In terms of structural interventions for sexual and intimacy problems, there are many possibilities. In fact, many of the behavioral/experiential tasks of standard sex therapy are intrinsically structural interventions. For example, therapeutic assignments to have dates or do sensual/sexual tasks validate and strengthen the spousal or couple subsystem. How a couple deals with such tasks may be considered an enactment whereby they bring in a detailed account of their responses for the therapist's further structural analysis and modifications. Consider what a powerful structural intervention is inherent in Masters and Johnson's (1970) two week, intensive, residential treatment format.

Communication-Interactional Sequence

One of the early forms of family therapy, drawing largely on general systems theory, cybernetics, and information theory, focuses on family communication. It encompasses the early phase of the work at the Mental Research Institute (MRI) (Bateson, Jackson, Haley, & Weakland, 1956; Jackson, 1967; Satir, 1967; Watzlawick, Beavin, & Jackson, 1967).

EARLY MODEL OF FAMILY COMMUNICATIONS

In this model, the most basic principle is that all behavior is communication: one cannot not communicate. Messages communicate not only information or content, that is, the "report" function, but also a "command" function, that is, how it defines the relationship of the communicants. As rules or patterns for communication (i.e., the relationship) evolve, these serve to maintain the system's balance or homeostasis. Because they are so effective at this, they are resistant to change. Nonetheless, rules must change as family conditions change and give way to new definitions of relationships. For example, couples who move beyond the courtship stage must typically find meaningful communication patterns in addition to the mutual accommodation and ignoring of problems that often characterize courtship.

In a given communicational context, relationships may be complementary, a pattern suggestive of inequality, or symmetrical, a pattern suggestive of equality. Of particular interest is communication which can lead to pathology or symptoms. For example, paradoxical communication involves a message that is intrinsically contradictory and inconsistent. One type is the double-bind message, which consists of a set of incongruent messages requiring a response that must inevitably fail and forbidding comment on the communication itself.

These major concepts formed the basis for the early form of communications family therapy, which aimed to change the family's problematic patterns of communication. Satir (1967), especially, is known for using a fairly direct approach by modeling and teaching clear communication and making explicit to the family their implicit rules.

Application to Sexual Dysfunction

Because there is an early example of this type of communications therapy applied to sexual dysfunction, this will be discussed before summarizing additional developments of the communications model.

Verhulst and Heiman (1979) were the first to apply a family therapy model to sexual dysfunction. They focus on the sexual interaction cycle as a communication sequence filled with meaning. Here a couple's sexual interaction refers to a process of "mutual influence, feedback, and communication"; these are conveyed through the language of physiological response and body and action language. The partners' individual characteristics influence what kinds of messages are sent and how they are received; thus, "certain sexual messages may incite fear or repulsion rather than arousal" (p. 24).

Based on studies in ethology, Verhulst and Heiman (1979) assert that certain interaction patterns that are part of all sexual interaction carry meanings; these include territorial, ranking order, attachment, and sensual exploration patterns. Any one of these patterns may come to dominate the sexual interaction process as "figure" while others recede into "ground." Such a dominant pattern may interfere with the balance necessary to move the sexual interaction in the direction of arousal, desire, and orgasmic release. Normal feedback processes allow for correction if one or both partners experience anxiety, fear, or disgust as part of one of the dominant patterns. For example, in a territoriality pattern, a wife may react defensively if she understands her husband's activity as trying to assert possession of her body.

The importance of Verhulst and Heiman's (1979) approach is the specific focus on the sexual interaction encounter itself as worthy of analysis as a communication sequence between partners. Therapeutic intervention, then, would aim to change the excessive or dysfunctional interactional pattern that prevents the mutual communication of desire and arousal, for example, negative meanings associated with excessive territoriality or attachment concerns that result in the mutual communication of such nonsexual emotions as fear or anger.

Their suggested interventions are quite straightforward, in accord with the early Satir communications approach and with standard sex therapy. The therapist teaches the couple directly about the sexual interaction cycle and informs them of their problematic interactional pattern that interferes with the natural sexual response. Suggestions are given to change the communication and meaning within the sexual interaction; thus a husband was taught to sense his wife's signals of territorial defensiveness, to slow down, and "let her guide him in some tender pleasuring" (Verhulst & Heiman, 1979, p. 25). In other words, intervention consists of identifying the problem as residing within the nonverbal communication of meanings during sex, and then teaching more effective communication for this context that allows the natural sexual response to emerge.

CYBERNETICS EMPHASIS IN FAMILY COMMUNICATION

Further developments in the communications model of family therapy drew on cybernetics, and this work essentially follows two directions. The first centers on the control function served by the interactional circularity of communication sequences. The second centers on the control function of meaning served by the observing system; this is more complex because it involves the system observing itself and then acting on its own observed activities or patterns.

The pragmatics of communication in terms of interactional circularity is exemplified in the work of Mental Research Institute (MRI) Brief Therapy (Watzlawick, Weakland, & Fisch, 1974). In addition to focus on the command message, also important is punctuation of a message, that is, the unique slant or bias on interpretation given to a communication by a participant. And most essential to intervention, the principle of *circular causality* calls for attention to the specific sequences of behavior that contain the problem. A basic assumption is that a problem is maintained by positive feedback loops; that is, a response to a behavior (presumably designed to remedy it) actually exacerbates and perpetuates it. Thus what started out as a solution to a life problem continues, though the solution is unsatisfactory.

The key systemic formulation derived from the MRI form of brief strategic therapy is that the client's complaint is manifested in an interpersonal interaction that, in itself, constitutes the problem-containing process. Therapeutic intervention aims to interrupt this process, which is posited to be a solution that failed and continues to fail because it consists of "more of the same." Focus centers on exact behavioral sequences in which the problem occurs, with the therapeutic goal of interrupting the sequence and finding a new solution of a different order. A strength of this approach is the minimizing or utilization of client resistance. In the MRI model, the linkage between the individual and system derives from viewing problems as manifested within specifiable behavioral sequences in which each individual moves in step with others to produce the dance of dysfunction.

The therapist uses whatever will work to interrupt an interaction pattern and produce a satisfactory solution. Following the dance metaphor, this could result from changing the music, one's step, who leads, the view of self as a dancer, the meaning of the dance, and so forth. Stopping the original problem cycle through the most parsimonious means is critical since this allows for a range of other solutions to emerge from the clients before the therapist becomes part of the cycle. The importance of the individual is also evident as the therapist promotes compliance by consciously devising frames for interventions that are consistent with individuals' unique qualities and perceptions.

One final point relevant to the communication-interaction sequence merits special emphasis. Utilization, mentioned above in reference to resistance, derives from Ericksonian (Haley, 1976) hypnosis, which is considered the precursor of strategic family therapy.

Using the communication concept of utilization, the therapist uses the client's unique qualities, especially ways of being, perceiving, and knowing, in order to tap the unconscious in effecting changes in thinking, feeling, and behaving. Utilization procedures, whether a so-called trance, use of metaphor, sensory focus, or mirroring, indirectly release existing potentials within the client to change what have become automatic and problematic patterns. Although others have a part in the repetitive patterns, effective interruption may result from changing the individual's part in it.

Major treatment steps in the brief therapy model include: letting the client know that therapy will be brief, obtaining a specific definition of a major complaint, making an estimate of the behavior that maintains the problem, negotiating concrete goals stated as minimum changes indicative of progress, devising and giving interventions, and termination (before the therapist too becomes part of the problem process). The therapist offers directives strategically in a low-keyed manner so as to minimize resistance, and uses paradoxical instructions if appropriate for certain clients (e.g., symptom prescription, restraint of change, etc.).

This approach to a system's communication, with emphasis on the principle of circular causality, should be highly relevant to the treatment of sexual and intimacy problems. One could, in general, specifically define the actual sexual dysfunction as the problem to be solved (assuming that this is the way the clients present it). Attention might center on communicational/behavioral sequences during problematic sexual encounters (including immediate behaviors leading up to them as well as during sex) in order to assess or estimate exactly what is the nature of the vicious interactional cycle that maintains the problem. This would be similar to Verhulst and Heiman's (1979) focus on the sexual interaction, except that they were concerned with meanings communicated, as opposed to the process whereby the symptom is contained within the circular interactional sequence.

Application to Sexual Dysfunction

Several sex therapists have recently used selected concepts from brief strategic therapy within the context of traditional sex therapy. Zilbergeld and Ellison (1980) and Rosen and Leiblum (1989) have, to some extent, incorporated the concept of the couple interaction process and techniques such as reframing and paradox. In addition,

LoPiccolo (LoPiccolo, 1991; LoPiccolo & Stock, 1986) has used the systems concept of homeostasis and symptom function to explain clients' ambivalence toward change and the technique of therapist neutrality to defuse resistance to change. These efforts represent a step toward integration.

A few family therapists have applied the full problem interaction or cybernetic model to sexual dysfunction. But these efforts too, as evidenced in the discussion below, fall short of meaningful integration.

In the first example, treatment does not stay focused on the sexual complaints, nor on analysis of the sexual encounters for discovery of the problem-containing process. Duncan and Parks (1988) propose a model of brief therapy that "integrates an individual, cognitive-behavioral approach with a strategic approach at both pragmatic and theoretical levels" (p. 151). Their rationale for integration stems from a process-constructive model (Duncan, 1984; Duncan & Fraser, 1987; Fraser, 1986) that allows for the theoretical integration by providing a conceptual framework which permits selective integration of different therapeutic models to match the particulars of a given client situation. Treatment may therefore involve diverse techniques selected in order to foster change in the service of therapy goals. The argument is that multiple views of reality exist, and, depending on the client characteristics, the therapist constructs the reality that will be most useful to achievement of therapeutic goals. Generally, this reality will be most useful if it matches the client's perceptions and conceptualizations of the problem.

Duncan and Parks (1988) state that the ultimate systemic goal of treatment is to interrupt the "problem-containing process" (p. 156). Cognitive-behavioral frames may be especially appropriate since they are complementary to and similar to a strategic perspective, and have proven effectiveness with certain problems. They speculate that the reason for the success of behavioral therapies is that they match clients' perceptions and concepts about problems.

The case example problems were "marital quarrels, difficulty communicating about sex, and sexual performance problems" (frequent erectile failure and lifelong premature ejaculation) (p. 157). There is no statement as to what the clients saw as their primary complaint, but apparently the therapist estimated that the marital quarrels were connected to the husband's sexual frustration. The initial interventions were aimed at changing this pattern of quarrels through reframing, symptom prescription, and restraint of change. When the quarrels stopped but the sexual dysfunctions continued, the therapist then applied a behavioral skills acquisition frame. The goal was to deal with the husband's anxiety; this was accomplished through relaxation training, sensate focus, communication training, and information on the impact of anxiety on sexual functioning. Therapy was considered successful when the couple indicated at session six readiness to terminate; intercourse had been accomplished, but the premature ejaculation remained unchanged.

Duncan and Parks' (1988) use of the MRI model with sexual dysfunction leaves many questions unanswered. Although they claim brief strategic therapy as the overarching theoretical framework into which cognitive-behavioral sex therapy techniques are attached, they do not demonstrate the application of the major intervention principles of brief therapy with the case. They offer no hypothesis about the nature of the "connection" between the marital conflicts and the husband's two sexual dysfunctions—neither linear nor circular. They do not state whether the marital quarrels were the "problem-containing" process that was maintaining the sexual dysfunctions or whether they were simply the first vicious cycle that therapy aimed to interrupt. Although the next interventions addressed the husband's anxiety and lack of arousal and attraction to his wife during sex, Duncan and Parks (1988) never formulated the sexual dysfunctions in process or interactional terms. Also unclear is whether the couple's goal (and a negotiated therapeutic goal) was to bring about a concrete behavioral change in the dysfunctions, and, if so, why remedy of the premature ejaculation was not included. It is unstated as well whether only one successful intromission was achieved, whether this was the designated goal indicative of sufficient progress, or whether the couple had other reasons for terminating at that point and requesting exercises to work on the premature ejaculation on their own. No follow-up information is offered, and thus no evidence that progress continued or that the premature ejaculation improved.

This detailed critique is necessary and justified when a treatment model is applied to new problem areas and when claims are made for its effectiveness. Duncan and Parks (1988) suggest that the brief strategic therapy framework was instrumental in the successful outcome, but the many questions raised above do not support this claim. In fact, Duncan and Parks (1988) acknowledge that the sensate focus introduced change into the context of the couple's sexual interaction. They also note that the acquisition of behavioral skills such as anxiety-management and sensual pleasuring offer "an equally plausible rationale for the successful outcome." They conclude that "the behavioral approach dictated much of 'what' was presented and the strategic dictated 'how' the couple was approached" (p. 159). Yet they maintain that the overarching theoretical framework responsible for outcome was brief strategic therapy. But without detailed information showing how they applied the major steps of this model to the clients' problem, one could just as well argue that the traditional sex therapy methods constituted the major framework.

The second example of brief strategic therapy applied to sexual dysfunction is a discussion in hypothetical terms, not of actual clinical application or of a case example. May and Bobele (1988) propose an interactional conceptualization of sexual dysfunction in the unemployed male professional. They cite "job loss, loss of self-esteem, depression, erectile failure, fear of failure, and impotency" as factors that affect each other and are affected in turn through feedback loops. This hypothesis seems removed from the typical focus of brief strategic therapy on specific behavioral/interactional sequences that contain the problem. The factors mentioned above represent different classes of phenomena (e.g., life events, individual attributes, and symptomatic responses). They do not comprise the specific behavioral/interactional sequence of two or more people that manifests "more of the same" type of solution being unsuccessfully applied.

The various interacting facets cited actually represent the etiological content of traditional sex therapy, and May and Bobele (1988) recognize this; however, their arguments to distinguish their model from sex therapy are simply not convincing. Departing from their model's ahistorical method, they recommend obtaining a complete sexual, physical, and marital history with the rationale of its being a "ritual" that can reveal useful information. They also claim distinctiveness from sex therapy because of the husband-wife-jobless context, but sex therapy has always considered contexts that could trigger a dysfunctional sexual response (e.g., the use of alcohol, lack of privacy, societal gender-role expectations, life crises, etc.). Finally, they devalue the importance of remedying the sexual dysfunction by reiterating that the goal of intervention is to "interrupt problem-maintaining behavior rather than to 'solve' the secondary impotence brought on by the husband's unemployment" (p. 261). This latter point curiously sounds like linear causality. And it also seems to confuse the reasonable client and therapeutic goal of improving sexual function with the therapeutic means for attaining that goal.

A final example is the cybernetic-systems approach to sexual problems presented by Sanders (1988) and Sanders and Tomm (1989). This is an integrative approach that, in fact, downplays its various theoretical components in favor of emphasizing the cybernetic second-order focus on the importance of the observing system.

There is acknowledgment that several domains are present in an interconnected way in sexual problems. These are the biological states, knowledge base, and behavioral repertoires of the individuals. These are essential components of traditional sex therapy, and they are classified as deriving from "lineal epistemology." Intervention with these domains may work for "a large number of sexual concerns, but it may be rather limiting when dealing with the more complex or 'resistant' concerns." For the latter, the goal of intervention, rather than specific behavior change, is instead "metachange—a change in the couple's ability to change" (Sanders & Tomm, 1989, p. 364).

Attention centers on the couple's relationship and the therapist's relationship to them. Sexual problems result from "a circular interaction process of repeated cycles of invitations to behave a certain way." These patterns also fit in to the overall process of a couple's relationship. Sanders and Tomm (1989) assume that with the more resistant cases "clients have a motivational problem of mobilizing . . . resources to deal effectively with their sexual difficulties" (p. 359). Rejecting psychodynamic concepts to explain human motivation, they attribute the problematic mutual invitations to behave sexually in ineffective ways to each person's socially derived self. But even this concept of self and its behavioral tendencies are attributed to cultural influences rather than to persons. For example, they refer to childhood proscriptions to sexuality or clients being in the grips of a family view about sex. These are ways of intentionally externalizing the problem, a way of emphasizing the "social interactional basis for the mental phenomena," rather than ascribing the expectations or beliefs to individuals (p. 366). Treatment relies heavily on therapist neutrality and circular questioning to enable the couple to discover opportunities to take an observer position and to see the impact of their own observations. The goal is for clients to discover their own ability to change.

This approach to treating sexual problems seems to fall into the typical dichotomy of saying that many sexual problems will benefit from what is essentially traditional sex therapy, whereas there are the "difficult problems" that require a cybernetic-systems approach. They do not make clear the reasons for this distinction or what therapy would look like for one or the other type of sexual dysfunction. It seems that cybernetic-systems theory is essentially reserved for resistant clients and severe dysfunctions such as desire disorders.

In summary, the communicational-interactional sequence as derived from cybernetic systems concepts is highly relevant to sexual dysfunction. The MRI brief therapy model, with its intense look at behavioral-interactional sequences that constitute the problem containing process, certainly affords an understanding of the self-maintaining, self-controlling processes of a circular interaction system. But the first two applications of this theory discussed above have not tapped into its unique potential. This model offers a lens for viewing and discovering the vicious cycle that is contained in the exact behavioral sequences surrounding the couple's typical sexual encounter in which dysfunction occurs. It may then be possible to isolate one or more aspects of the sexual interaction sequence as targets to change and so interrupt the process. It can be applied to other of the couple's nonsexual interactional sequences *if* these are believed to contribute to the specific sexual/intimacy problem that therapy aims to remedy.

The systemic concept of the problem-interactional sequence definitely has a place in integrative systems therapy. But the therapist's skill in identifying the problem-containing process and in devising interventions will obviously influence whether a meaningful change takes place.

Individual/Family-of-Origin Interface

Each of the previously discussed facets of the family system constitute a piece of the whole. Each of the respective treatment models focuses on its single facet as the critical point of intervention for changing the presenting symptom. That is, therapy aims to impact on sociocultural linkages or themes, or on family structure, or on a communication-interactional sequence. But if a given focused intervention does not bring desired therapeutic results, applying "more of the same" may be an obvious systemic mistake.

A totally different perspective can be achieved by putting a different lens into the therapeutic camera. Possibly a broader view of context or an in-depth view could make a difference. For example, in the structural concept of boundaries, which may range from enmeshed to disengaged, several legitimate questions arise. It is obvious that these extremes affect the relationship bond negatively, but what do these terms mean in regard to individuals? And how are individuals involved in maintaining these extreme patterns? The answers are not contained in the specific focus of structural family therapy. Enmeshment and disengagement carry unacknowledged meanings that derive from theories of individual development.

The various dimensions of the family system are abstractions based on analysis of the behaviors of individuals with each other. Thus when we posit an "enmeshed couple relationship," we have analyzed individuals behaving in interaction with each other to arrive at this assessment. It is valid to ask what this pattern provides for each individual as well as what it provides for the relationship. When systems theorists negate such individual concepts as development and personality, then certain words that they use (cannot escape using) are rendered meaningless and empty. The theorist knows the meaning but does not acknowledge it because it does not fit the singular focus of the model.

Let me illustrate by going back to the cybernetic-systems approach to sexual problems discussed previously in the section on the Communication-Interaction Sequence (Sanders, 1988; Sanders & Tomm, 1989). There is a stated rejection of psychodynamic concepts to explain clients' "motivational problem of mobilizing . . . to deal effectively with their sexual difficulties" (Sanders & Tomm, 1989, p. 359). The preference is to stay focused on the couple's relationship and on the therapist's relationship to the clients. The individual as an emotional and psychological system is intentionally bypassed except for acknowledgment of social self that obtains sexual beliefs and expectations from society.

Certain terms are used that seem devoid of meaning if their relevance to individual motivation is simply negated. For example, *sexual mutuality* is an ideal that refers to each person's experiencing of self and the other as having a desire to be sexual with the other and actively choosing to participate in intimate interaction within a context of "*emotional and physical vulnerability*, with *trust* that one will not be taken advantage of by the other" (Sanders & Tomm, 1989, p. 349) Sanders (1988) also equates *intimacy* to this quality of emotional and physical vulnerability in the context of trust. Sanders (1988) refers to his work with a couple, stating: "My hypothesis was that by trying to get them to be more *intimate, I was intensifying fears and feelings that they were not sure they could handle*" (pp. 81-82, emphasis added).

All of the italicized words imply individual feelings, expectations, and motivations. Yet the only explanation of the individual permitted is that of a social self that takes in social sexual myths such as the patriarchal assumptions about men and women. This view is essentially the same as Masters and Johnson's (1970) linear explanation whereby society's sexual stereotypes lead to spectator anxiety, which leads to dysfunctional sexual behaviors. The difference is that in the cybernetic approach, it is the mutual interactions of the social selves of each partner, filled with societal myths, that lead to the invitations to behave in problematic ways. This explanation leaves unanswered basic questions about both sexual and intimacy needs, why these should trigger individual emotional reactions such as fears, and why people react differently to societal myths in formulating the social self.

Believable human meanings for these concepts come out of complex individual developmental processes. In the cybernetic-systems analysis, the terms are simply present but not adequately accounted for. An explanation of the ingredients in intimate human relationships is available in object relations theory: intimacy can be frightening because it is the deep sharing of self with another, and one can both desire and fear this intense experience at the same time. These ambivalent emotions connect to the person's first relationship with the primary caretaker, and subsequent adult intimate/sexual relationships are often unconsciously experienced as an opportunity for both the delights and dangers of merger with another. In the above discussion based on cybernetic-systems concepts, terms such as intimacy, mutuality, and vulnerability are empty. Only developmental and personality concepts give them meaning.

In working with sexual distress, it is essential to have concepts that explain the interface between the individual and the family of origin. A number of theorists have made significant contributions to understanding of the individual in the family system. Concepts from Bowen's (1978) family systems theory and from object relations theory (Kahn, 1989; Scharff, 1988) are highlighted here, although other multigenerational/psychodynamic models share a similar thrust (Boszormenyi-Nagy & Spark, 1973; Framo, 1982; Sager, 1976).

FAMILY SYSTEMS THEORY

Bowen's (1978) model is greatly respected for its elegant linking of psychodynamic and systems thinking (Aylmer, 1986). It permits attention to symptoms as resulting from the interactive influences of each partner's self-system, the couple-nuclear system, and the extended-family system (family of origin). Within the self-system are the critical factors of development, personality, and family of origin programming. Stressor or nodal events in the extended family system are associated with the timing, persistence, and intensity of marital conflict. Such problems, however, may also arise out of the couple-nuclear system as a result of unrealistic expectations or reciprocal reactive triangles (interactional patterns that stabilize the dyad during stressful periods through the involvement of a third person or influence).

The family, by virtue of its nature and functions, embodies both emotion and intellect. These qualities are also central to individual functioning. *Differentiation of self* refers to the process that occurs as the individual is able to experience a balance of reason and emotion, which enables one to resist being overwhelmed by the emotional reactivity of his or her family. Without this balance, when individuals marry, their own nuclear family will reflect a high degree of emotional fusion manifested as either overcloseness or as distance. These problematic conditions connect to other processes that produce family and individual dysfunction. *Triangles* become the means of coping with emotional tensions when dyads do not directly face and resolve their issues. A triangle simply refers to the dyad's incorporating a third person (or other source) to lower anxiety and promote system stability. *The family projection process* refers to the mechanism for passing on to a favored or vulnerable child, through intense focus, the legacy of a poorly differentiated self. As a child matures and attempts to cope with this intense emotional fusion with a parent and the impaired sense of self, the young person may remain physically fused with the family, or *emotional cut-off* may seem a solution. With the former, the person remains physically close and overinvolved; with the latter, the person flees the family. Either option, however, denies the dysfunctional emotional bond and the need to resolve it.

This brief summary can only suggest the systemic importance of these concepts to a couple's sexual/intimate relationship. Because partners with fairly similar degrees of self-differentiation tend to mate, relationship patterns emerge that are a function of their interlocking psychic development. Thus the potential is there for extremes in coping with one's emotional reactivity—either through demands for overcloseness or for distance. The sexual/affectional relationship often becomes the stage for the playing out of this psychic drama. The linkages between the individual and systems are powerful and obvious in this conceptual framework.

Therapy based on this model is often long term; typically it involves sessions with the couple and with individual partners. Much of the therapeutic change process emphasizes helping each partner to focus on self, stop projection-blame, and change long-standing dysfunctional roles within his or her extended family. This process promotes awareness of how the individual acts out similar roles in the couple relationship and frees the person to behave more rationally and less reactively. A variety of techniques could be appropriate, but the therapist's style is one of detached rationality for the process of assisting partners to increase their differentiation from their families of origin. The latter condition is necessary for a healthier nuclear family. The genogram is a critical tool for assessment and treatment.

The genogram is a schematic means of obtaining and ordering information about three generations of the family and its emotional processes. It follows a family-tree format and notes important data such as age, sex, marriages, births, divorces, deaths, other critical family events, and their dates. The construction of the genogram encourages accuracy and objectivity on the part of the family as a beginning step to balance emotional reactivity. For the therapist, it provides a picture of the family's structure, themes, and emotional processes that guides the treatment process.

Application to Sexual Dysfunction

Several recent publications attempting to integrate systems thinking and sex therapy draw from Bowen's (1978) theory, but also from the intergenerational concepts of Framo (1982) and Boszormenyi-Nagy and Spark (1973). These efforts address the intergenerational transmission of problematic sexual values, concerns, and loyalties.

Hof and Berman (1986, 1989; also Berman & Hof, 1987) propose that sexual dysfunction may result from a couple's collusive interpersonal interaction that maintains each others' roles in or loyalties to the family of origin; thus the symptom functions to protect each other from change. They have developed the sexual genogram as the primary tool for exploring "issues of sexuality in the structure and belief system of the family of origin" (Hof & Berman, 1989, p. 308). The sexual genogram elaborates on the basic genogram by attending specifically to family sexual history and issues, especially secrets.

In one case, the therapist's etiological explanation for the man's premature ejaculation was that this symptom allowed him to remain loyal to the family script, namely, that men in the family were ineffective; it served to keep him in his place because he was otherwise quite successful. This legacy interlocked with his wife's anorgasmia, which gave her a control that she had lacked as a child when she was molested by her father and grandfather; this symptom also maintained her repression of some pleasurable childhood sexual contacts with a brother. This explanation reveals both partners as unconsciously colluding to protect each other from changing their individual family legacies, which are typically manifested as roles and needs.

Berman and Hof's (1986) treatment approach, which incorporates the intergenerational etiology of sexual dysfunction, appears quite variable. Their writings center on explaining the sexual genogram, not on its integration with sex therapy. They continue to maintain the distinction between sex therapy and family therapy as they recommend standard sex therapy if a couple openly acknowledges a sexual dysfunction and is ready to discuss sex (Berman & Hof, 1987). In such cases, the therapist may develop a short version of the sexual genogram to aid conceptual understanding. The complete genogram is recommended for impasses in therapy. Here, the partners work on their individual sexual genograms and speculate about them. Ultimately, they explore them with the therapist to uncover the family connection to the sexual problem. The therapist then integrates this understanding with traditional sex therapy components to resolve the problem.

Weeks (1987) proposes a multicausal model for explaining inhibited sexual desire and a "systematic program of treatment" (p. 194) that incorporates individual, interactional, and intergenerational perspectives. A full assessment of marital issues is necessary (this process and the genogram are not covered since these topics appear as earlier chapters). In addition, assessment encompasses detailed information on the history and nature of the inhibited sexual desire; however, a rating of desire is obtained only from the symptomatic partner. The focus is on assessment of negative sexual self-talk and treatment though cognitive restructuring. Although Weeks (1987) states the intent to integrate, he essentially leaves this task for the reader to accomplish.

It remains unclear how Weeks' (1987) integrated treatment program proceeds. Moreover, his handling of the cognitive material covered seems quite nonsystemic. For example, the desire level of the non-symptomatic partner is not obtained, and that partner's role in treatment is initially defined as one of helpfulness. Further, the cognitive intervention centers on the female partner's lack of desire and on her negative self talk that connects to the current relationship and the family of origin. But an individual session with her partner centers on how he experiences the sexual problem, not on assessment of mutual contribution to the dysfunctional sexual interaction. It seems that a family systems view of the interlocking dimensions of the couple problem would appear in the cognitive approach. For example, the therapist could explore the desire level and the sexual self-talk of the nonsymptomatic partner to discover his or her complementary legacy from the family of origin. The cognitive therapy was geared strictly to changing the symptomatic partner. This method sharply contrasts to Zilbergeld and Ellison's (1980) earlier use of systems theory to conceptualize desire dysfunction not as an individual attribute but as the result of discrepancies between partners' desire levels.

The overall process of therapy presented by Weeks (1987) remains unexplained, and no complete case summary is provided to demonstrate the process or method of integration. So the degree of integration of family systems with standard sex therapy methods appears to be modest.

OBJECT RELATIONS THEORY

As does Bowen's (1978) family systems theory, object relations theory represents a bridge between family therapy and psychoanalysis. Object relations theory centers on a necessary facet of the family system that has, until recently, been largely ignored. A meaningful family systems perspective must encompass a way of understanding the individual's developmental history (Kahn, 1989; Luepnitz, 1988; Scharff, 1982; Slipp, 1988).

Object relations theory provides an explanation of unconscious experience and learning (from infancy and early childhood) that carry into adulthood. This theory posits that relatedness and relationship are instinctive and central to the individual's identity. The centrality given to relationship places this theory within the systemic paradigm. The vestiges of the earliest relationships carry over into adult relationships. They manifest through projective identification, which is inherently both an intrapsychic and an interactional process. The individual's projective identifications stemming from the quality of nurturance within the family set up relatively stable patterns for subsequent relationships. Projective identifications play a part in the process of mate selection and in the continuing relationship between partners. The systemic element is thus further evidenced in the process of collusion whereby mates unconsciously participate in each other's projective identifications.

Object relations theory centers on the origin and meaning of interpersonal relationships. The early parent-child relationship is a prototype for all subsequent bonding. For the child's "true self" to emerge, the primary relationship must provide "good enough" nurturance. This allows for both appropriate symbiosis and subsequent separation and individuation that result in a cohesive sense of self and a secure identity. This self constitutes the basis for the capacity to experience and enjoy with a partner sensual and sexual satisfaction, as well as feelings of caring and being cared for, loving while giving love, and tolerating and forgiving. On the other hand, deprivation in that first relationship leads to a "false self" which, in adult life, experiences sexual/emotional encounters with fears of loss of self, or of abandonment, or of annihilation. These unconscious fears trigger a range of defensive responses that block satisfaction of sexual/intimacy needs.

The intrapsychic processes stemming from deprivation in the earliest caregiving relationship center on splitting off the bad or unsatisfying object, repressing it, and introjecting this hate of the object as a part of the ego. Consequently, strong feelings, expectations, or images, both negative or idealized, are then often projected onto others as the person seeks to establish intimate relationships. The process takes on added systemic properties if collusion or reciprocal projection exchange is elicited. Here partners unconsciously "accommodate by accepting and identifying with the projective identifications from the other" (Nichols, 1988, p. 54).

Partners with impaired capacities for intimacy often gravitate toward each other and mate with the unconscious expectation of healing old wounds—the partner will be the ideal parent who will meet all needs. It is as if partners strike a deeply unconscious deal with each other as "each person is dealing with a part of the other that the other cannot acknowledge is present" (Nichols, 1989, p. 54). But their interlocking psychic needs are likely to be at odds and go unmet. A couple's problems with intimacy and sexuality may be on the order of minor annoyances, or they may be so severe as to impact on other dimensions of their relationship and on the family system.

Application to Sexual Dysfunction

Talmadge and Talmadge (1986) incorporate object relations and systems theories to arrive at an integrative conceptual understanding of desire disorders. They emphasize the mutuality and stability of the relationship system that evolves as partners unconsciously collude to recreate their experience with the original love object/caretaker. Both partners expect the fulfillment of interrelated needs for bonding, nurturing, affection, and sexual pleasure; and the courtship stage supports the fantasy of the partner as the perfect caretaker. Sexual desire problems may emerge when a couple cannot move beyond this stage to incorporate the real partner, ambivalences, and negative feelings. Instead of confronting and resolving these inevitable elements of an intimate relationship, the result may be withdrawal, lack of desire, or an empty, mechanical interaction.

Intimacy, on the other hand, encompasses an intense closeness that reveals innermost selves, "trust, interdependence, vulnerability, power, mutuality, and the knowing and seeking of self." With such closeness comes the risk of remembering "old pain from violations of trust and oneness in early development. . . . Marital success requires tolerance for regression in the partners, who must make room for their childlike needy selves to emerge in mutual dependence." A satisfactory intimate and sexual relationship allows partners to move flexibly between a stance of mutuality (characterized by equality) and the parent-child stance (characterized by regression). Thus it allows for a high degree of "closeness without merger" (Talmadge & Talmadge, 1986, p. 8).

In terms of treatment, Talmadge and Talmadge (1986) follow a highly eclectic approach derived from Gestalt/experiential psychotherapy, systems techniques, and sex therapy. It can encompass: straightforward information about stages of intimate relationships and mutual projections; assigning behavioral tasks to introduce new behaviors; reframing; paradoxical directives; promoting experiential awareness of feelings; training in effective communication; and use of the client-therapist interaction for modeling genuineness, self-disclosure, and confrontation. Both individual and conjoint sessions are appropriate since an implicit goal is that individual progress toward separateness and responsibility will foster a healthy dyadic relationship. Case examples illustrate an array of techniques used within the overriding object relations/systemic view of the desire disorder. Talmadge and Talmadge (1986) definitely make a contribution toward the integration of family systems theories with sex therapy.

Another recent integrative treatment for sexual problems draws on general psychoanalytic concepts, especially with regard to the blending of sex and aggression. Goldner (1989), too, argues for a theoretical base that can account for the simultaneous internal and relational levels of the sexual experience. The proposed model incorporates a psychoanalytic perspective and gender-based societal structures within the systemic problem-interactional framework. She believes that sex can become structured according to powerful gender stereotypes to serve as the medium through which individuals attempt to heal narcissistic injuries. When this happens, the result is that sex loses its mutually playful and pleasurable quality and a vicious sexual and relationship pattern emerges that guarantees the continued existence of sex as a pseudosolution that maintains the problems at both the internal and relationship levels.

Goldner (1989) presents a case in which the couple's sexual relationship consisted of the male's insistence on including a third partner for his female partner during their sexual encounters. This arrangement satisfied his voyeuristic and her exhibitionistic needs as well as supported a sado-masochistic sexual and overall relationship structure. The psychoanalytic perspective explains how the need to bond can become distorted through the "eroticization of hostility." Societal gender structures figure in this distortion as society eroticizes gender cliches in a way that connects them to sexual passion. Thus the couple's "gendered, sexualized scripts reciprocate so that his male training in forbidden looking meshes with her female knowledge of herself as someone who is secretly to allow what she must appear to forbid." The problem-interaction system takes over as their interaction becomes a "game"; that is, the type of sex that they have becomes a pseudosolution to reverse, for him, "the narcissistic injury of his sense of sexual exclusion and masculine insufficiency" and to reverse, for her, her sense of "invisibility and marginality" (Goldner, 1989, pp. 39-40).

The "solution" could not resolve the problem of power within the couple's sexual and overall relationship. After each sex act, he was left with intensified doubts about his masculine selfhood, and her role as a sex object left her with intensified feelings of invisibility. These feelings played out in symmetrical fashion as each partner "upped the ante" to create more bizarre activities and behaviors. Goldner's (1989) integrative approach results in a sophisticated understanding of the complementary interaction of individual unconscious psychosexual development, societal structures, and systemic relationship and problem patterning. Intervention likewise can encompass diverse strategies.

Object relations and intergenerational family systems theories enable us to capture a facet of the family unavailable through the other systemic lenses discussed in this chapter. This lens focuses on a couple's interpersonal interaction as a stable, mutually interlocking pattern that evolves out of each partner's development in and/or legacy from the family of origin. The result is reminiscent of a film with flashbacks or dream sequences in that it shows the connection of current interaction to past history. Sexual and intimacy disorders, then, may be explained as emanating from the interface between the individual and developmental and intergenerational dimensions. Patterns or behaviors associated with these dimensions operate unconsciously or out of awareness. Also explicit are standards of healthy individual and relationship functioning that are rooted in psychodynamic theories.

The epistemological basis for inclusion of individual dynamics as central to the family system is the same as that offered for inclusion of the sociocultural context. The broadest theoretical framework—general systems theory—accommodates this perspective as well as others. No family therapy theory has the market on the "truth," and all theories emerge out of a given sociocultural context and the theorist's construction of reality. Beyond this systemic/constructivist rationale, ethical principles such as "truth" and "justice" may also serve as standards for evaluating theories. That is, does the theoretical model permit an understanding of the breadth as well as the depth of human experience that would foster meaningful service to client? And does the model appear just to the extent that the therapist would accept its use for himself or herself as client?

Conclusion

This chapter has identified four broad facets of the family system that are cornerstones of integrative systems therapy for sexual distress. The family-societal interface, family structure, communication-interactional sequence, and the individual/family-of-origin interface are elements that define some of the major schools of family therapy. But the singular focus of each does not mean that each is looking at different phenomena; they simply use different theoretical tools (lenses) to capture the immediate focal point of interest.

References

Aylmer, R. C. (1986). Bowen family systems marital therapy. In N. S. Jacobson & A. S. Gurman (Eds.), *Clinical handbook of marital therapy* (pp. 107-148). New York: Guilford Press.

Bateson, G., Jackson, D. D., Haley, J., & Weakland, J. H. (1956). Towards a theory of schizophrenia. *Behavioral Science, 1,* 251-264.

Berman, E. M., & Hof, L. (1987). The sexual genogram—Assessing family of origin factors in the treatment of sexual dysfunction. In G. R. Weeks & L. Hof (Eds.), *Integrating sex and marital therapy* (pp. 37-56). New York: Brunner/Mazel.

Bertalanffy, L. von. (1968). *General systems theory: Foundation, development, applications.* New York: Braziller.

Boszormenyi-Nagy, I., & Spark, G. (1973). *Invisible loyalties.* New York: Harper and Row.

Bowen, M. (1978). *Family therapy in clinical practice.* New York: Jason Aronson.

Duncan, B. L. (1984). Adopting the construct of functionality when it facilitates system change: A method of selective integration. *Journal of Strategic and Systemic Therapies, 4,* 58-63.

Duncan, B. L., & Fraser, J. S. (1987). Buckley's scheme of schemes as a foundation for teaching family systems theory. *Journal of Marital and Family Therapy, 1,* 299-305.

Duncan, B. L., & Parks, M. B. (1988). Integrating individual and systems approaches: Strategic-behavioral therapy. *Journal of Marital and Family Therapy, 1*(2), 151-161.

Fish, L. S., Fish, R. C., & Sprenkle, D. H. (1984). Treating inhibited sexual desire: A marital therapy approach. *American Journal of Family Therapy, 12*(3), 3-12.

Framo, J. (1982). *Explorations in marital and family therapy.* New York: Springer.
Fraser, J. S. (1986). Integrating system-based therapies: Similarities, differences, and some critical questions. In D. E. Efron (Ed.), *Journeys: Expansion of the strategic-systemic therapies.* New York: Brunner/Mazel.
Goldner, V. (1989). Sex, power, and gender: The politics of passion. In D. Okun & B. F. Kantor (Eds.), *Intimate environments: Sex, intimacy, and gender in families* (pp. 28-53). New York: Guilford Press.
Goodrich, T., Rampage, C., Ellman, B., & Halstead, K. (1988). *Feminist family therapy: A casebook.* New York: Norton.
Haley, J. (1976). *Uncommon therapy: The psychiatric techniques of Milton H. Erickson, M. D.* New York: Norton.
Hartman, A., & Laird, J. (1983). *Family-centered social work practice.* New York: The Free Press.
Hof, L. (1987). Evaluating the marital relationship of clients with sexual complaints. In G. R. Weeks & L. Hof (Eds.), *Integrating sex and marital therapy* (pp. 5-22). New York: Brunner/Mazel.
Hof, L., & Berman, E. M. (1986). The sexual genogram. *Journal of Marital and Family Therapy, 1,* 39-47.
Hof, L., & Berman, E. M. (1989). The sexual genogram: Assessing family of origin factors in the treatment of sexual dysfunction. In D. Kantor & B. F. Okun (Eds.), *Intimate environments: Sex, intimacy, and gender in families* (pp. 290-320). New York: Guilford Press.
Jackson, D. D. (1967). Aspects of conjoint family therapy. In G. H. Zuk & I. Boszormenyi-Nagy (Eds.), *Family therapy and disturbed families* (pp. 28-40). Palo Alto: Science and Behavior Books.
Kahn, M. D. (1989). Through a glass brightly: Treating sexual intimacy as a restoration of the whole person. In D. Kantor & B. F. Okun (Eds.), *Intimate environments: Sex, intimacy, and gender in families* (pp. 54-73). New York: Guilford Press.
Laszlo, E. (1972). *The systems view of the world.* New York: George Braziller.
LoPiccolo, J. (1991, May 4). *Post-modern sex therapy.* Paper presented at the annual meeting of the American Association of Sex Educators, Counselors, and Therapists, St. Louis, MO.
LoPiccolo, J., & Stock, W. (1986). Treatment of sexual dysfunction. *Journal of Consulting and Clinical Psychology, 54*(2), 158-167.
Luepnitz, D. A. (1988). *The family interpreted: Feminist theory in clinical practice.* New York: Basic Books.
Masters, W. H., & Johnson, V. E. (1966). *Human sexual response.* Boston: Little, Brown.
Masters, W. H., & Johnson, V. E. (1970). *Human sexual inadequacy.* Boston: Little, Brown.
May, J. L., & Bobele, M. (1988). Sexual dysfunction and the unemployed male professional. *Journal of Sex and Marital Therapy, 1*(4), 253-262.
Minuchin, S. (1974). *Families and family therapy.* Cambridge, MA: Harvard University Press.
Nichols, M. (1984). *Family therapy: Concepts and methods.* New York: Gardner Press.
Nichols, W. C. (1988). *Marital therapy: An integrative approach.* New York: Guilford Press.
Regas, S. J., & Sprenkle, D. H. (1984). Functional family therapy and the treatment of inhibited desire. *Journal of Marital and Family Therapy 1,* 63-72.

Rosen, R. C., & Leiblum, S. R. (1989). Assessment and treatment of desire disorders. In S. R. Leiblum & R. Rosen (Eds.), *Principles and practice of sex therapy* (pp. 19-47). New York: Guilford Press.

Sager, C. J. (1976). *Marriage contracts and couple therapy.* New York: Brunner/Mazel.

Sanders, G. (1988). Of cybernetics and sexuality. *Family Therapy Networker, 12,* 38-41, 79-84.

Sanders, G., & Tomm, K. (1989). A cybernetic-systemic approach to problems in sexual functioning. In D. Kantor & B. F. Okun (Eds.), *Intimate environments: Sex, intimacy, and gender in families* (pp. 346-380). New York: Guilford Press.

Satir, V. (1967). *Conjoint family therapy.* Palo Alto, CA: Science and Behavior Books.

Scharff, D. E. (1988). *The sexual relationship: An object-relations view of sex and the family.* New York: Routledge, Chapman & Hall.

Slipp, S. (1988). *The technique and practice of object relations family therapy.* Northvale, NJ: Jason Aronson.

Slowinski, J. (1984). Reflections on sex therapy: An interview with Harold I. Lief and Arnold Lazarus. *Journal of Sex Education and Therapy, 1,* 13-21.

Talmadge, L. D., & Talmadge, W. C. (1986). Relational sexuality: An understanding of low sexual desire. *Journal of Sex and Marital Therapy, 1*(1), 3-21.

Taggart, M. (1985). The feminist critique in epistemological perspective: Questions of context in family therapy. *Journal of Marital and Family Therapy, 11,* 113-126.

Verhulst, J., & Heiman, J. (1979). An interactional approach to sexual dysfunction. *American Journal of Family Therapy, 7,* 19-36.

Watzlawick, P., Beavin, J. H., & Jackson, D. D. (1967). *Pragmatics of human communication.* New York: Norton.

Watzlawick, P., Weakland, J. H., & Fisch, C. (1974). *Change: Principles of problem formulation and problem resolution.* New York: Norton.

Weeks, G. R. (1987). Systematic treatment of inhibited sexual desire. In G. R. Weeks & L. Hof (Eds.), *Integrating sex and marital therapy* (pp. 183-201). New York: Brunner/Mazel.

Woody, J. D. (1989). The reality of an integrative sex therapy. *Journal of Sex & Marital Therapy, 1*(1), 62-73.

Zilbergeld, B., & Ellison, C. (1980). Desire discrepancies and arousal problems. In S. Leiblum & L. Pervin (Eds.), *Principles and practice of sex therapy,* (pp. 65-101). New York: Guilford Press.

Zilbergeld, B., & Kilmann, P. R. (1984). The scope and effectiveness of sex therapy. *Psychotherapy, 1*(3), 319-326.

5

Integrative Systems Therapy: Introduction to the Model

> But before I treat a patient like yourself I need to know a great deal more about him than the patient himself can always tell me. Indeed, it is often the case that my patients are only pieces of a total situation which I have to explore. The single patient who is ill by himself, is rather the exception.
>
> T. S. ELIOT, from *The Cocktail Party*

The psychotherapy literature in the past decade reflects an increasing willingness to use multiple theories and techniques. Research indicates that from one third to one half of clinicians identify their mode of practice as eclectic. This trend is expected to continue. Rather than seeking a puristic epistemological basis for integration, most therapists draw from diverse theories because they accept the salience of specific concepts (Norcross, 1987). For example, Lazarus (1981) incorporates various techniques within an overall cognitive-behavioral framework. And, more recently, Luepnitz (1988) finds logic in blending feminist, psychoanalytic, and systems concepts.

Distinctions in the meanings of eclecticism and integration are often debated. Norcross (1987) prefers the term *eclecticism* and argues that it should be prescriptive and systematic. *Prescriptive eclecticism* refers to selecting theory and treatment to match the client's specific problem or characteristics based on the expectation of effectiveness as supported by clinical experience and/or outcome research. *Systematic eclecticism* refers to having a design or method for selecting interventions (again based on support) that can be taught and replicated. Another important distinction is that of *synthetic eclecticism*, which calls for an integration of diverse theories, not just a method of selecting techniques. The term *integration* is essentially equivalent to synthetic eclecticism, because integration refers to "incorporation of parts into a whole" (Norcross, 1987, p. 6).

The term *integrative* is used throughout this book to encompass the above three meanings. The proposed model of integrative therapy (IST) is *prescriptive* in that the theory and treatment were selected for their relevance to the range of sexual distress. The model is *systematic* in having a method for selecting theory and interventions that can be taught and duplicated. And the model is *synthetic* in the attempt to incorporate diverse contemporary theories into a whole.

An integrative systems therapy for sexual distress must also make sense on a pragmatic level—that is, appear valid to clinicians who actually work with various types of sexual problems. The nature of sexual distress points to the need for a holistic understanding of the problem in the context of its interface with societal, family, interpersonal, and individual dimensions. The terms *holistic* and *interface* are critical to the goal of integrating concepts and strategies at a deep level, rather than simply applying first one treatment approach and then another. The latter has, in fact, been "standard" practice: that is, first marital therapy for relationship problems, then sex therapy for sexual dysfunction or complaints, then individual therapy if the first two are not effective.

In contrast to the "standard" practice, the IST model provides an explanation that is rich because it potentially accounts for the interaction (mutual influencing) of the various dimensions of the problem. Consider the example of a couple with the complaint of their ritualized sexual interaction, which consists of the husband's verbal domination and demeaning of his wife during the sex act. As an individual each partner experiences the sexual distress on a physiological, emotional, cognitive, and behavioral level. Both may be conscious about the well-intentioned beginnings of this self-maintaining interactional pattern that now is a problem. It may embody basic structural elements characteristic of their overall relationship, such as enmeshment. Moreover, these may be congruent with societal structures and themes, such as stereotyped gender roles. At the same time, the distressful sexual interaction may embody unconscious dimensions of the personalities and self-structures of both partners, which manifest as vestiges from the individual-family of origin interface. These operate systemically to maintain stability in the couple's present relationship as well as in the specific behavioral sequences that constitute the problem.

Having a view of the potentially interacting dimensions of the problem takes us beyond a simple diagnosis of sexual sadism, or a relationship problem, or expected but unfortunate fallout from societal structures and themes. With a holistic conceptualization of the problem, it becomes possible to understand the interaction of all of these factors and to devise truly integrative treatment strategies—those that might impact simultaneously on several dimensions of the problem.

This chapter has four purposes. First, it sets forth an epistemological position and basic assumptions that serve as the foundation for an integrative systems approach to intimacy and sexual dysfunctions. Second, it lays out the general principles of the model. Third, it illustrates in detail how the components of the model apply in assessing a case of sexual dysfunction. And, fourth, it provides a preview summary of the four stages of therapy, each of which is subsequently covered in a separate chapter.

Foundations for Integration

Most therapists are highly eclectic in clinical work and probably selectively integrate concepts and techniques via intuition. The goal here is to set forth a more formal rationale. The epistemological base for IST derives from both theory, namely general systems theory, and from ethics, both general and professional ethics.

GENERAL SYSTEMS FRAMEWORK

General systems theory, because of its highly abstract level, provides a suitable metatheoretical paradigm for integration. It allows for attention to both ground and figure. Context is an inherent or core element in a system, and is determined flexibly according to one's focal point. Because of current controversies in family therapy, the context most in dispute is the social environment (which can encompass social institutions and structures, as well as assumptions and values that are inherent in language, culture, and history).

A related assumption in general systems theory is the reality of an observer/participant selecting a viewpoint. This means that the theorist or therapist exists in the same context that he or she is viewing. Thus when a theorist develops a theory, it does not constitute a neutral or objective analytical tool. There is no answer to the question of its "truth." A more relevant question is "What function is the selected theoretical language to play within the human arena?" (Constantine, 1989, p. 123). With perspectivism, we must resort to another level of experience—values and ethics—to answer that question and to arrive at a standard for judging theory.

ETHICAL THEORY

Ethical theory rescues us from the morass of pure relativism (Erickson, 1988; Woody, 1990). First, from general ethics, the principle of social justice offers a basis for social living that applies to all persons. This principle calls on people to act only in ways that they are willing for others in the society to act (Rawls, 1971). Second, professionals are bound by additional ethical principles by virtue of their obligation to serve the welfare of others.

The therapist is thus ethically obliged to provide service that he or she believes will benefit the client. This standard applies to the selection of theories that guide professional activity. This selection will, by necessity, reflect to some extent the therapist's values (including social values as well since the therapist is part of the same social/historical context as the client). Two guidelines for the ethical selection of theory might be: "truth" and "justice."

First, "truth" here might refer to the theory's usefulness in accounting for the complexity of human experience sufficient to foster the helping process. We can tap in to this complexity through the general systems metatheory. It encompasses diverse views of behavior; but since no one theory of therapy takes in this whole picture, drawing from several theories is necessary.

Second, the principle of "justice" serves as a standard for judging the moral dimension of social relationships, which many theories ignore. Does the theory allow for consideration of social justice in relationships? And returning to the therapist's obligation to clients to use "good" theory, the principle of justice also applies. For example, if we did not know what role we might play in society (sex, position, status), would we endorse a given theory and therapy to be used by others (possibly on us)?

Calling upon ethical standards can serve as a reminder that a theory is not reality, but merely one way that professionals explain human behavior in order to help people. All theories are limited. Feminists have repeatedly pointed out the shortcomings of those family therapy models that center on process and claim neutrality on content and context (Taggart, 1985). For example, the interactionalist model conceptualizes family violence as a circular process, a view that ignores the reality of power and the suffering of victims. Only recently have proponents of this view begun to confront the complexity of the issue rather than defend the original position (Dell, 1989).

With this epistemological framework, integration of theoretical models is justified if it fosters understanding of the complexity of a given client or type of problem and if it reflects a valuing of the client that is equivalent to one's own valuing of self. The therapist has to make these latter judgments. And they, too, inevitably depend upon not only professional competence but also upon the therapist's personal character and moral vision.

PRELIMINARY PRAGMATIC ASSUMPTIONS

The holistic nature of experience is an argument for conceptual integration. Theory divides human functioning into behavior, affect, cognition, interaction, and so forth. But this does not mean that people experience problems or make changes according to these singular facets. And even though a given technique is oriented to a single facet, such as behavior therapy, this does not necessarily mean that, if a client changes, the change was brought about by intervention on the intended target. Theorists take human behavior apart in order to simplify it, but therapists have to find ways to put it back together. Integration of therapeutic models is a way of doing this.

The commonalities underlying the strategy of different theoretical models support conceptual integration. First, there are many generic processes within the various types of therapy that are common in all effective treatment. Norcross (1987) has placed these processes into three broad categories: support, learning, and action factors. Second, one therapeutic method may foster the goals of another (whether intended or not). For example, Lazarus has noted that clients may experience "spontaneous insight" in association with behavior therapy (Powell, 1987). More recently, Duncan and Solovey (1989) have reported a client's attaining spontaneous insight through doing strategic tasks, but labeled it "client-ascribed meaning." They have sparked a debate, however, by asserting that "client-ascribed meaning" is different from "therapist-ascribed meaning," such as a therapist's interpretation to promote insight. Others do not see the necessity for such fine distinctions. Thus Slipp (1989) asserts that the process in question is insight and that it benefits the client. The same type of semantic hair-splitting appears in Sanders and Tomm's (1989) preference for the term "outsight" over "insight" (rejected because of its psychodynamic connection) to refer to clients' gaining understanding about their part in circular patterns in relationships.

Such distinctions, in view of the holistic nature of human experience, serve the goal of maintaining theoretical consistency rather than that of helping clients. Regardless of the preferred terminology in the above, client learning was the generic factor. And it is associated with positive outcomes in treatment, as are support and action factors The various theories simply use different techniques for promoting learning, support, and action.

The nature of client change supports conceptual integration. Achieving meaningful change is a recursive process consisting of the interaction of many facets of experience. Clients will vary on the dimensions that are part of this process: for example, degree of "stuckness," readiness to change or use help, and degree of progress in finding one's own solutions. This latter point is important because we must assume that most couples or families who never seek therapy struggle on the trail to finding solutions and arrive at them either with a creative burst of energy or through trial and error plodding. Given the range of potential factors relevant to change, it is possible that some clients could benefit from a singular therapeutic strategy (e.g., empathic listening, behavioral modification, a paradoxical intervention, or cognitive restructuring, etc.), whereas others might need a more comprehensive or integrative treatment. A client's success may not be due to a singular technique targeting the "source" of the problem. It may come from an element of treatment, or it may be that the total treatment boosts a solution process already in progress.

Distinctions between content and process are not a barrier to conceptual integration, nor are they useful for moving the client on the road to change. Systems therapists often emphasize this distinction. For example, Todd (1986) cautions that the systemic perspective may be lost if the therapist becomes "immersed in the particular content" (p. 94) rather than attending to the interactional patterns.

With sexual distress, I would caution against denying or diminishing the importance of sexual content. That approach on the part of the therapist can play into cultural taboos and stereotypes about sex and so maintain "more of the same" type of interaction in which clients may already be engaged. Such a stance of denial on the part of the therapist constitutes an intervention. Once the therapeutic system is underway, everything the therapist does has intervention power—not just carefully designed tasks or directives.

Because of the physiological component, the content of sexual problems is truly different from the content in which other types of couple problems are embedded. In a couple's sexual encounter, one goal is for partners (usually both) to have physical contact and exchanges in order to experience pleasurable physiological responses—desire, arousal, orgasm. When there is a dysfunction, one or more of these physiological responses is absent. When there is sexual dissatisfaction, the physiological responses may occur, but evaluations of the encounter or overall relationship are negative.

Sexual distress is not the same as a couple's problems in value conflicts, quarreling, or communication. These latter areas of dispute do not have a similar physiological component involving focused sensual/sexual exchanges. A partial analogue might be found in the disturbed physiological processes due to eating disorders, but these do not involve a mutual sensual exchange with a partner. Sexual dysfunctions have an impact, of course, beyond the physiological; emotions, cognitions, behavior, and the couple's and their family's overall relationship may be affected.

The therapist obviously cannot observe sexual problems in order to determine process, although observation is possible with couple quarrels, communication problems, and so on. This may be the reason that some systems therapists prefer to focus on another relationship difficulty or pattern hypothesized to be linked to the sexual problem. These may very well be important, but they do not negate the validity of attending to the sexual interaction in which the problem is manifested. One can use various systemic lenses on the sexual content to discern interactional patterns, but it is necessary to deal with that content. It is not, however, always necessary to use a strictly "systemic" technique to effect a systemic change. As asserted throughout this book, traditional sex therapy methods, often labeled as content-oriented, have systemic properties and can impact on systemic processes.

A final point about sexual content centers on the therapist's decisions on when and how to explore sexual detail. There can be no simple guideline for these judgments. Family therapists seem hesitant on this issue. Sanders (1988) assumes a pervasive reluctance on the part of clients to deal with their sexual lives and a high degree of sexual naivete. Perhaps this view stems from the fact that much of his clinical experience has been with Canadian clients, who may be more reserved than Americans. Weeks (1987) cautions against probing into sexual content before joining with the client, but does qualify this by noting that joining may require a few seconds or a few sessions.

Sensitivity is necessary in discussing sexuality, but not all clients hold culturally based negative attitudes toward sex. Many extenuating factors unique to each client can influence the attitude toward sexual material. For example, the salience of the sexual problem, personal comfort level with sex, and motivation for solution could render many clients more ready to discuss sex than their therapists. The clinician's own competence and comfort in dealing with sex and its place in the preferred theoretical model of treatment also influence decisions about if, when, and how to explore sexual content.

Basic Principles

There are 10 broad principles that guide the IST model. They appear in summary fashion below but are explained further, along with case examples, in subsequent chapters.

1. IST is relevant to a wide range of sexual distress, including dysfunctions; sexual complaints; and concerns about sexual relationships, obsessive-compulsive patterns, sexual-body image, object choice, gender identity, and affectional preference. This view contrasts with several recent efforts which have applied systems theory only

for desire disorders or for clinical impasses in traditional sex therapy. Treatment for incest, however, is beyond the scope of this book since this complex family problem requires intensive and extensive multidisciplinary treatment and interagency consultation.

2. IST incorporates traditional sex therapy concepts and techniques, categorized here as the Cognitive-Behavioral Dimension, one of the five major components of the model. However, the rationale for and the strategies derived from sex therapy are integrated to promote congruence with systems theory. IST pursues and elaborates the systemic potential of the techniques in conjunction with the other conceptual dimensions within the model.

3. IST accepts the immediate sexual distress as the problem to remedy (if presented as the primary complaint or if it emerges as a significant complaint in intimacy disorders that the client wants addressed). But because of the multitheoretical base, IST accommodates a flexible approach to problem definition. The problem may be defined as a sexual symptom in terms of an individual's undesired response or as a couple symptom in terms of a defeating interactional pattern or as both. On the other hand, with some situations, the problem may be defined, not as a symptom, but more globally as the need for understanding, insight, or decision making involving the sexual distress. It is necessary early on to formulate the problem and elicit specific client goals. Obviously, goals may change, evolving towards greater specificity or towards encompassing broader issues. Throughout, the therapist assists the client to identify outcomes indicative of progress.

4. Focusing on sexual content is necessary and congruent with an overall systems perspective that centers on process, patterns, and relationships. The therapist guides the client's report on this content according to which systemic perspective is needed. Initially, for purposes of diagnostic accuracy, the content explored centers on problematic sexual behaviors, and the sensations, images, emotions, and cognitions associated with them.

5. Focusing on and tracking the problematic sexual interaction is critical. Sexual interaction refers to the complex behavioral/communicational sequence of the typical sexual act or encounter that contains the sexual complaint. The term *sexual interaction* thus captures a molecular view of the problem, as distinguished from a molar

view, such as the couple's "sexual relationship" or "overall relationship" or "typical interaction pattern."

6. Flexibility in the use of concepts and techniques is essential. Given the uniqueness of client situations and each therapeutic system, the therapist needs flexibility in assessment and in selecting and devising treatment strategy. IST readily affords that flexibility.

7. Structure for the process of therapy, as well as flexibility, is provided by conceptualizing treatment in stages, each of which poses certain therapeutic challenges. If these are met successfully, therapy can proceed. If not, the therapist will likely feel confused, perhaps identifying the impasse as resistance.

8. The components from the different theories are incorporated at each stage of therapy to varying degrees to guide both etiological understanding and treatment strategy. One concept may dominate at a given stage while others are simply present more as infrastructure for the therapist's clinical thinking. Case examples in subsequent chapters illustrate the diversity of these potential combinations and guidelines.

9. The conceptual components for IST are the cognitive-behavioral problem paradigm (under which traditional sex therapy fits), family-societal interface, family structure, communication-interactional sequence, and individual/family-of-origin interface. These were discussed in Chapters 3 and 4. Table 5.1 briefly summarizes these components. In the following section, separate assessment hypotheses based on each component are offered for a case of sexual dysfunction and then integrated to provide a comprehensive etiological understanding of it.

10. Therapy is conceptualized as a series of four broad stages. Each stage presents tasks and challenges for the therapist. The stages are (a) the therapeutic system, (b) initial assessment and early interventions, (c) refocusing and power interventions, and (d) maintaining progress and terminating. The numbering suggests a sequence, but elements from several stages are, in fact, often telescoped in a given session. For example, while early sessions may emphasize building the therapeutic system, this task pervades all stages. It is also possible that stage three may not be necessary. And, as clinicians know only too well, therapy often ends before planned termination takes place.

TABLE 5.1 Conceptual Components

Cognitive-Behavioral Dimension (Traditional Sex Therapy)	*Problem-Interactional Sequence*	*Family-Societal Interface*
Sexual symptom as problem to remedy	Communication/behavioral sequences containing and maintaining the problem	Sociocultural factors and embedded structures
Assesses: problem history, relationship(s) and life stressors		Impact of gender-based structures and themes
individual's biological social, sexual, developmental, psychological history, especially cognitions and reinforcement	Problematic sexual encounter as interactional sequence consisting of physiological, behavioral, and psychological communication sequence	Impact of family linkage to social institutions Interventions: may derive from any model but should reflect sensitivity to these factors and the wholistic quality of client's life
Interventions: information/education, cognitive-restructuring, experiential/behavioral sensual and sexual tasks	Problem contained within a vicious circular interaction that began as an attempted solution	*Individual/Family-of-Origin Interface*
Family Structure Life cycle and events	Related couple/family interactional sequences may connect to sexual problem	Failures in differentiation: emotional fusion; family legacies (roles, triangles, loyalty conflicts, emotional reactivity)
Structural adaptation and failures Couple intimacy subsystem boundaries: enmeshed/disengaged; alliances and coalitions; power	Interventions: reframing, restraint of change, prescription of symptom, straightforward and paradoxical directives to interrupt sequence	Object-relations history: "self" emerges from the quality of primary nurturing relationship; determines capacity for intimacy and sexual fulfillment
Parental/executive subsystem boundaries: hierarchy, alliances, coalitions;		Defensive stances to protect impaired self due to narcissistic rage or fears of engulfment or abandonment
Interventions: enactments and other in-session restructuring techniques; tasks to restructure		Interventions: rational therapeutic style, genogram, interpretation, others consistent with goal of increased rationality or cohesive self

Using the Model Components for Assessment

How can the various components outlined in Table 5.1 fit together to provide a coherent framework for understanding the cause and maintenance of sexual distress? Each dimension guides thinking from several perspectives about the nature of the problem. And while this is always speculative, these understandings point toward certain treatment methods. This does not mean that we must use the strategies from each method. The therapist must still evaluate and select these to fit the circumstances of the client situation.

General systems theory forces attention to the interaction of factors and circular causality. Table 5.1 above merely lists the possible explanations to explore. Going beyond this, Figure 5.1 below suggests the circular interactional patterns among the dimensions that could contribute to a sexual or intimacy problem. No single factor is necessarily determinative of a disorder, but a number of negative factors in various dimensions could interact to overdetermine the likelihood of sexual disturbance. For example, with a desire disorder, it is likely that the configuration of contributing factors would, no doubt, differ for various clients with that dysfunction, although there might be similarities in some dimensions.

Some of the possible interactions among the elements in Figure 5.1 can be noted. For example, both the individual/family-of-origin interface and societal-family interface encompass development through time. These developmental pieces can be said to be present within the other more focused problem and relationship dimensions since one's history and current evolution are present where the individual is present. Imagine planning to present an assessment with an overhead projector. We could record on each of five transparencies five different assessments according to each dimension in Figure 5.1. Each one of the transparencies could be placed on top of the other to constitute a total assessment picture. Although this act makes for a concrete image of combining the various insights obtained, it is simply additive, not integrative, since it does not capture the systemic, interactive reality. It does not show how the various parts are connected, nor the process or structure of the whole. The most we can do is to put one transparency at a time into the projector in order to obtain that singular perspective of the problem. Integration must take place through the

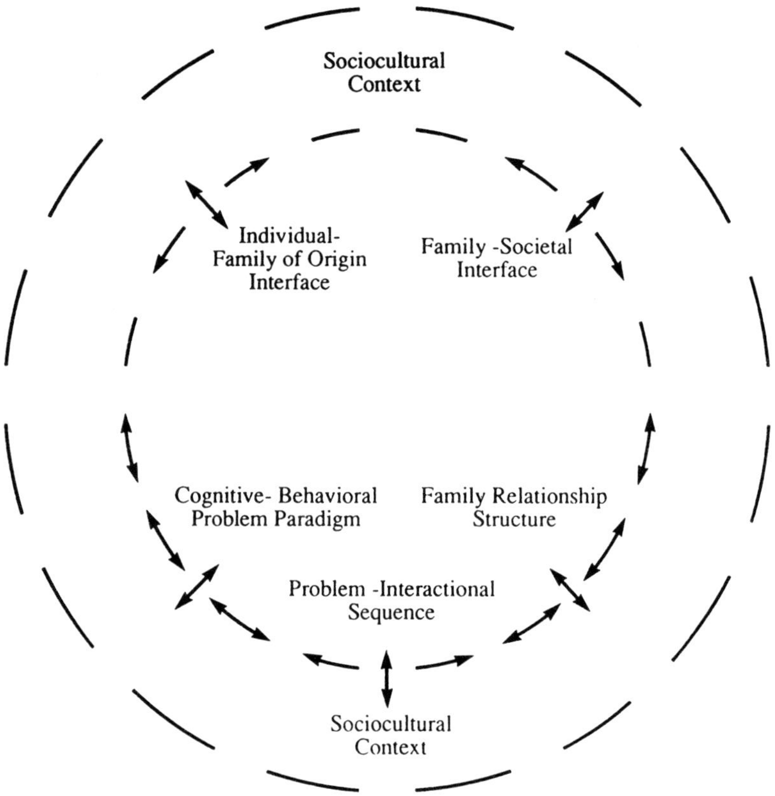

Figure 5.1. Interacting Dimensions Relevant to Etiology

therapist's mental processes of conceptualizing the pieces of the problem holistically and systemically.

The systems principle of equifinality applies here. Equifinality refers to the process whereby an open system "may attain a time-independent state independent of initial conditions and determined only by the system parameters" (Bertalanffy, 1968, p. 18). This means that the process, not necessarily initial causes, dictates outcomes. A variety of beginnings could result in the same outcome, and the same beginning could result in a variety of outcomes.

To illustrate, the terms "normal" or "problematic" might be used to describe a given dimension with regard to a client's intimate experience, but the factor labeled does not remain static or totally predictive of functioning in another dimension. For example, within the individual/family-of-origin interface, consider a young woman who has had a "normal" developmental/personality history, which gives her a good start in life. But, as a teenager, she becomes a victim of rape. Many intervening factors besides the individual developmental dimension could impact on how she internalizes this event and whether it impairs her capacity for intimacy and sexual satisfaction in a subsequent relationship. The outcome would also involve other factors such as her interactions with any present or future partners in her voluntary sexual relationships and all the qualities which those persons bring, as well as the nature of those relationships. Thus process can take over to produce a given outcome.

Figure 5.1 uses arrows to show interaction and multidirectionality to capture the mutual influence of the different dimensions. This figure attempts to suggest the continuing influence on current functioning of one's past history, as represented in individual and family development, and also the influence of current functioning in changing individual and family structures.

To further illustrate Figure 5.1, the following discussion of a case presents five separate assessment hypotheses to explain the couple's sexual distress. A final assessment statement aims to conceptualize the problem holistically and systemically.

In the case of Denise and Dave below, the assessment process begins with consideration of the family-societal interface, especially gender-based structures and themes, and then proceeds with the other dimensions in clockwise direction of the arrows. This dimension places the couple in the present time, where the problem exists, and within a broad social context. One might choose to start with another dimension. This analysis is done to illustrate the potential problem explanations conveyed in Figure 5.1, not to suggest how to conduct the assessment in therapy or how to make assessment or treatment decisions. The last section of this chapter on the stages of therapy touches on this, and remaining chapters cover it in detail.

FAMILY-SOCIETAL INTERFACE

In the family-societal interface, gender-based themes and societal linkages are important. Denise and Dave, although they have been married for 3 years, have yet to accomplish many of the tasks of the stage of early marriage. Denise, 26, has no desire for or interest in sex, gets no pleasure from it, and is not orgasmic. They are thinking of starting a family, but she is hesitant because she questions the stability of their marriage due to their sexual problems; this concern led her into therapy. Denise is successfully employed in a management position, whereas Dave, 27, has changed jobs several times, is currently in sales (which he dislikes), makes less money than Denise, and works part-time as a flight instructor (an activity he does enjoy). Besides concerns about sex and careers, they have other problems involving societal linkages. The relationship with Denise's family of origin is somewhat stressed due to Dave's being of a minority race (although of a higher class status than her family). They also have conflicts because of the amount of time Dave spends at the fixed base air facility and because his friends from there drop in freely at their home. They disagree about money, with Denise managing it and complaining about Dave's excessive spending; they are purchasing a home. The sexual problem is but one of several this couple is having in creating a marital unit with appropriate boundaries and sufficient cohesion to meet life's challenges as a team and to meet each other's emotional and sexual needs. The fact that they are an interracial couple may be an added but unacknowledged stressor around the question of having a child.

On the basis of the family-societal interface assessment alone, treatment might aim to foster an overall better adjustment to the tasks and roles of early marriage as a way of impacting on the sexual problem. Thus the sexual distress is broadly defined as but one of many problems the couple has in making a satisfactory adjustment to the institution of marriage.

Other information, however, suggests that this understanding based on the family-societal interface is not sufficient. Denise and Dave were a couple for 5 years prior to marriage, presumably sufficient time to adjust to each other. They went off to college together and lived together the last year, but during this long courtship Denise permitted no sexual activity or intercourse between them. This fact suggests the validity of focusing on Denise's sexual attitudes, cognitions, and so on (the cognitive-behavioral dimension), but before doing this, I want to look at another dimension—the couple's family structure.

FAMILY STRUCTURE

In terms of family structure, Dave and Denise appear to be disengaged in many areas of their relationship. Dave is gone from home a lot (two evenings a week at his regular job and Fridays and Saturdays at the flight school). Moreover, they do not share similar interests, nor do they attempt to compensate with quality time when they are together. Denise complains about this and Dave's friends being around, but she also likes her time alone—not cooking, watching television whenever she wishes, and knowing that Dave's long hours minimize the possibility of his requesting sex. She appears to be the overfunctioning partner (in career, economic base, and maturity), while he is underfunctioning (in these areas). She, however, attributes her success to him because he pushed her to go to college. Her symptom of inadequacy in the sexual area may serve to balance the relationship and keep her from totally overshadowing Dave.

Intervention according to this assessment of relationship structure would aim to decrease their disengagement by restructuring the couple boundary and other activities that produce separateness. Note that the structural focus does not negate the previous insights gained through the assessment of the family-societal interface.

COMMUNICATION-INTERACTIONAL SEQUENCE

Taking an even more circumscribed perspective, we look to the communication-interactional sequence for this couple's typical sexual encounter. They have sex once, possibly twice a week. Dave no longer initiates more than this, because he knows Denise dislikes sex. He "puts up with her," and they may even joke about it—she is fondly known as the "bitch" in their household. If they go without sex for a week, it is no longer a joking matter. Dave argues about it, and she agrees to intercourse. Denise's goal is simply to get it over. She permits no caressing, no intimate kissing, no oral sex (all of this repulses her); and she does not caress or pleasure him either. She accommodates him for intercourse, which is sometimes initially uncomfortable. Afterwards, they go to sleep, and start over again the next day with the same pattern. The pattern occurs even when Dave tries to set a romantic mood by cooking a special dinner. The pattern is one of avoidance of sex, eventual argument, obligatory sex, and equilibrium.

Intervention according to this understanding of the problem would aim to interrupt the vicious cycle containing the problem, that is, change the steps in this dismal dance. This perspective might also focus on other interactional sequences believed connected to the sexual interaction sequence. Note again, this understanding does not negate the validity of the previous insights captured through different lenses.

COGNITIVE-BEHAVIORAL PROBLEM PARADIGM

Using the cognitive-behavioral problem paradigm (typical in traditional sex therapy) uncovers Denise's early and continuous learning of negative sexual attitudes and avoidance of sexual behavior. Coming from a Catholic family, she was drilled, not only in Catholic school but by her mother, about the negatives of sex. She recalled a sex education film in the seventh grade as traumatic, "a bad memory." She did not date until age 18 when she met Dave. Her parents were affectionate to each other but not toward their six children. Another event powerfully reinforced the early learning. She and Dave had intercourse after about a year of dating, and she was terrified that she was pregnant. Once she learned that she was not pregnant, she ended all sexual and affectionate contact with him, and this avoidance pattern defined their relationship for the next 5 years. She obtained birth control pills 3 months before they were married. Then, when they first had intercourse she "hated" it and has ever since. This analysis suggests a powerful conditioning of fear and anxiety responses to sex that continues to be reinforced both by her successful avoidance and by the negative sexual encounters when they take place. Dave's sexual learning was just the opposite. His family was very open about sex and expressive of emotion. He enjoys all aspects of sensuality and sexuality, and has given Denise books on sexuality to read, which she also avoids.

Intervention based on this understanding would aim to extinguish Denise's phobic response to sex and alter the many accompanying faulty cognitions. A variety of cognitive-behavioral techniques could be used, many of which are common in traditional sex therapy. Note that this understanding can be viewed as a close-up of the previous interactional sequence that magnifies the role of each person's learned schemas in the interaction.

INDIVIDUAL/FAMILY-OF-ORIGIN INTERFACE

Focusing on the dimension of individual-family of origin interface reveals rigid, interlocking roles for this couple that stem from experience in families of origin. Both of Denise's parents were alcoholic in her youth (they are currently divorcing). As a result, she became the "take charge" person in her family and came to trust only herself and her own efforts. Low self-esteem, however, led to social isolation and she is still a loner. Her life centers on work and proving her worth. Dave grew up in a family that provided affection as well as material benefits and opportunities for fun and leisure. He has had many hobbies and seeks out new and different experiences. He is best at playing. It appears that when they met during their late teens, they fulfilled each other's unconscious ideal partner fantasy. Now, the idealized projections of certain qualities have become thorns in their sides. To Denise, Dave seems like her "little boy" to whom she is not even attracted. To Dave, Denise seems a worrying, bitchy mother who threatens to take away all his pleasures. Yet their dependence on the relationship is strong because each partner completes the other's incomplete self, and it protects both from changing in the unique areas in which each needs to grow.

Intervention based on the understanding that the sexual problem is an outgrowth of this intergenerational relationship configuration would promote self-differentiation and building of a secure identity for each partner. These emotional gains would modulate the automatic roles and rigid family legacies that characterize the present relationship. Note that this understanding connects present and past family relationships, patterns, and interactions and connects conscious and unconscious functioning. This assessment focus centered on unconscious process, whereas the two previous assessment dimensions looked closely at behavior for its reinforcement potential and at interactional sequences for their self-maintaining circularity.

All five dimensions were applied to Dave and Denise's problem to illustrate the conceptual assessment tools, though not necessarily a preferred sequence for using them. Nonetheless, we can now posit a comprehensive formulation of the problem that incorporates interaction and circularity of the dimensions.

Sexual dysfunction appears to be an overdetermined prospect for Denise. Her learned fear of sex combined with her family of origin legacy of low self-esteem, lack of trust, and social isolation left her deprived of intimacy—until she met Dave. With his expansive, affectionate, expressive, and fun-seeking qualities, he was able to overcome her isolation tendencies, and become the person who met her needs for emotional closeness. And she, with her practical, hard-working character, met his unconscious need for an anchor to complete his similarly insecure identity. The traumatic experience of a feared pregnancy reinforced the fear of sex. Her subsequent avoidance of sex and Dave's acceptance of the rules of the courtship set the stage for Denise's continued aversion to sex and the stabilizing of a dysfunctional relationship structure and dysfunctional sexual interaction pattern. They remained arrested in identity development and differentiation as a result of the homeostasis provided by several dimensions of their relationship and the symptom.

All five conceptual dimensions were used to illustrate diverse explanations of a sexual problem, but this is not intended to reflect the process of therapy. Carrying out this type of assessment, if deemed necessary, takes place in the context of various stages of treatment, each of which poses complex challenges for the clinician. As noted previously, the four stages of IST are: the therapeutic system, initial assessment and early intervention, refocusing and power interventions, and maintaining progress and terminating.

Preview of the Stages of Therapy

This chapter ends with a listing of the tasks of all four stages of IST. Although not discussed at this point, this framework alerts the reader to what is yet to come. Each of the next four chapters deals with the processes within a single stage and provides detailed case examples.

Stage 1: The Therapeutic System challenges the therapist to accomplish the following:

1. Assess the client's suitability for IST.
2. Join with the client.
3. Promote client expressiveness and ventilation.
4. Center on the client's view of the problem.
5. Elicit the client's expectations of therapy.
6. Consolidate the therapist's professional credibility.

Stage 2: Initial Assessment and Early Interventions challenges the therapist to accomplish the following:

1. Process information from inventories and scales.
2. Define the problem to be remedied.
3. Negotiate a therapeutic contract.
4. Formulate an initial assessment of problem content and process.
5. Apply initial interventions.
6. Assess the impact of early interventions.

Stage 3: Refocusing and Power Interventions challenges the therapist to accomplish the following:

1. Obtain other conceptual perspectives of the problem.
2. Incorporate these into a pragmatic assessment that encompasses interaction of various factors maintaining the problem.
3. Validate the initial problem focus and client goals or redefine and renegotiate.
4. Devise "power" interventions that could potentially impact on several interacting factors involved in maintaining the problem.
5. Match strategy and intervene according to the strength of the therapeutic system (including current client characteristics) and negotiated problem definition and goals.

Stage 4: Maintaining Progress and Terminating challenges the therapist to accomplish the following:

1. Stay attuned to the client's changing reality to anticipate future barriers.
2. Involve the client in planning for strategies to maintain progress.
3. Attend to termination issues such as tempering the therapeutic alliance and giving and receiving credit.
4. Evaluate therapy in accord with the diversity of the IST model.

References

Bertalanffy, L. von. (1968). *General systems theory: Foundation, development, applications.* New York: Braziller.

Constantine, L. L. (1989). Furniture for firewood: Blaming the systems paradigm. *Journal of Marital and Family Therapy, 15*,(2), 111-113.

Dell, P. F. (1989). Violence and the systemic view. *Family Process, 28*(1), 1-14.

Duncan, G. L., & Solovey, A. D. (1989). Strategic brief therapy: An insight-oriented approach? *Journal of Marital and Family Therapy, 15*(1), 1-9.

Erickson, G. D. (1988). Against the grain: Decentering family therapy. *Journal of Marital and Family Therapy, 14*, 225-236.

Erickson, G. D. (1989). Linear hisses and systemic cats. *Journal of Marital and Family Therapy, 15*,(2), 123-126.

Lazarus, A. A. (1981). *The practice of multimodal therapy.* New York: McGraw-Hill.

Luepnitz, D. A. (1988). *The family interpreted: Feminist theory in clinical practice.* New York: Basic Books.

Norcross, J. C. (1987). Introduction: Eclecticism, casebooks, and cases. In J. C. Norcross (Ed.), *Casebook of eclectic psychotherapy* (pp. 3-18). New York: Brunner/Mazel.

Powell, D. H. (1987). Commentary: Demonstrating therapeutic eclecticism. In J. C. Norcross (Ed.), *Casebook of eclectic psychotherapy* (pp.239-241). New York: Brunner/Mazel.

Rawls, J. (1971). *A theory of justice.* Cambridge, MA: Harvard University Press.

Sanders, G. (1988). Of cybernetics and sexuality. *Family Therapy Networker, 12*, 38-41, 79-84.

Sanders, G., & Tomm, K. (1989). A cybernetics-systems approach to problems in sexual functioning. In D. Kantor & B. F. Okun (Eds.), *Intimate environments: Sex, intimacy, and gender in families* (pp. 346-380). New York: Guilford Press.

Slipp, S. (1989). A differing viewpoint for integrating psychodynamic and systems approaches. *Journal of Marital and Family Therapy, 15*(1), 13-16.

Taggart, M. (1985). The feminist critique in epistemological perspective: Questions of context in family therapy. *Journal of Marital and Family Therapy, 11*, 113-126.

Todd, T. C. (1986). Structural-strategic marital therapy. In N. S. Jacobson & A. S. Gurman (Eds.), *Clinical handbook of marital therapy* (pp. 71-105). New York: Guilford Press.

Weeks, G. R. (1987). Systematic treatment of inhibited sexual desire. In G. R. Weeks & L. Hof (Eds.), *Integrating sex and marital therapy* (pp. 183-201). New York: Brunner/Mazel.

Woody, J. D. (1990). Resolving ethical concerns in clinical practice: Toward a pragmatic model. *Journal of Marital and Family Therapy, 1*(2), 165-178.

Part Two

The Process of Therapy

6

The Therapeutic System

Hope implies process . . . a going forward, a confident search.

KARL MENNINGER, from *The Vital Balance*

As a conceptual framework, integrative systems therapy (IST) has much to offer in building the therapeutic system. It allows the flexibility needed to accommodate the many client variables that influence whether a client becomes engaged in therapy. The first goal is for the client to gain sufficient respect for and trust in the clinician so as to continue with treatment. Each of the various theoretical components of IST has its unique strengths for engaging clients, and they all share certain other commonalities as well. A major contribution from systems theory is the emphasis on the interactional nature of the therapeutic system. The actions and reactions of all the players—therapist and client(s) alike—make up its quality. Another contribution centers on the concept of resistance. Systemic thinking sees this as the client's unique way of participating and as a normal product of the therapeutic context. Having several theoretical models to draw on allows the therapist to monitor his or her early actions and reactions to accommodate the client's productions, including resistance, in order to promote a viable therapeutic system.

Development of the therapeutic system gets underway with the first contact with the client and continues through the end of treatment. Typically, the first session or two are especially critical for this goal. Six major challenges accompany this stage of treatment. They are (a) assessing suitability for therapy, (b) joining with clients, (c) promoting client expressiveness, (d) centering on the client's view of the problem, (e) eliciting client expectations, and (f) consolidating professional credibility. Although the following treats each challenge separately, they are clearly all interrelated processes.

Assessing Suitability for Treatment

As indicated in Chapter 1, sexual distress can encompass a broad range of problems and issues; so it is necessary to judge the client's suitability for IST. This approach can take two broad tracks in defining the problem with the client. The first track is to formulate the sexual distress as a symptom, that is, as a chronic or recurring individual or couple pattern of behavior, or both, and to directly do therapy aimed at remedying or changing this symptom. The second track is to formulate the sexual distress as a condition calling for client exploration, insight, or decision making around the problem. Although these are not mutually exclusive problem definitions, one or the other typically dominates the direction of treatment at a given point.

Screening for suitability takes into account two major issues. First, is the client ready to commit sustained effort to therapy? Second, is some treatment format other than outpatient therapy indicated by the specific form of the client's sexual distress?

COMMITMENT TO THERAPY

Judging a client's commitment to therapy is not a simple process, because the therapist has some responsibility to elicit this and inspire hope. But it is often clear after one session that the client is not serious about engaging in therapy. It may be that the person came initially to obtain relief from an emotional crisis. And one session may, in fact, have restored some degree of equilibrium or provided understanding of the problem or fostered a decision to go no further with therapy.

The case of Terrence illustrates this point:

> Sixty-seven years old and widowed for 1 year, Terrence had cared for his terminally ill wife for the last 2 years of her life. He had recently entered a limited live-in relationship with Tamara, a 60-year-old woman, and had experienced erectile difficulties in attempting intercourse. He spoke in the first session about his love for his wife, the wonderful sexual and marital relationship they had had, and his continuing closeness to his children and grandchildren and his elderly brothers and sisters. He also revealed his lack of trust in Tamara and his disapproval of her values, her conflictual relationship with her children, and her prior lifestyle, which had included three marriages. The session ended with the suggestion that he bring in his new partner (she was quite willing) for further problem assessment. Although Terrence agreed to this, he did not return to therapy. A phone call several weeks later revealed that he had moved out of Tamara's apartment.

Commitment to therapy may not be forthcoming if one or both partners attends to obtain a forum for announcing the desire to separate or divorce. At this point, one or both may be certain of not wanting further treatment. The therapist can offer to help evaluate further the potential for the relationship or to help negotiate the decision.

When a couple shows tenuous commitment to each other and to therapy, and perhaps not much hope, still IST may be appropriate, though it may be necessary to negotiate limited treatment goals. It is usually risky to plunge into directly working on the sexual distress, but several options may be possible that take into account their tentativeness. Will they accept a brief trial period of good will and effort to test whether commitment is possible? Will they accept a trial period of therapy, within the separation format, focused on helping them face their problems and perhaps rekindling some positive sentiments towards each other? Is there a minor or short-term goal they could work on that might influence the present negative set about the relationship? These options can foster a discovery of whether a part of themselves still cares about the partner and the relationship.

This strategy aims to show respect for the relationship as well as for the deeply negative emotions and thoughts that persons may experience in the face of severe intimacy problems. Sometimes one lands on a creative option that sparks the interest of both partners and allows them to begin work on the relationship in a tentative manner. For other clients, however, this is not possible.

Therapists sometimes walk a tightrope when it comes to deciding on a couple's suitability for therapy directed to remedying intimacy problems. It is valid to respect the couple unit and search out its remaining strengths, but also legitimate to respect partners as individuals if they wish to leave an oppressive relationship or seek help in reaching a decision about it. Individual therapy that focuses on these latter goals may also address, to some extent, sexual distress and intimacy issues, but not necessarily in the context of resolving them in the present relationship.

NEED FOR OTHER TREATMENT

The second critical question in assessing suitability is whether some treatment other than outpatient therapy is indicated. In dealing with sexual distress, it is necessary to screen for physical, psychiatric, or other conditions that suggest a different treatment would be more effective. Not only may the client need referral for sexual dysfunctions and disorders, but medical intervention may be the treatment of choice.

Organic factors figure significantly into several sexual dysfunctions—especially dyspareunia and erectile disorders. Even if organic etiology has not been established, in cases where previous extensive sex therapy or psychotherapy has not helped, the clinician must carefully evaluate options before proceeding with further psychotherapy.

The case of Sam and Sara, both 55, illustrates the validity of considering treatment options:

> Sam and Sara were referred by a urologist for therapy for Sam's lifelong and global premature ejaculation. The urologist was considering having Sam use the penile injection Papaverine. Used to treat erectile dysfunction, the drug provides an erection that will last for 1 or 2 hours. In Sam's case, the injection would not stop the premature ejaculation, but would permit a sustained erection nonetheless that would allow a longer period of intercourse. Early in the first session, the couple reported that they had had 3 years of sex therapy several years before. It had brought no improvement, and they said they simply did not "have the heart" to undertake more therapy. Their strong relationship, characterized by a high degree of intimacy and good communication, suggested that they would make a good adaptation to the penile injection regime. A trial of this treatment was recommended to the

urologist. Several months later, the couple reported complete satisfaction with the medical treatment.

A final point about screening for suitability for IST pertains to treatment for incest and for sex offenders. These problems, though involving sexual distress, are not covered here precisely because their complexity demands more treatment options than are typically offered by the solo practitioner. Effective treatment usually calls for teams, encompasses both individual, family, couple, and group (and sometimes inpatient) formats, and demands extensive interagency consultation and referral. An integrative treatment approach is certainly indicated for these problems but is beyond the scope of this book. (See Trepper and Barrett [1989] for a systemic treatment of incest.)

Joining With Clients

Structural family therapists deem "joining" necessary because of the assumption that family members (or at least some) will normally be skeptical about therapy and the need for the whole family to be present. But joining is necessary regardless of whether the client is an individual, couple, or family, because it bridges the gap between the therapist's readiness to help and the client's understandable ambivalence about getting help. Joining is the effort to connect with the client, not only at the beginning, but throughout treatment. The therapist pursues this goal by emphasizing the elements of his or her personality and experience that are congruent with those of the family (Minuchin, 1974).

Both knowledge and skill and the therapist's personhood and character are vital to joining with clients. Basic skills include the ability to center on clients: to hear their unique perceptions and experiencing of their problems. The client-centered skills of empathy and unconditional positive regard certainly contribute to this process. With couples, it is necessary to elicit each person's account of the problem and give them the leeway to relate to each other in their typical manner. It is very common at the beginning of the initial session for one to say to the other: "Do you want to start?" or "I'll start" or "You go first." Accepting their opening moves and accommodating to these maneuvers promotes joining. We can also observe whether these interactions reflect significant relationship patterns; but a therapist's snap judgments, generalizations, or premature intervening invite client resistance.

The case of Ann and Adam (cited in Chapter 1) exemplifies this type of accommodation. During the first session, as Ann was talking about their long history of sexual incompatibility, she revealed that she had been sexually molested by a neighbor when she was 7 years old. She had never told this to Adam or anyone else. She was understandably emotional. Adam remained aloof and unresponsive to her even at this point, though it was obvious that she wanted a supportive response from him. This communication exchange was, in fact, indicative of their typical interaction pattern, but for the therapist to comment on it or challenge it at this early stage would not have contributed to joining with Adam.

The therapist's demonstrated competence in the areas of sexuality and intimacy can also aid the joining process. This comes through as we are able to stay knowledgeably and comfortably focused on identified sexual issues. Knowing how and when to ask for elaboration and description is critical. The therapist needs to believe genuinely that sex is a positive force in life, but at the same time to show appreciation for the difficulties and challenges of living together intimately. Bypassing or failing to explore sexual content as a normal aspect of a couple's relationship does not inspire confidence in the therapist's ability to help.

Demonstrating competence with sexual problems can be especially demanding when a sexual disorder is the issue. First, it is vital to show acceptance and compassion for the person, although the sexual disorder may involve attitudes and behavior personally repugnant to the therapist. Then, with couples, one must convey understanding of the partners' typically divergent views on the relevance of the sexual disorder. For example, Harry and Helen sought therapy when she discovered the feminine attire that he used in cross-dressing. Shocked and distraught, Helen had given him the ultimatum to get help and discontinue the cross-dressing or the marriage would be over. Harry, on the other hand, while understanding her reaction, was initially unclear about the meaning of his behavior and what he wanted to do about it. It was important to understand both partners' reactions to the problem and to reframe these as strengths. For example, Helen's reaction reflected her strong commitment to Harry and their life together, and Harry showed his devotion by not making an empty or shallow promise.

Promoting Client Expressiveness and Ventilation

Clients facing sexual problems may experience a range of emotions. Some readily acknowledge their confusion, pain, and hurt, whereas others are reticent, tentative, and guarded. Partners will often interact with each other in the session around their conflicting views and feelings about their problem. It is imperative to appreciate the immediacy of these expressions and exchanges and determine strategy. Early on it is valid to promote expressiveness in order to convey that no views or feelings are off limits for therapy. Allowing individuals to ventilate previously disallowed feelings may also free them to tap into positive sentiments.

The therapist remains the ultimate judge of the potential impact of these processes. It is necessary to monitor partners' unbridled blaming and attacking, because these may damage hope, trust, and commitment to work on the problem. Sexual and intimacy problems present some special issues. For example, with desire and sexual aversion disorders, it is wise to explore details of the symptomatic partner's reactions in individual sessions, because these may encompass responses of disgust, nausea, and total abhorrence of the partner's sexual overtures. The same approach is often indicated with sexual affairs. Although the partner knows of the other's infidelity, the revelation of details of the affair in a conjoint session can further damage the nonoffending partner's self-esteem and commitment to improve the relationship. In the case of Ann and Adam, in her fury and rage at Adam's infidelity and refusal to give up his affair, Ann pushed him for details: "What does your girlfriend do in bed with you? Tell me exactly and I'll do it too." Allowing her to continue in this vein or Adam to respond to her demand would not benefit the therapeutic system or prospects for effective treatment.

When sexual disorders, such as paraphilias or a gender identity disturbance, are a factor in a couple' sexual distress, the therapist needs to decide whether individual sessions would be most appropriate for partners to deal with the details of their feelings and cognitions surrounding the specific disorder. The individual format can give either partner the opportunity to express feelings of sexual interest or desire, explore thought patterns, or provide details of sexual history that might not be appropriate for conjoint sessions. Regardless of the nature of the sexual distress, most therapists want the flexibility of having individual sessions if needed.

Moving to an individual format when a couple has initially come together for therapy is a major decision. The risk is great for the therapist to develop a coalition with one of the partners and compromise the couple therapy. For this reason, it is critical to know why one is having the individual sessions and to negotiate the purpose of these sessions with the couple and how this fits with their overall goal for therapy. Most important is having a clear understanding; without this, the client may assume total confidentiality applies (Haas & Malouf, 1989). Although some marriage and family therapists strongly adhere to a position of "no secrets" of any kind, others believe that complexities around confidentiality should be anticipated in couple therapy and clearly negotiated (Karpel, 1980; Margolin, 1986). In this vein, one viable policy is to state that the therapist will have the final judgment on whether any content of individual sessions is critical to the couple's problem and needs to brought back to conjoint sessions. Otherwise, the therapist risks the loss of power to work honestly and effectively with the couple system. The disadvantage, of course, is that this type of position may cause an individual to be less than candid. But this disadvantage is preferred over the therapist's loss of power in the original therapeutic system.

Centering on the Client's View of the Problem

It is easy to refer to the client's view of the problem as if that is a singular entity. Even with individuals, there may be divergent views; with couples, differences in defining the problem is typical.

The first contact, which is usually by phone, allows the therapist to begin focusing on the client's view of the problem. Clients also often have preferences for how they want to approach the problem. One individual in a marriage or committed relationship often makes the first contact and may state the intention to start with individual therapy. Clinicians tend to have strong opinions on this issue and to rule out opposing views. It is prudent first to explain the value of seeing both partners for the initial session. But then the therapist should listen and evaluate. The decision may be to encourage the person to discuss the possibility of conjoint therapy with the partner, or to accept the person's immediate view of the problem, such as "This is something I want to explore by myself," or "This is something I think is mostly my problem," or "My partner is totally opposed to therapy and will not come in."

This flexible approach has advantages that outweigh disadvantages. It fosters the building of the therapeutic system by accepting the client's perception of the problem. It conveys respect for the couple relationship while not denying that same respect to the partner as an individual. And it opens the door for developing a therapeutic system that may evolve to include the partner.

Once in the initial session, centering on the client's view is best accomplished by theoretical flexibility of the part of the clinician. Flexibility here refers to being guided by a theoretical base that is inclusive and holistic rather than exclusive and narrow in focus. Rigid adherence to a single theory in the initial session may lead to premature channeling of the client's perception of the problem to a facet that fits the theoretical model but forecloses a full exploration of the client's views and goals.

The IST approach gives the client the lead in describing the problem. The therapist guides the description but with the goal of initially seeing the large picture. This contrasts with the therapist's guiding of description in order to center in on a singular theoretical model and approach to the problem (which will likely come later). With the IST model, the therapist is open to hearing many views of the problem instead of cutting off or rechanneling views that do not fit a preferred theory. For example, clients have described a sexual dysfunction, all at once without any guidance, in terms of behaviors, emotions, thoughts, their past history, current stressors, traumatic events, current intimate relationship, and their history with their parents and other family members. Many readily offer, without being asked, their theory as to why they have the problem. Allowing clients to describe fully their perceptions of the problem not only builds the therapeutic system but provides information that will be useful in designing therapeutic interventions. We need to know what solutions they have tried on their own, how these worked, and whether they have had prior professional help. The following case vignette suggests the importance of the client's being able to express freely her views of the problem.

> Janet, 35, wanted to start individual therapy to deal with her lack of sexual interest and desire and inability to have an orgasm. She was committed to her marriage and loved Jim, her husband, and he was willing to be involved in therapy, but she wanted to come in alone first. The problem had begun 12 years before on their wedding day. She had enjoyed sex with Jim during their courtship and engagement. She had many theories about the problem and had tested and rejected most of them. Moreover, several years before the couple had had 8 months of sex therapy from another therapist. Janet was very vocal about this. She had hated the sensate focus exercises and was disgusted by the masturbation assignment. Another task in the prior therapy had her confront and express anger and other negative emotions to her mother. This process, Janet said, was very damaging and practically ruined her relationship with her mother. Accepting Janet's preference to come in alone and listening fully to her views fostered a therapeutic system that needed to be different from that in her previous therapy. Allowing her to express her strong opinions and attitudes without challenging these conveyed that she was the expert on what she experienced. It was important not to force her and the problem into a particular theoretical mold but to use her perceptions and experience in developing goals and designing strategy.

Eliciting Client Expectations for Therapy

Cognitive behavior therapy gives much emphasis to eliciting client expectations for therapy, and this ingredient is incorporated into IST. Cognitive therapy aims to shape attitudinal sets conducive to the client's accepting and carrying out his or her roles and responsibilities in therapy. But before doing this, it is essential to know the client's expectations. More generally, all therapeutic approaches must inspire an attitude of hope for improvement and belief in one's ability to change. The latter is not due to any one strategy but emerges with an overall viable therapeutic system.

Typically, client expectations will be fairly congruent with IST, because most people expect therapy to remedy their complaint as well as to discuss their relationship(s), details of the intimacy or sex problem, and their sexual and past histories. When expectations are somewhat off target, it is necessary to address this gap. Ideally, the therapist initially accepts the expectations while also attempting to bring them into alignment with the IST model without raising client resistance. For example, in the case of Janet above, though not stated directly, she expected that this therapy would offer something different from what she had had before. And, in fact, this was possible with the IST model, because it gives importance to the client's perceptions and past and current attempts at solutions, and to avoiding "doing more of the same."

Some clients expect the therapist to provide a professional opinion on whether they are "normal," or really have a problem. For example, "Is my sexual desire (or masturbation, etc.) really abnormal?" Also common is the expectation that therapy will "fix" the symptomatic partner or "do magic" so that no one has to work on the problem or change. These expectations usually disappear as respect for and trust in the therapist develops and the client becomes open to persuasion, information, or reframing.

Clients with sexual dysfunctions often do not really know what to expect of sex therapy or how it works. This means that they expect an explanation, and, beyond this, reassurance that the therapist is competent to treat sexual problems and will treat them in an ethical and professional manner. Sex therapists also occasionally get inquiries from persons looking for or expecting therapy to provide a "hands on" experience, such as through a sexual surrogate. Such situations call for immediate clarification of what sex therapy is and is not. Masters and Johnson (1970) used sex surrogates for a brief time for male clients without partners, but discontinued this early on following a lawsuit. Although this procedure has sparked lay interest, sex therapists have rarely endorsed it or used it because it carries many ethical and legal risks. (Ethical issues are discussed in detail in Chapter 10.)

If a client's expectations appear strongly antithetical to or incongruent with the therapeutic process, the clinician may still attempt to resolve the disparity. But if this is not possible, termination and referral may be the only solution. The case below illustrates this rare situation.

> Ken, a 46-year-old divorced man, sought treatment for lifelong premature ejaculation. In the initial session he was critical of the therapist's questions about the history of the problem and his previous relationships and marriage. Empathic responses and explanations about the

reason for the questions had no impact. He continued in an argumentative, hostile manner stating that he did not want therapy that would explore his history or personality. Not only was the therapist unable to bridge the gap in expectations, but the lack of reasonable client compliance foreclosed the possibility of a therapeutic system. The session ended with mutual agreement that they would not work together, and the therapist gave referral information.

As client expectations of therapy become clear, and these are acknowledged or dealt with, if necessary, the therapist in many ways models what the therapeutic process is and the nature of the collaborative relationship. This modeling in itself is a powerful intervention for inspiring the client's expectation for a solution and belief in his or her own ability to change. But this attitude of hope also flows from meeting the other challenges of the therapeutic system: joining, promoting client expressiveness and ventilation, centering on the client's view of the problem, and consolidating professional credibility.

Consolidating Professional Credibility

Cognitive-behavioral therapy specifically notes the importance of the therapist's expertise in building the client's positive expectations and readiness to take on the client role and responsibilities. Working with the IST model demands considerable expertise. And the critical step toward consolidating professional credibility is to achieve this competence through study, clinical experience, and supervision. The first component is the comprehensive human sexuality content, both knowledge and attitudes, including a thorough assessment of one's own personal sexual attitudes and issues. Then comes proficiency in the cognitive-behavioral methods of treating sexual dysfunctions and disorders. Add to this a broad understanding of marital therapy, especially the systemic conceptualizations and skills relevant to family structure, problem-interactional sequences, and the individual-family of origin interface. This diversity of knowledge, theory, and skill needs to be integrated within the clinician's personal/professional identity so as to allow for a humane, holistic, and ethical approach to sexual and intimacy problems.

The therapist with this degree of expertise will not have to work at consolidating professional credibility but will see it evolve as a viable therapeutic system comes into being. This whole process cements the client's trust in and respect for the clinician's ability to help.

During the early period of building the therapeutic system, the therapist needs to be wary of providing "expert" advice, information about sexuality, or correction of the client's sexual/marital myths. All of these may be appropriate interventions at some point, and they can be offered in many ways—formally, informally, indirectly, and so forth. But it is necessary to judge whether the therapeutic alliance is strong enough for moving in this direction or whether information and education is what the client needs at the moment. Yet it is possible to begin planting the seeds of accurate sexual information during this stage by mixing them with responses that convey empathy, acceptance, and caring. For example, to a woman who has no interest or desire for sex but who participates as a duty: "You must feel a lot of anger and disgust when you decide to go ahead and have intercourse and you know your body isn't ready, you're not lubricated, and it's going to be uncomfortable." This is an indirect way of planting the seed for the client to receive information that may be offered more directly later. Some women do not have the information that lubrication is necessary to make intercourse comfortable, if not arousing. But others who know the facts do not, for various reasons, use a lubricant, although they do choose to have intercourse. Giving this type of information or advice before the client will be receptive to it is not a demonstration of expertise.

More than any specific technique, it is the personal/professional character of the therapist, armed with the IST model, that consolidates professional credibility. There is a certain humility that leads to close listening and realization that each person's problem is unique. There is appreciation for the fact that needs for closeness and sexual expression are not easily met; they can get distorted and produce homeostatic individual and relationship patterns. There is no rush to oversimplify a human problem with many dimensions. Clients come to trust the professional who wants a full account of how they experience and live the problem.

Clients often report that a previous therapist's approach was insulting, simplistic, sexist, and so forth. For example, a young couple saw a counselor about the wife's lack of desire and avoidance of sex. The "professional response" they received was that this was a common reaction of women, and they were advised to shower together as a way of increasing her sexual interest. Both partners felt insulted by this advice.

The competent professional is not paralyzed by understanding sexual and intimacy problems on several levels. The IST model provides for an integrated assessment-intervention stage that gets underway in the first session and results in clear therapeutic goals and tasks (this stage is discussed in Chapter 7). Allowing for a broad inquiry into the many dimensions of the problem not only consolidates professional credibility and the therapeutic system but also supplies the raw material for creating initial assessment hypotheses and intervention strategies.

Conclusion

Building the therapeutic system begins with the first contact with the client. Although efforts toward this goal may be greater in the first few sessions, they do not end there. Moreover, in actual practice, this stage is not distinct from initial assessment and early interventions. With the first client contact, we also inevitably begin to assess and intervene simply by virtue of the therapeutic relationship. Chapter 7 goes further into this realm.

References

Haas, L. J., & Malouf, J. L. (1989). *Keeping up the good work: A practitioner's guide to mental health ethics.* Sarasota, FL: Professional Resource Exchange.

Karpel, M. (1980). Family secrets: I. Conceptual and ethical issues in the relational context. II. Ethical and practical considerations in therapeutic management. *Family Process, 1,* 295-306.

Margolin, G. (1986). Ethical issues in marital therapy. In N. S. Jacobson & A. S. Gurman (Eds.), *Clinical handbook of marital therapy* (pp. 621-638). New York: Guilford Press.

Masters, W. H., & Johnson, V. E. (1970). *Human sexual inadequacy.* Boston: Little, Brown.

Minuchin, S. (1974). *Families and family therapy.* Cambridge, MA: Harvard University Press.

Trepper, T. S., & Barrett, M. J. (1989). *Systemic treatment of incest: A therapeutic handbook.* New York: Brunner/Mazel.

7

Initial Assessment and Early Interventions

> Do you think it is easy to change?
> Ah, it is very hard to change and be different,
> It means passing through the waters of oblivion.
>
> D. H. LAWRENCE, from "Change"

Integrative Systems Therapy (IST) aims to account for the complexity that takes place in clinical work. Much of the literature on therapeutic approaches does just the opposite. It oversimplifies the richly creative, eclectic, and often serendipitous process of psychotherapy in order to promote a singular theory of human behavior and change.

The second stage of IST, initial assessment and early interventions, presents many challenges. Most basically, the therapist must impose a structure on the interaction that will generate both a tentative understanding of the problem and initial intervention ideas. It is a paradox, however, that this structure must also permit considerable flexibility in the therapeutic interaction.

Just as integration of the various conceptual dimensions that contribute to IST began in the first stage of building the therapeutic system, successfully meeting the challenges of stage two also reflects the several conceptual bases. In general, this stage requires from one to four sessions.

Drawing on the photographic metaphor, the overall goal is to obtain a two-dimensional picture of the client's sexual distress. By the end of the first session, something akin to a Polaroid snapshot of the problem emerges. It captures the gestalt, but does not attend to posing subjects or arranging details of the surroundings, and so on. Nonetheless, such a snapshot enables the therapist to undertake intervention in that first session. While probably obvious to experienced therapists, it merits repeating that distinctions between assessment and intervention are quite arbitrary. Intervention begins when the therapy hour begins.

Even in the first session, the therapist pursues and stays aware of systemic dimensions of the problem, although these may not necessarily be the focus of the interaction. This awareness is present more as ground in the snapshot, while the content of the sexual problem constitutes the figure in the forefront. Yet if one begins exploration of the problem-interactional sequence in the first session, then certain systemic aspects of the problem come into focus.

The six major challenges of this stage of therapy are: (a) processing information from inventories and scales; (b) defining the problem to be remedied; (c) negotiating a therapeutic contract; (d) formulating an initial assessment of problem content and process; (e) applying initial interventions; and (f) assessing the impact of initial interventions. While the following discussion treats each separately, they are all clearly interrelated processes.

Processing Information From Inventories and Scales

Numerous standardized inventories and scales are useful in the assessment of sexual distress, and some of these may be used more or less routinely, especially with clients presenting with sexual dysfunctions and sexual disorders. Always at issue in using such measures is the amount of time required for administration and scoring, whether specialized professional credentials are required, and the cost for clients. This section briefly notes a few of these standardized instruments and also presents a scale specifically developed to measure the couple sexual interaction system.

PERSONALITY AND RELATIONSHIP INVENTORIES

The presence of individual psychopathology can be a factor. Two research reports found that between 30% and 50% of sexual dysfunction patients merited a concurrent DSM III Axis I/II diagnosis (Derogatis, Meyer, & King, 1981; Fagan, Schmidt, Wise, & Derogatis, 1988). Another found that a "majority of patients with inhibited desire had a past history of at least one major episode of depression" (Rosen & Leiblum, 1989, p. 27). Heiman and Grafton-Becker (1989) recommend assessment of current depression as well as subclinical depressive symptoms; they routinely use the Brief Symptoms Inventory (Derogatis, 1977) to assess psychiatric symptoms.

The Minnesota Multiphasic Personality Inventory (MMPI-2) could also prove useful for measuring psychological distress (Butcher, 1990; Graham, 1990). Standardized assessment data contribute to the total assessment process, which enables the clinician to develop a treatment plan or recommend other intervention. If used, psychodiagnostic test results are not processed in a linear fashion as an explanation of the sexual distress. Standardized testing is simply a mechanism for intense focus on an individual's thinking, emotions, and behavior. Thus it can be seen as one piece of the individual-family of origin interface, that is, a measure of personality. The clinician integrates this with other assessment data in designing interventions.

For measuring the couple or family relationship, the therapist should consider the use of at least one objective inventory. The Dyadic Adjustment Scale (DAS) (Spanier & Thompson, 1982) takes only 5 to 10 minutes to complete and is appropriate either prior to or following the first session. It can augment assessment of relationship structure and themes based on data obtained in interviews. Other self-report relationship scales may serve a similar purpose, for example, the Family Adaptability and Cohesion Evaluation Scales (FACES) (Olson & Portner, 1983), and the Marital Satisfaction Inventory (Snyder, 1983).

With clients who are only tenuously engaged in the therapeutic system or with other circumstances, the clinician must evaluate the potential overall benefits of using formal assessment measures and determine a time frame for using them that will produce the desired therapeutic effect. Such clinical judgment is illustrated in the following vignette.

Ned (26) and Nancy (23), married for one year, were referred by a physician for premature ejaculation. Living in a rural area, they would have to drive 5 hours for the scheduled 2-hour appointment. The DAS was mailed along with directions for completing and bringing it to the first session. At the end of the first session, they were not asked to do a personality inventory. They had put forth great effort even to obtain therapy, both had heavy work schedules, and it seemed advisable to have them devote their limited free time in the coming weeks to the first assigned at-home experiential tasks.

SEXUALITY SCALES AND INVENTORIES

A number of inventories specifically provide measures of sexual symptoms, practices, interaction, attitudes, and so on. Because of the explicit nature of many of these scales, clinical judgment is necessary to determine if and when such measures can contribute to the assessment of a given client's sexual distress.

The Derogatis Sexual Functioning Inventory (DSFI) (Derogatis & Melisaratos, 1979) is a self-report measure that provides scores on ten domains of an individual's sexual functioning. These include: information, experience, drive, attitudes, psychological symptoms, affects, gender role definition, fantasy, body image, and sexual satisfaction. A clinical psychometric profile adds to the utility of this instrument.

The Sexual Interaction Inventory (SII) (LoPiccolo & Steger, 1974) is a self-report inventory that measures sexual adjustment and sexual satisfaction for heterosexual couples. Items cover frequency of sex, the range of sexual behaviors, pleasure derived, knowledge of partner's preferred sexual activities, self-acceptance, and acceptance of partner. A clinical profile based on eleven scales is obtained.

The Multiphasic Sexual Inventory (MSI) (Nichols & Molinder, 1984) is a self-report measure of a wide range of psychosocial characteristics of sex offenders. Scales encompass atypical sexual behaviors, sexual deviance, sexual dysfunction, sex knowledge, and attitudes toward treatment.

Since sexual inventories contain explicit sexual themes, it is usually wise to become familiar with the client before using these. The therapist then has a sense of what type(s) of sexuality inventories are needed and whether the client could benefit from such measures and respond honestly. Some clients, even before the initial therapy session, can honestly answer sexual inventories while others first need time to develop trust in the therapist and a commitment to treatment. The latter is often true of clients with inhibited desire, sexual aversions, and paraphilias.

The Sexual Interaction System Scale (SISS) (Woody & D'Souza, 1991) was developed for use with couples experiencing sexual dysfunction or sexual dissatisfaction. It is an integrative assessment tool in that it draws from several conceptual dimensions that make up the IST approach. The purpose of the SISS is to obtain measures of the sexual interaction system that is typical of a couple's recent sexual encounters. Specifically, it provides a measure of each partner's perception of that system and an overall score of the couple's sexual interaction system.

The SISS draws on several sources for its conceptual base. Items aimed at measuring sexual dysfunction derive from Kaplan's (1979) tri-phasic model of the sexual response cycle, which is also the basis for the DSM III-R (1987) diagnostic classifications of the sexual dysfunctions. Also included are items relevant to two additional stages of sexual response, sexual interest and evaluation of the experience. Zilbergeld and Ellison (1980) have posited these additional stages as well as the view that all stages of the sexual response may be autonomous and independent of each other.

Items that measure the interactional system draw on two theory bases. A major source is Verhulst and Heiman's (1979) explanation of a couple's sexual response as an interactional communication process. Specifically, the whole process of sexual arousal and sexual satisfaction is mediated through communications which take place through: (a) physiological language (sexual phenomena evident through physiological processes); (b) body language (posture movements, facial expression, spontaneous sounds, and so on); and (c) action language (the action of doing something to one's partner). The final concept is that of the interaction pattern set up by the partners' cognitive evaluative and emotional reaction following the sexual encounter. Because these reactions would be evident, an interactional pattern likely emerges and contributes to the emotional tone of the couple's overall relationship and to the tenor of the next sexual encounter. Typical patterns would be those of closeness and affection versus distancing and avoidance.

Table 7.1 contains items that comprise the SISS. A full discussion of the rationale, administration, scoring, and reliability and validity studies for the scale is available elsewhere (Woody & D'Souza, 1991).

TABLE 7.1 Items From the Sexual Interaction System Scale

	Circle Appropriate Response					
	Rating					
Item	*None/ Never*					*High/ Always*
1. I am interested in sex—willing to get involved, either initiating or responding to partner's initiating	1	2	3	4	5	6
2. I experience desire—fantasies or sensation leading to initiating sex activity or responding with desire	1	2	3	4	5	6
3. I insist on or force sex on unwilling partner	1	2	3	4	5	6
4. I become aroused in sex activity (female becomes lubricated; male has erection sufficient for intercourse)	1	2	3	4	5	6
5. I experience increasing pleasure and excitement, and wish to continue sex activity	1	2	3	4	5	6
6. I worry about the success of my sexual performance	1	2	3	4	5	6
7. I get sensual pleasure from caressing my partner's body	1	2	3	4	5	6
8. I freely touch and caress my partner's genitals (sexual organs)	1	2	3	4	5	6
9. I show caring and affection during sex	1	2	3	4	5	6
10. I get sensual pleasure when my partner caresses my body	1	2	3	4	5	6
11. I feel disgust or revulsion during most sexual activities	1	2	3	4	5	6
12. I see sex as an opportunity for shared pleasure	1	2	3	4	5	6
13. I see sex in terms of my need for release of sexual tensions	1	2	3	4	5	6
14. I express complaints or negative feelings during sex	1	2	3	4	5	6
15. I enjoy kissing as part of the sexual encounter	1	2	3	4	5	6

TABLE 7.1 (Continued)

	Circle Appropriate Response					
	Rating					
Item	*None/ Never*					*High/ Always*
16. I enjoy different sensations during sex—touches, sounds, sights, smells, tastes	1	2	3	4	5	6
17. I engage in verbal conflicts during sex	1	2	3	4	5	6
18. I withdraw and stop participating in sex	1	2	3	4	5	6
19. I find sex pleasurable and act to increase my arousal and pleasure	1	2	3	4	5	6
20. I enjoy oral stimulation of my genitals by my partner	1	2	3	4	5	6
21. With actions and/or words, I do what it takes to make sex pleasurable for both of us	1	2	3	4	5	6
22. I feel loved and valued during sex	1	2	3	4	5	6
23. I enjoy providing my partner with oral stimulation of genitals	1	2	3	4	5	6
24. I experience orgasm (climax) during the sexual encounter	1	2	3	4	5	6
25. I attempt to control and dominate during sex in ways my partner dislikes	1	2	3	4	5	6
26. I take action to increase my partner's sexual satisfaction	1	2	3	4	5	6
27. Female has persistent or recurring genital pain with intercourse. (Males, also give your opinion.)	1	2	3	4	5	6
28. Male does not become erect or loses erection when starting intercourse. (Females, also give your opinion.)	1	2	3	4	5	6
29. Female has vaginal contraction (vagina closes and penis cannot enter) thus preventing intercourse	1	2	3	4	5	6

(Continued)

TABLE 7.1 (Continued)

	Circle Appropriate Response					
	Rating					
Item	*None/ Never*					*High/ Always*
30. Regardless of type of stimulation, female's orgasm is greatly delayed or does not occur. (Males, also give your opinion.)	1	2	3	4	5	6
31. Male ejaculates too quickly—before, upon, or soon after penetration and before he wishes to. (Females, also give your opinion.)	1	2	3	4	5	6
32. Male is unable to have orgasm or ejaculate through intercourse. (Females, also give your opinion.)	1	2	3	4	5	6
33. I feel sexually satisfied by the sexual experience when it is over	1	2	3	4	5	6
34. I feel emotionally close and affectionate toward my partner during sex	1	2	3	4	5	6
35. I feel saddened and disappointed by the sexual experience	1	2	3	4	5	6
36. I participate in sex from duty to meet my partner's sexual needs	1	2	3	4	5	6
37. I participate in sex for closeness or affection	1	2	3	4	5	6
38. I participate in sex in order to feel normal	1	2	3	4	5	6
39. I participate in sex to avoid my partner's rejection or anger	1	2	3	4	5	6
40. I see the sexual encounter overall as a good or positive experience	1	2	3	4	5	6
41. I show warmth and affection toward my partner after sex	1	2	3	4	5	6

TABLE 7.1 (Continued)

	Circle Appropriate Response					
	Rating					
Item	*None/ Never*					*High/ Always*
42. I feel angry and distant from my partner as a result of sex	1	2	3	4	5	6
43. I feel my partner is too possessive of my body during sex	1	2	3	4	5	6
44. I withdraw emotionally from my partner as a result of sex	1	2	3	4	5	6
45. I criticize or blame my partner for several days after sex	1	2	3	4	5	6
46. I have bad feelings toward my partner for several days after sex	1	2	3	4	5	6
47. For days after sex, I avoid my partners attempts at closeness or affection	1	2	3	4	5	6
48. For days after sex, I avoid sexual advances or situations	1	2	3	4	5	6
49. I see sex adding positively to our overall nonsexual relationship	1	2	3	4	5	6
50. I fake orgasm or pretend sexual satisfaction	1	2	3	4	5	6
51. I am happy with our sexual relationship	1	2	3	4	5	6
52. I see sex adding positively to our overall nonsexual relationship	1	2	3	4	5	6
53. I desire sex more frequently than we engage in it	1	2	3	4	5	6
54. Our overall relationship makes it easy for us to have a good sexual relationship	1	2	3	4	5	6
55. I don't think we communicate well about our sexual needs, wishes, and satisfaction	1	2	3	4	5	6
56. I would like more variety in our sexual activities	1	2	3	4	5	6

Defining the Problem

The therapist uses various methods to meet the challenge of defining the problem to be remedied. Typically, clients who seek a specialist in sexuality are ready to be quite direct in presenting the sexual dimensions of the problem. Other clinicians may, however, see clients who are not ready to acknowledge a sexual problem: They may talk around the problem or test the therapist's willingness or competence to deal with sexual material. Yet, even when the client is direct in acknowledging some type of sexual distress, the therapist must still elicit and define the exact problem to be remedied.

Several therapeutic strategies help to meet this challenge. As suggested above, the SISS is useful in the process of diagnosing the presence and severity of a couple's sexual dysfunction or dissatisfaction. Within the interview format, however, direct questions and probes encourage the client to provide necessary details about the sexual problem. These too add to the formulation of a precise diagnostic description of the sexual distress. It is critical to determine whether a client experiences more than one symptom, and with couples, whether both partners experience symptoms of sexual distress. For example, if the presenting problem is a husband's cross-dressing, it is important to discover whether either partner is sexually dysfunctional or dissatisfied with their sexual relationship. So the SISS might be appropriately used even if the immediate presenting problem is not a specific dysfunction or dissatisfaction in the sexual relationship.

The context of direct questions must also accommodate the need for appropriate empathy, affirmation, and encouragement of client self-exploration. Clients can be permitted to become somewhat tangential, since the therapist with a systemic bent will have a framework for processing much of this material. For example, the client often freely reveals, without being asked, current situational or family issues and other problems that may connect to the sexual distress. Thus problem definition takes place within both a directive and nondirective interview strategy and via data from inventories and scales. This mix promotes an initial decision on a specific problem to be remedied and ideas about its breadth and depth. Arriving at this critical understanding makes it possible to proceed to the next challenge, which is to begin analysis of the problem content and process by drawing on conceptual dimensions that make up IST.

Problem definition was relatively straightforward in the case of Ned and Nancy cited above. The couple's DAS scores revealed good relationship functioning. The interview, as well as their SISS results, produced agreement that premature ejaculation was the source of their sexual distress. No other dysfunctions were identified for either partner.

In other client situations, however, problem definition is not so straightforward nor singularly focused. Some problems contain several salient and interrelated dysfunctions that emerge within the initial session. These alert the therapist to the need to explore various facets of the problem before narrowing it or prioritizing its components.

The exact nature and meaning of a given "problematic" sexual behavior can be quite diverse, even controversial. For example, there could be several explanations for the presence of homosexual activity on the part of a married man. Similarly, transvestism may reflect fetishistic expression, a coping mechanism for anxiety, gender dysphoria, or a rejection of the culture's rigid limits on masculine and feminine expression. Clearly, problem definition presents a challenge; however, the multitheoretical base of IST promotes a refined understanding of the nature of the sexual distress.

The case of Paul (48) and Penny (46) exemplifies numerous difficulties as well as ambivalence about which problem to focus on and about their commitment to each other and to therapy. Both had had unsatisfactory first marriages, and their present relationship was conflictual in many areas. Both, however, shared a strong commitment to their family; they had two children from their marriage and two from Penny's first marriage. One of her children was in treatment for chemical dependency, and the other was emotionally cut off by Penny. She harbored considerable anger and lack of trust toward Paul as a result of learning several years before of his anonymous homosexual encounters while he was away on business trips. Their most immediate concern was Paul's inhibited orgasm: he was unable to have an orgasm intravaginally or in the presence of his wife through any type of stimulation. This symptom and the resulting sexual distress for both partners complicated their other marital and family difficulties, which also included significant family-of-origin issues. There were also ethical issues to consider in defining the problem that centered on Paul's homosexual encounters and their relevance to his affectional preference. In this case, some assessment of various problem components was conducted before determining the problem that would become the focus for intensive assessment and treatment.

Negotiating a Therapeutic Contract

Negotiating the therapeutic contract requires the ability to explore and elicit not only the client's verbalized goals but those that may remain unverbalized. People are not eager to volunteer extensive information about their hopes for their sexual relationship. But it is necessary to probe sensitively for unspoken (and often unrealistic) expectations of the treatment. For example, with premature ejaculation, couples may expect that the male's increased control will provide his partner an orgasm through intercourse. In one such case, the partner, upon questioning, stated her wish to have "earth-shaking orgasms with intercourse." Since a large majority of women do not attain orgasm through intercourse, regardless of how long it lasts (Kaplan, 1989), further negotiation toward more realistic treatment goals was needed. To illustrate further, with a couple presenting sexual distress due to a husband's cross-dressing, the treatment goal could range from enabling his wife to understand and accept his behavior to his giving up the practice entirely. The therapist needs a thorough understanding of the various types of sexual distress and their impact on individual and relationship functioning in order to help clients arrive at viable treatment goals.

The case of Paul and Penny above suggests the complexity that can characterize the negotiation process. The therapist had doubts about the couple's overall commitment to each other. Moreover, there was much conflict between them surrounding their everyday marital and family routines. Most important was the meaning of Paul's anonymous homosexual encounters. Nonetheless, both partners avowed their interest in and desire for sex with each other. They became aroused, Penny was orgasmic with various types of stimulation, and Paul enjoyed all aspects of their sex activity. The only negative factor was that Paul's inability to ejaculate left them with feelings of disappointment and hopelessness. Paul emphatically stated that he was not interested in a gay identity, explaining that he had had a year of individual therapy devoted to this topic and to his becoming familiar with the community's gay culture. The couple agreed that their goal was for Paul to become able to have orgasm with Penny. They believed this change would improve both their sexual and marital relationship.

Negotiating this therapeutic goal raised several ethical concerns for the therapist: to be sensitive to the client's dignity and right to self-determination; to promote the welfare of both partners; to carefully evaluate theory and practice relevant to the couple's problems; to consider the sociolegal ramifications, including the possibility of a client complaint about the therapy provided; and to be aware of personal/professional identity issues that could impact on therapy with these clients and their type of problem.

The nature of this case called for conscious consideration of these ethical concerns in negotiating therapeutic goals. Final determination of the treatment goal evolved from several concrete steps that were presented to the couple: (a) further assessment would be necessary before moving toward any treatment goals; (b) the therapist explained the theoretical controversy about treatment for so-called "dissatisfied homosexuals"; (c) after the assessment, the therapist's level of expertise was clarified and offered to help them toward their goal of remedying the inhibited orgasm; (d) they were informed of other specialized sexuality centers that could be resources; (e) it was agreed that a referral would be made at any time that either the clients or therapist decided the treatment plan was not appropriate or not effectively helping them; and (f) they were told that the therapist would judge whether any content from individual sessions should be brought to couple sessions.

Negotiating the therapeutic contract with clients experiencing sexual distress is typically not this complex. Nonetheless, the process demands sensitivity because of the nature of sexuality. Sexual ignorance and myths are pervasive and can unconsciously influence the judgment of both the clients and the therapist. The practitioner's personal values and biases can subtly influence treatment goals. There is no singular standard of what constitutes "healthy sexuality"; so one must guard against imposing arbitrary standards for client goals. For example, some clients simply want some improvement in their sexual relationship, not an overhaul of this dimension in their lives. The client's values, preferences, and ideas about therapeutic goals and progress must count in this process (Heiman, 1986). In cases with obvious potential ethical or legal issues, the therapist may wish to have clients sign the treatment contract.

As stated previously in Chapter 6, IST, because of its multitheoretical base, accommodates to two possible tracks in defining the problem and negotiating the therapeutic contract. The first track is to formulate the sexual distress in terms of a symptom to remedy or change in some way. This is possible when the individual or couple is committed to changing the symptom. The second track that is possible with IST is to formulate the sexual distress as a condition calling for client exploration, insight, and/or decision making. This track is appropriate when the individual or couple is unclear about their understanding or intention regarding the sexual distress. The multitheoretical base of IST allows pursuit of either track to accommodate the range of client and problem characteristics that appear in actual practice. Explaining these as separate tracks, however, does not mean that they are parallel and never cross or merge. Two case vignettes illustrate the different directions the therapeutic contract can take.

After 4 years of marriage, Roger (26) had confided in his wife Rhonda (23) that he cross-dressed. They sought therapy after about a year of trying to cope with this issue. Both were distraught over what Roger's behavior meant for their relationship and future in their rural community. Clear couple goals did not emerge: Roger hoped therapy would enable Rhonda to accept and participate in his cross-dressing during their sexual relationship, but Rhonda could not accept this as a goal for treatment. Goals for individual therapy were agreed upon: Roger would explore in depth the meaning of his cross-dressing and its connection to his desire to "go public." Rhonda would deal with her faltering self-esteem and evaluate her options both within and outside of the marriage.

In another situation of cross-dressing, the treatment contract negotiated would directly focus on altering aspects of the symptom. Chapter 6 mentions the case of Harry and Helen in which Helen gave an ultimatum that unless Harry discontinued the cross-dressing, the marriage would be over. After considering various options, Harry asserted a commitment to eliminating the cross-dressing. Both partners desired this change and wanted it to be the focus of therapy. This treatment focus was supported by the initial assessment of the problem behavior based on results from the DAS and MMPI and analysis of the cognitive-behavioral and problem-interactional components of Harry's cross-dressing pattern.

Assessment of Problem Content and Process

It should be obvious from the discussion thus far how the various challenges of stage three of IST, discussed separately here, are part of a singular process and do not proceed in any simple, step-by-step sequence. In the above mentioned case of Penny and Paul, with the dysfunction of inhibited male orgasm, the problem had many interacting facets. All of these were considered to some extent before defining the problem of focus. On the other hand, with Nancy and Ned's problem of premature ejaculation, although the first session revealed potential relationship and family-of-origin stressors, these were minor; so the premature ejaculation was defined as the problem.

As the therapist and client begin to agree on the problem definition, then a more intensive assessment gets underway. Because IST can accommodate two broad tracks in problem definition, the direction of the intensive assessment will vary. If it is possible to formulate the sexual distress as a symptom to be remedied, then that goal and therapeutic contract dictate the process of the intensive assessment and early interventions. On the other hand, if the sexual distress is formulated in terms of the client's need for understanding, evaluation, insight, and decision making, then a different process of assessment and early intervention takes place.

ASSESSMENT OF SEXUAL DISTRESS AS SYMPTOM

With many cases, the judgment is that treatment will focus on relieving or altering the symptom. Assessment continues then with this goal in the forefront. Two components in the IST model are most useful at this point, namely, the cognitive-behavioral dimension (exemplified in traditional sex therapy) and the problem-interactional sequence (derived from strategic therapy). [See Chapter 5, Table 5.1 for the overview of the conceptual components of IST.]

These two approaches fit together well both conceptually and pragmatically (Duncan & Parks, 1988). They are both symptom-focused, center on the here and now, and aim to remedy the problem. Both approaches focus on careful analysis of communication and behavior. Finally, interventions from both use directives, coaching, and homework tasks. The therapeutic goals are also similar in aiming to alter or interrupt an existing behavioral/communication pattern and replace it with something different.

There are many ways to proceed with this initial assessment challenge. Most basically it involves eliciting information through inventories, interview methods, observation of the client in therapeutic interaction, and client reports of assigned selfmonitoring tasks. These data are then used to formulate a more precise assessment of the symptom, which dictates the early interventions used.

THE COGNITIVE-BEHAVIORAL CONCEPTUAL FRAMEWORK

The Sexual Interaction System Scale (SISS) has already been discussed in terms of its contribution to problem definition. But with regard to the couple's sexual encounters, it also reveals the degree of positive vs. negative behavioral exchange and types of reinforcement contingencies, the presence of negative emotional respondents and evaluative cognitions, and the presence of aversive pain or phobic reactions in a partner.

Following the cognitive-behavioral legacy of sex therapy, the clinical interview continues to elicit information for assessing the defined sex problem. Addressed specifically are: (a) each partner's health and physical condition; (b) description and history of the current sex problem; (c) each partner's sexual knowledge, attitudes, beliefs, and current and preferred sexual activities; (d) each partner's sexual, relationship, and marital history; (e) current life events; and (f) specific cognitions, behaviors, emotions, fantasies, and so on involved in the couple's problematic sexual encounters.

This comprehensive collection of case information permits a formulation of the problem in terms of cognitive-behavioral theory as illustrated in the following discussion of the problem of premature ejaculation presented by Ned and Nancy.

Ned's premature ejaculation was lifelong in that he believed he had had the problem since his late teens. He had not had any other sexual partner except his wife, and the problem had been present from their courtship through the current first year of the marriage. Ned indicated that he was also "fast" with masturbation, and having a second intercourse with his wife following an initial episode of premature ejaculation did not significantly or consistently affect the problem. Neither partner was currently on medication, though Ned had a long history, since childhood, of a peptic ulcer. Throughout the years, he had taken numerous medications, including Tagamet (cimetidine hydrochloride), which has been implicated in loss of sexual desire (Kaplan, 1983), and Reglan (metoclopramide hydrochloride), which has numerous central nervous system side effects (Physicians' Desk Reference, 1991; Drug Interactions and Side Effects Index, 1991) but none documented as impacting on sexual function. The couple had continued to engage in intercourse, although infrequently, since the problem led them, especially Nancy, to avoid affectionate as well as sexual overtures. Their sexual relationship was characterized by the following pattern: long periods of no sex, Ned's eventual initiation of sex, Nancy's reluctant participation, anxiety and expectation of failure by both, efforts to keep Ned's arousal level down, ejaculation before or upon penetration, and disappointment and emotional withdrawal by both partners. The present sexual interaction constituted an emotionally painful, and thus aversive, situation for both partners. They experienced negative emotions and expectations about their sexual activity, they avoided affectionate and sexual stimuli, and they had a generalized cognitive set of hopelessness about their sex life and future relationship. Both also harbored negative evaluations about Ned's personal adequacy and held him responsible for the problem.

This cognitive-behavioral assessment expands on the more generalized concept of "performance anxiety" (Masters & Johnson, 1970), though it certainly includes that. And it also differs in not positing etiology as stemming from societal sexual myths that emphasize performance. Because the problem appeared to be lifelong and global, Ned's anxiety was not based on a societal myth that overemphasizes male sexual performance. His anxiety was based on his own sexual response pattern. He had long held a negative view of his sexual adequacy, which was likely a factor in his not having had any other girlfriend or sexual partner except his wife. When the premature ejaculation then continued in sex with his wife, just as it had during masturbation before marriage, Ned's anxiety escalated. And it was further intensified by his knowledge that Nancy had had other "adequate" male sexual partners.

PROBLEM-INTERACTIONAL SEQUENCE FRAMEWORK

Moving beyond the cognitive behavioral framework to the problem-interactional sequence, one finds considerable congruence and linkage between the two. This model allows setting into motion the above descriptions of cognitions, emotions, and behaviors to tease out an interactive pattern in which a proposed solution, in fact, constitutes the problem.

The information for this pattern clearly emerged from Ned's and Nancy's responses on the SISS and from the interview data. The couple's construction of the problem led them to a solution which consisted of avoiding affection, arousal, and sex. But when this failed, the second line of defense was to attempt to inhibit arousal in both partners so as to inhibit Ned's arousal. This solution was doomed to fail because Ned, in fact, required very little sexual stimulation for orgasm and ejaculation. His routine "fast" response was no doubt overdetermined by several factors (including a possible organic-based low threshold for ejaculation). Yet the couple continued to try to inhibit his arousal; and when premature ejaculation occurred, they would withdraw from each other again, thereby beginning "more of the same," (i.e., attempting to inhibit Ned's sexual desire and arousal). And so the vicious cycle continued.

No doubt the presence of painful emotions and negative cognitions triggered by their aversive sexual encounters would also support their pattern of withdrawal from each other and avoidance of affection as the solution to continue. Thus these two initial assessments based on cognitive-behavioral and problem-interaction concepts are complementary and congruent with regard to explaining the symptom. Early interventions in the case of Ned and Nancy are discussed in the final section of this chapter.

ASSESSMENT OF SEXUAL DISTRESS IN TERMS OF NEED FOR INSIGHT

The initial process of defining the problem and negotiating the therapeutic contract often produce the judgment that treatment will not directly focus on remedying the sexual symptom. Instead the sexual distress appears to call for client understanding, insight, and decision making. Further intensive assessment is then directed toward these goals. In fact, the following discussion illustrates how assessment constituted a major part of the content of the therapeutic process.

Reconsider the case of Roger and Rhonda discussed above. Roger's cross-dressing was not defined in terms of a symptom for therapy to alleviate or change (i.e., the behavior or the couple's interaction around it). Rather, the sexual distress was defined in terms of the crisis created in their lives. They needed understanding of the behavior, of the impasse in their relationship, of the potential for their marriage, and of their individual needs and options for fulfilling these. It was assumed that increased understanding would help them cope with and resolve the crisis. Individual sessions would allow full exploration of apparently different immediate needs and goals for therapy, with the expectation that they would share their insights privately as well as in projected couple sessions.

The course of further assessment and early interventions with each partner was highly integrative. For purposes of illustration, the following analysis is not comprehensive but suggests the relevance of reinforcement, interactional, relational, and individual-family of origin components in assessment of, as well as intervention with, both partners.

Exploring the meaning of his cross-dressing was the focus for Roger's confrontation of self, identity, and the future direction of his life. Therapy aimed to affirm him in his journey toward self-understanding and decision making. Various theoretical concepts proved useful in offering explanations and interpretations for him to consider. Cognitive-behavioral and problem-interactional analyses centered on the current manifestation of the behavior.

The cross-dressing was a powerful reinforcer in two ways: as a negative reinforcer, it relieved painful, conflicting feelings about his gender identity; and the whole sequence of cross-dressing was reinforced positively because it culminated in sexual satisfaction through masturbation (usually, although occasionally in the past through intercourse and orgasm with his wife).

In terms of the problem-interactional sequence, originally, Roger's secret led to feelings of distance from Rhonda; as these intensified through their mutual distancing, Roger would use time alone to dress in the effort to gain relief. Once relief was obtained through this means, the secret loomed larger in his perception of the limits of their intimacy; and the cycle continued. Once Roger revealed the secret, however, Rhonda's alienation did, indeed, increase. Although she attempted for a while, prior to therapy, to incorporate his dressing into their sexual relationship, this was aversive for her (though reinforcing for Roger). She then withdrew emotionally, and willingly made herself absent (or did so at his subtle suggestion) so that he could have time alone to dress; and the vicious cycle continued.

It is important to emphasize that these analyses were offered to enhance their understanding, not to use as a basis for changing the behavior or interactional pattern. They did not agree on any desired direction of change. Further conceptual explorations were directed toward the structure of the couple's relationship and their individual personalities and self-structures within the family-of-origin interface.

Socially, both partners had status within their families and community through educational and professional achievement and through marriage. Most of their energies throughout the marriage had centered on career development, a goal that was tied into their long history of enmeshment and completing each other's identities through the relationship. Roger's cross-dressing began very tentatively in puberty and increased when he went away to college. Due to extreme shyness, he had never dated until he returned home to finish college at age 19 and began dating Rhonda, who was 15. She essentially grew up with Roger and his family, because her own parents were constantly separating during this period. They married when she was 18, and she credited Roger and his family with much of her achievement. Other siblings in her family were similarly, if not more, successful, because the mother expected this, although she had not provided accompanying support or affection.

Roger's and Rhonda's identities and self-structures were so interlocked with the legacies from both families of origin that individuation and separation had collusively been blocked. Understandably, neither wanted their impasse over Roger's cross-dressing to lead to divorce. Yet both had found that their effort to incorporate it and still have a satisfying marriage had not succeeded.

Although therapy was brief (2 couple sessions and 3 individual sessions each), they gained in insight and began the process of individuation, although they had reached no decision about the marriage. Roger came to understand his behavior as reflecting significant gender dysphoria: even prior to therapy he had begun to seek information on transvestism and transsexualism, and he raised in sessions the possibility of his relocating and further exploring and expressing his femininity. Rhonda acknowledged that meeting Roger's needs negated her own needs for intimacy and sexual fulfillment: she stopped the effort to participate in his cross-dressing and asserted the belief that she could live without him if they came to a decision to separate or divorce.

Applying Initial Interventions

Previous sections mention the two broad tracks that the therapy contract may take. One aims to remedy the symptom directly, whereas the other aims to promote client understanding, insight, decision making, and so on. The two tracks are not mutually exclusive, but it is often beneficial and necessary to specify the immediate primary direction. In some cases, both client and therapist understand that increased insight may be the best vehicle for eventual remedy of the sexual distress, although no one may know at the beginning what the remedy might consist of.

Having said this, I believe the reality is that therapy can indeed encompass both dimensions in that both "action" and "insight" can synergistically operate to remedy the symptom.

The discussion that follows on early interventions centers on the case of Ned and Nancy, in which the treatment contract called for direct alleviation of the symptom of premature ejaculation. The interventions clearly reflect the "action" focus, but they also encompass the integrative richness of IST. Hence their influence was also expected to enhance client understanding and insight. Slipp (1989) supports such a position in arguing that strategic interventions can clear a path for a client's journey toward insight.

Ned and Nancy were seen initially in a 2-hour session, part of which included brief individual meetings with each partner sandwiched between two conjoint meetings. The therapeutic contract called for a second session in 5 weeks with telephone contacts during this period. This format was undertaken to deal with the barrier of a 5-hour drive to therapy during extreme winter conditions. I believed the integrative conceptualization of treatment would increase chances for this format to work.

Four broad groupings somewhat arbitrarily categorize the many interventions that place took during the session. These are: (a) reframing the problem, (b) preparing clients to accept and undertake the at-home behavioral/experiential task, (c) enhancing success with tasks, and (d) presenting tasks.

Reframing is not simply a singular intervention resulting from a therapist's verbal reconstruction of the problem. It can come about in many ways other than the therapist's "positive connotation" or "ascribing noble intentions." Moreover, the therapist needs to sincerely believe in the reframing, and not offer it merely as "a strategic ploy" (Nichols, 1984, p. 544). Although the following account may sound like a therapist's monologue, it was not. The various reframes evolved from interaction with the clients and were the outcome of numerous techniques.

During the course of the session, the problem of premature ejaculation was decatastrophized and normalized; it was no longer a shameful secret but became instead a discussable problem that affects many men. Its causes were reframed from Ned's personal inadequacy or particular "weirdness" to a composite of what might be called the couple's "damn bad luck" (de Shazer, 1983). This reframe came about as explanations mentioned many elements potentially contributing to it: an organic factor such as a low threshold for ejaculation, lack of learning to discriminate genital sensation, the negative impact of the vicious cycle of Ned's anxiety during sex, and the couple's attempted solution that added another vicious cycle.

The above reframes and other interventions left them with a view, not of a couple at odds, blaming, and negating their sexuality, but instead, of a team inspired with new hope to play a good game. Their sexual needs were affirmed; and sex was reframed from a dreary urge and obligation to a positive pleasure, especially sensual pleasure, and as an experience that could contain many arousing activities other than the pursuit of intercourse and orgasm.

Throughout the session, various interventions prepared Ned and Nancy for the stop-start assignment (explained in detail in Chapter 3) even before I decided to assign it. For example, I elicited and tuned into their sexual attitudes, values, and their range of sexual practices. Informal information was mentioned that normalized and reinforced partners' taking turns, pleasuring each other, and engaging in sensual stimulation that did not include intercourse. These behaviors seemed congruent with their values. Other informal sex information touched on men's learning through sexual experience to discriminate genital sensations, especially the premonitory sensation that signals the inevitability of ejaculation. This information would surface again in the assignment.

Showing both partners equal attention conveyed that their joint effort would be required. As I explored their daily routines and schedules, I was also judging their ability to give time to the tasks and planting seeds for their making the commitment. I clarified their expectations of therapy to be sure these would mesh with the sexual-sensual tasks under consideration. Some of their comments about their own childhoods, families of origin, and their courtship suggested their belief that these issues might be involved in the problem. I did some brief developmental and family history to assess these factors; this also allowed me to evaluate if their beliefs in family causation would create a negative attitude toward the task under consideration. In answering their direct questions about prognosis, I emphasized that clinical research offers a good prognosis when the couple faithfully carries out the tasks as directed. Many interventions served to prepare the couple to accept and undertake the at-home assignments.

There is really a continuum from this effort to the next category of interventions designed to enhance success of the initial assigned task. An integrative conceptualization of therapy contributes greatly to this process. Many factors can conspire to produce failure; so it is necessary to defuse as many of these as possible.

With Ned and Nancy, I explored in the brief individual sessions for factors that might interfere with their doing the assigned stop-start task. When I learned of Ned's opposition to the optional first stage of masturbation in the stop-start learning exercises, I presented the assignment without this stage. However, the fact that I accommodated to his values on this could increase his commitment to the task. I raised other questions to elicit potential resistance to the assignment. The couple committed to a schedule of three times per week for the assignment in spite of their extremely long work hours that left them with very little time together. Many clients fail to do assignments because the therapist presents them in a hurried or unclear manner. The verbal directions were augmented with a copy of several pages from Kaplan's (1989) book on premature ejaculation that is directed to a lay audience. These printed directions, covering only the stages they were to do, enhanced success by reinforcing the therapist's directions, consolidating professional credibility, validating the selected treatment approach, and providing them with a concrete reminder of the therapeutic alliance.

The final category of interventions, presentation of the tasks, should contain carefully crafted and precise directions geared to match unique client and problem characteristics. Assigning at-home sensual-sexual exercises requires the therapist to be comfortable in giving explicit directions. It may be helpful to intersperse some informal sex education with the assignment. Ned and Nancy were to complete the first three stages of the stop-start exercise during the coming 5-week period: manual stimulation by partner; manual stimulation with lubricant by partner; and intromission via female superior position, with "quiet vagina" and the male controlling movement. Detailed directions also clarified when they would be ready to move to each stage and the importance of making telephone progress reports to the therapist after they completed each stage.

It is important to be very clear on task instructions. Because of the nature of sexual material, client or therapist assumptions and anxieties can lead to misunderstandings. I emphasized that there was to be no intercourse during Ned's "learning" period, except as permitted by the third stage of the exercises. When both partners seemed surprised by this, it became clear that they needed further information and explanation. I explained that it was necessary to stop their typical negative pattern with intercourse to permit a positive learning process to begin; interspersing the two would be incongruent. The exercises would promote the goal of increased control, which would then make possible the later goal of full intercourse. They appreciated the explanation, understood, and agreed that they would not engage in intercourse before the third stage. It should be noted that prohibiting intercourse, even without other assignments, is appropriate in other types of sexual distress to interrupt aversive or self-defeating problem-interactional cycles.

The next point of emphasis for them was that the learning process would take time and likely involve some trial and error. This is similar to restraint of rapid change, a strategic technique which has proved effective in countering client resistance. Ned was told to expect miscalculation and ejaculation before the fourth time, and so on. The overall goal in telling a client to expect error is to defuse resistance and tendencies to obsess about performance on the tasks. This latter tendency can result in a new negative pattern of anxiety.

Finally, the task was presented in language to convey that sensual pleasure is possible and desirable for both partners. A reminder was given for Ned to be attentive to his wife's desire for sexual satisfaction and orgasm and pleasure her at some other time than when they were doing the stop-start exercises. I pointed out the importance of his being selfish and enjoying the opportunity to focus only on his own genital sensations during the exercises. The directions essentially contained many "hypnotically embedded" suggestions for the couple's enjoyment, shared intimacy, and expectation of success.

The early interventions applied with Ned and Nancy illustrate what can take place during this process within the IST framework. Drawing from diverse theoretical explanations and strategies enables the therapist to construct interventions to accomplish several goals. The therapeutic process described above was clearly aimed at direct remedy of the symptom. At the same time, it contained many elements that started this couple on the journey toward insight into sexuality, intimacy, their relationship, and themselves.

Assessing Initial Interventions

Once an initial general strategy is underway, careful monitoring of progress is a given. This permits judging the client's response to treatment and whether the strategy is addressing the problem as predicted. The therapist can then decide whether the initial assessment is on target and whether to continue or change directions.

When a major part of the early intervention consists of client homework, review of this in subsequent sessions is essential. New treatment decisions will depend on: whether the client carried out the task; whether the client carried out the task and how (followed, ignored, or embellished instructions); reactions to the task; and the overall outcome with regard to its expected impact on the problem. Client responses to at-home sensual-sexual tasks can be quite variable. The unexpected often occurs, and the challenge of ongoing assessment and devising strategies continues.

The assignment of client homework can serve several purposes. It can provide further data for diagnosing, defining, and treating the problem. It can be a part of a comprehensive treatment plan that encompasses problem alleviation as well as client insight, with homework figuring in at various stages of the plan. Or it can be the primary vehicle for addressing and remedying the symptom. Obviously there is much to review and evaluate if assigned tasks are part of early intervention.

In-office therapeutic processes may be the chosen initial strategy for treating a client's sexual distress. Judging the immediate impact of this strategy is a more nebulous and fluid process than getting the client's response to a homework assignment. Consider such techniques as the sexual genogram, the therapist's empathy, interpretations, rational explanations of personality or couple relationship patterns, fostering new relationship contracts, or experiential or utilization methods. A basic issue is how much time to allow for client gains before facing up to the critical questions. What is the client reaction? Is understanding or insight emerging? Is the client expressing satisfaction with therapy and a sense of progress? Is the therapeutic alliance strengthening? Under these circumstances, one can easily put off the challenge of assessing the initial treatment strategy. With homework tasks, however, the feedback is built in, comes in a concrete form, and is not easily ignored.

Recall the case of Ned and Nancy. After the initial session, assignment of the stop-start exercises was to be the primary vehicle for alleviating the problem. Feedback came in the form of assigned phone contacts with the therapist. In this case, the intervention was continued because the couple reported doing the exercises as directed, a positive response to them, and a confident mood about continuing. The same response with subsequent stages of the assignment further validated proceeding with this strategy.

In another case cited earlier, the initial intervention was quite different. Janet, 35, had lost her orgasmic ability as well as interest in and desire for sex on her wedding day. She experienced aversive reactions to all sexual activity. Because she had had a negative reaction to prior sex therapy that included sexual-sensual tasks as well as the suggestion to confront her mother, my assessment called for a very different intervention. Treatment would center on building a strong therapeutic alliance that would permit exploring her sexual distress in the larger context of her current life roles, marital relationship, and identity and self-structure stemming from her family of origin and subsequent intimate relationships. The primary therapeutic strategy was to provide a safe environment for her to express intensely painful feelings of shame, disgust, numbness, emptiness, and rage. This plan proved essential and effective for the subsequent several directions that therapy eventually took to resolve the problem.

Conclusion

Many challenges face the therapist during the stage of initial assessment and early interventions. IST makes no pretense of offering an easy formula for treating sexual distress. On the contrary, the therapist has to face up to the complexities of sexual and intimacy problems. This means being prepared to define the problem and negotiate the treatment through a filter of keen sensitivity to the client's unique situation and goals. It also means having a theoretical base that accounts for the several dimensions that may figure in sexual distress. Being a multitheoretical approach, IST allows for initial assessment and treatment to take several directions, that is, toward a goal of direct remedy of the symptom, a goal of insight and decision making, or perhaps both. But this stage is merely a starting point that also demands validation, revision, or elaboration of the initial strategy map so as to keep on track in the therapeutic journey.

References

American Psychiatric Association. (1987). *Diagnostic and statistical manual of mental disorders* (3rd ed., revised). Washington, DC: Author.

Butcher, J. N. (1990). *MMPI-2 in psychological treatment.* New York: Oxford University Press.

Derogatis, L. (1977). *SCL-90-R: Administration, scoring and procedures manual.* Baltimore, MD: Clinical Psychometrics Research.

Derogatis, L. R., & Melisaratos, N. (1979). The DSFI: A multidimensional measure of sexual functioning. *Journal of Sex & Marital Therapy, 5*(3), 244-281.

de Shazer, S. (1983). *Keys to solution in brief therapy.* New York: Norton.

Drug interactions and side effects index. (1991). Oradell, NJ: Medical Economics Co., Inc.

Duncan, B. L., & Parks, M. S. (1988). Integrating individual and systems approaches: Strategic-behavioral therapy. *Journal of Marital and Family Therapy, 1*(2), 151-161.

Fagan, P. J., Schmidt, C. W., Wise, T. N., & Derogatis, L. (1988). Sexual dysfunction and dual psychiatric diagnosis. *Comprehensive Psychiatry, 29*(3), 278-284.

Graham, J. R. (1990). *MMPI-2: Assessing personality and psychopathology.* New York: Oxford University Press.

Heiman, J. (1986). Treating sexually distressed marital relationships. In N. S. Jacobson & A. S. Gurman (Eds.), *Clinical handbook of marital therapy* (pp. 361-384). New York: Guilford Press.

Heiman, J., & Grafton-Becker, V. (1989). Orgasmic disorders in women. In S. R. Leiblum & R. C. Rosen (Eds.), *Principles and practice of sex therapy* (pp. 51-88). New York: Guilford Press.

Kaplan, H. S. (1979). *Disorders of sexual desire and other new concepts and techniques in sex therapy.* New York: Brunner/Mazel.

Kaplan, H. S. (1983). *The evaluation of sexual disorders.* New York: Brunner/Mazel.

Kaplan, H. S. (1989). *PE: How to overcome premature ejaculation.* New York: Brunner/Mazel.

LoPiccolo, J., & Steger, J. C. (1974). The Sexual Interaction Inventory: A new instrument for assessment of sexual functioning. *Archives of Sexual Behavior, 3*,(6), 585-595.

Masters, W. H., & Johnson, V. E. (1970). *Human sexual inadequacy.* New York: Little, Brown.

Nichols, H. R., & Molinder, I. (1984). *Multiphasic Sex Inventory Manual.* Tacoma, WA: Author.

Nichols, M. (1984) *Family therapy: Concepts and methods.* New York: Gardner Press.

Olson, D. H., & Portner, J. (1983). Family adaptability and cohesion scales. In E. E. Filsinger (Ed.), *Marriage and family assessment: A sourcebook for family therapy* (pp. 299-315). Beverly Hills, CA: Sage.

Physicians' desk reference. (1991). Oradell, NJ: Medical Economics Company.

Rosen, R. C., & Leiblum, S. R. (1989). Assessment and treatment of desire disorders. In S. R. Leiblum & R. C. Rosen (Eds.) *Principles and practice of sex therapy* (pp. 19-47). New York: Guilford Press.

Slipp, S. (1989). A differing viewpoint for integrating psychodynamic and systems approaches. *Journal of Marital and Family Therapy, 1*(1), 13-16.

Snyder, D. K. (1983). Clinical and research applications of the Marital Satisfaction Inventory. In E. E. Filsinger (Ed.), *Marriage and family assessment: A sourcebook for family therapy* (pp. 169-189). Beverly Hills, CA: Sage.

Spanier, G. B., & Thompson, L. A. (1982). A confirmatory analysis of the Dyadic Adjustment Scale. *Journal of Marriage and the Family, 44*, 731-738.

Verhulst, J., & Heiman, J. (1979). An interactional approach to sexual dysfunction. *American Journal of Family Therapy, 7*, 19-36.

Woody, J. D., & D'Souza, H. (1991). *The Sexual Interaction System Scale: A measure for use in Integrative Systems Therapy for sexual distress.* Unpublished manuscript.

Zilbergeld, B., & Ellison, C. R. (1980). Desire discrepancies and arousal problems in sex therapy. In S. R. Leiblum & R. C. Rosen (Eds.), *Principles and practice of sex therapy* (pp. 66-101). New York: Guilford Press.

8

Refocusing and Power Interventions

> The passion which unites the sexes . . . is habitually spoken of as though it were a simple feeling, whereas it is the most compound, and therefore the most powerful, of all the feelings.
>
> HERBERT SPENCER, from *The Principles of Psychology*

Nowhere is the complexity of clinical work more evident than in the middle stages of treatment. Integrated systems therapy (IST) acknowledges this reality.

The IST model assumes that it is valid to obtain various conceptual perspectives of the client's problem. But it also demands that the therapist synthesize the various hypotheses generated into a systemic explanation that can account for the interaction of several dimensions. This means that an essentially "polyoptic" approach must become transformed in the clinician's mind to a wholistic but pragmatic view of the problem.

The challenges of this stage of IST are highly related, not discrete. It is not relevant to describe them in a stepwise manner since the process is recursive and complementary. Stated simplistically, this means that as new information obtained validates, corrects, and refines previous views, these ongoing changes give way to yet different avenues for continuing the same process and for the intervening that may already be consciously underway.

Aspects of this stage, rather than steps, may include: (a) obtaining new conceptual perspectives of the problem, (b) incorporating these into a holistic yet pragmatic assessment that encompasses interaction of factors maintaining the problem, (c) validating or redefining the initial problem focus and client goals, (d) devising "power interventions" that could potentially impact on interaction involved in maintaining the problem, and (e) matching strategy and intervening according to the strength of the therapeutic system and negotiated problem definition and client goals.

Instead of covering each of these aspects separately, this chapter begins with a general discussion of the process and illustrates with an extensive analysis of two cases.

The Process

Refocusing is typically routine in refining the assessment of a client's sexual distress. Simply put, it permits additional perspectives of the problem as the therapist uses different conceptual lenses from those initially placed in the assessment camera. Refocusing is not done simply because the initial assessment or early interventions prove inadequate for the job; they are usually starting points. In fact, some shifting around of focus plays a part in arriving at early treatment ideas. For example, the initial assessment of Ned and Nancy (the couple with the problem of premature ejaculation) discussed in Chapter 7, also included a quick scan of the couple's relationship and self structures evolving out of their families of origin. This glance, though limited, increased appreciation of the kind of people they were, their characters, and their family legacies. Although each carried some scars, these did not seem immediately significant to the symptom or its remedy; nonetheless, this awareness figured into the precise design of the intervention.

Refocusing does not require the therapist to implement the treatment techniques associated with each of the different conceptual lenses. For example, one can explore and attempt to impact on intergenerational patterns without necessarily using the entire treatment strategy associated with an intergenerational approach to family therapy.

The major purpose of refocusing in IST is to design more powerful interventions. As refocusing promotes deeper understanding of the problem, and especially of its interactive elements, this appreciation can set off a creative process that generates interventions expected to affect multiple dimensions of the problem. It is the impact on multiple factors or on a critical interactive linkage that defines "power interventions."

Describing power interventions is difficult precisely because the most important element is the therapist's creative process. They evolve out of what each therapist has within. This process encompasses not only knowledge and appreciation of human sexuality and of human behavior, the ability to synthesize conceptual understanding, but also such personal/professional qualities of the therapist as character, identity, and moral vision. These qualities are brought to bear in a unique manner on each client situation. There can be no simple formula for this creative process.

This point bears emphasis because it states an obvious but often unacknowledged truth about effective therapy. More things are wrought by the creative process than are accounted for in treatises espousing a singular model of treatment. Devising and delivering therapeutic strategies, if the process can be so crassly described, comes out of the therapist's ability to blend conceptual knowledge, personal/professional identity, and commitment to each client as a unique person in the context of the therapeutic encounter. It is this complex concoction, always with the "cooks's special secret ingredients" thrown in, that gives way to effective therapy. There is no simple recipe for all to follow.

Given this account of how power interventions emerge, what forms can they take? Their power is not inherent, but derives only from their effect. The therapist generates a strategy and believes that it might remove the barrier to the client's desired goals. But until there is evidence of impact, we cannot call them power interventions. This is not to suggest that a so-called power intervention "cures" or "reverses" the problem. A more apt description is that it serves as a catalyst in getting the client moving in the right direction. The client senses a breakthrough or an accomplishment and can move into an upward spiral.

The impact of an effective power intervention can be either dramatic or routine. The exact manifestation may reflect the client's character and perceptual style as much as anything. Some clients report an intense emotional or intellectual experience, an almost altered state of consciousness, a deep insight, or radical behavior change. Others may simply report a steady, satisfying progress, as if not wanting to overstate their achievement.

The exact form that a power intervention takes will vary. It can, in fact, derive from any of the five conceptual dimensions that make up IST or from other therapy models as well. It can be a unified, integrative intervention composed of several techniques from different conceptual dimensions. It can be a single technique that embodies linkages with different theoretical understandings. Regardless of its exact form, as the therapist imagines it, constructs it, and delivers it, the final product will be uniquely tailored to understandings of the specific client situation. The thinking behind the intervention is that it will have a multiple or synergistic impact on the problem, that it will set up a chain reaction in the direction of solution. Thus what might appear on the surface to be primarily a "sex therapy," or cognitive-behavioral, task may have been structured to be a power intervention.

An example may illustrate this. On occasion, I have recommended to a couple and given directions for them to discuss at home in a rational manner the realities of separation or divorce: problems it could solve or worsen; living, property, financial arrangements; care and custody of children; contacts with each other; social or dating relationships, and so on. The intended goal of such an assignment could depend on whether the couple had been flippantly threatening divorce or had never overtly acknowledged this option. Nonetheless, this assignment might be designed as a power intervention. It could stimulate response for each partner at the cognitive, behavioral, and emotional levels, It could promote a deeper awareness of self and of ongoing connections to families of origin. It could interrupt a problematic communication-interaction pattern. And it could expand awareness of the power of the social context that is unleashed when a couple separates or divorces. A word of caution—since there are risks with this intervention, the therapist must believe that it can help with the client's own stated impasse and with their treatment goals.

Because of the anticipated multiple impact, power interventions usually have a paradoxical element. For example, as a client is enabled to experience intense primary emotion that fosters empathy for self and partner, attributions change, and partners become more rational (Greenberg & Johnson, 1986). Or a seemingly simple technique of prohibiting sexual intercourse is expected to have multiple impact and create a rippling effect that eventually makes possible more and

TABLE 8.1 Elements of Power Interventions

1. Primary activity focus—client activity or therapist activity.
2. Matched to client qualities and/or view of reality.
3. Congruent with immediate problem definition.
4. Aimed to achieve a specific therapy goal.
5. Based on therapeutic strategy with proven effectiveness.
6. Designed to maximize impact on interacting or multiple system factors.

better sex. This is not a reference to a simple paradox such as symptom prescription. In fact, because of the nature of sexual symptoms, symptom prescription for most forms of sexual distress is generally not indicated. There are usually interrelated physiological, emotional, behavioral, and interactional elements creating a negative cycle. To simply direct clients to carry out the sexual symptom within a certain time frame or to intensify the symptom reflects a lack of understanding of the various contributors of sexual dysfunction.

In spite of the need to flexibly define power interventions for sexual distress, it is possible to identify elements that must be considered in formulating a power intervention. It might be said that the therapist and client co-create the intervention, because the client is obviously integral to the therapeutic system out of which it evolves. Table 8.1 lists the elements that characterize a power intervention.

The first and overarching factor is the activity focus—whether the intervention will center primarily on the client's activity (especially tasks) or on the therapist's activity in session. While this division is somewhat arbitrary, it is offered as a practical guideline. Second is the emphasis on designing the intervention to match the client's unique qualities or view of reality. The third element is that the intervention is, in fact, congruent with the immediate definition of the problem. The fourth element is that the intervention be aimed to achieve a specific therapy goal that is central to the overall goal of treatment. The fifth element is to build the intervention around a therapeutic strategy with established clinical effectiveness; thus it might draw from proven strategies from any of the major conceptual components that make up IST. And, sixth, the intervention contains the potential to impact on more than one system factor involved in the problem.

In summary, the most critical element in devising the intervention may be the conscious framing to match the client's particular view of reality (Duncan & Parks, 1988). And the most critical element in defining its success may be that it enables the client to reframe some facet of the problem that makes possible new solutions (Weeks & L'Abate, 1982).

Rather than proceed further in academic terms, a detailed case analysis, which appeared in an earlier publication (Woody, 1989), will hopefully better suggest the importance of process in the stage of refocusing and power interventions. It reflects both the planful and evolving integration described throughout this book. Following this, another case example illustrates a different type of refocusing and power intervention.

Case Analysis 1

Treatment consisted of four couple sessions, eight individual sessions with the wife, and six individual sessions with the husband. Many interventions, obviously, took place, but only a few are highlighted here. A strong therapeutic relationship made possible the specific strategies discussed.

> Allie, 26, and Andrew, 34, requested therapy for sexual problems that began shortly after their marriage 9 months before (her first and his second). They had several interrelated complaints. The first was painful intercourse for Allie (attributed to endometriosis) and her loss of interest in and desire for sex ("I don't want to be touched," "I hate it," "It's disgusting"). These sexual dysfunctions had apparently led to other complaints about their relationship. Andrew expressed anger at Allie's controlling his sexual expression and at her criticism of his desire for sex. Both were concerned about the pervasive tension in their relationship (especially at bedtime) and about their arguments over sex, Allie's mechanical participation, and Andrew's jealousy.
>
> Prior to entering therapy, one operation for endometriosis had brought some relief from the pain, which was worst during ovulation and prior to her menstrual period. Her doctor had mentioned as a treatment option using a drug to induce menopause. Allie was extremely upset by this because they wanted to have children and she had been trying to get pregnant since the marriage. Allie saw her husband's sexual desire as excessive, claiming that he used sex as a cure-all for anxieties. Andrew disputed this, saying that he enjoyed the emotional closeness that sex affords. Both reported much closeness and affection between them at times other than during sex. Allie said that she was

orgasmic and that Andrew was a considerate lover interested in her pleasure. She also mentioned that she became sexually active at an early age and previously enjoyed sex.

Allie's sexual problems began about 2 years before, while she was still involved with Zack, a man with whom she had lived for several years. She was already ending this relationship when she met Andrew. Within a few weeks she and Andrew planned to marry. Because of living in different states, their courtship of a few months consisted of phone contacts and a few weekends together. Andrew said his jealousy started because Allie stayed emotionally (though not sexually) involved with Zack right up to their marriage. Moving to her husband's locale, where he was a professional, Allie sold her share in a small business, but had to make several trips back and forth during the first months of their marriage. Her absences, along with their sexual problem, continued to fuel Andrew's jealousy. At the time of treatment, Allie was not employed, expressed satisfaction with being a homemaker, and was getting underway with some artistic interests.

Allie's goals were to stop the tension between them and Andrew's jealousy, while Andrew's goals were to stop the arguing and bad feelings and to have a more compatible sexual relationship.

By the end of the first session, I had tentatively adopted a systemic assessment that called for interruption of the immediate interaction pattern around sex since this was having extremely negative effects on each individual and on the total relationship. Their respective pursuer-distancer roles maintained both Andrew's feelings of being controlled and high desire for sex and closeness, as well as Allie's feelings of disinterest and disgust with sex. Dyspareunia and hypoactive sexual desire seemed appropriate diagnostic descriptors for Allie, with some uncertainty about whether she was experiencing sexual aversion.

Two initial straightforward directives were designed to disrupt the pattern while intruding least into their life. They were (a) to spend intimacy time, talking and sharing, out of the bedroom; and (b) each evening to decide between them, out of the bedroom and before going to bed, whether or not they would have sex. The therapist's decision to assume any degree of control over a couple's sex relationship is a critical, value-ladened judgment. Such an intrusion should be carefully evaluated for its impact on each partner and on the developing therapeutic relationship. Given the foregoing, an individual session was scheduled for each during the next 2 weeks.

The individual sessions were productive in further refining the assessment and continuing treatment. Each reported improvement in the relationship and having had sex 3 days in a row, with Allie noting some pain the third day. Apparently, the first directive had accomplished the goal of interrupting their typical interaction pattern leading to unpleasant sex and subsequent relationship tension. From focusing on the individual-family of origin interface, the following emerged as significant.

Allie had a history of extensive alcohol abuse, starting at about age 13, and she had also tried various drugs. On her own she had quit using alcohol 4 years before and weaned herself from marijuana 2 years ago. She was proud of her achievement, but also stated that she "fears" her past and "can't imagine being without Andrew." Being the eldest and only daughter in a middle-class family with two younger brothers, Allie expressed resentment at having had more homemaking and caretaking responsibilities than her brothers. But she also acknowledged her argumentativeness and rebelliousness against family values through her alcohol and drug use and early sexual activity (age 13), which she regretted. She had remained on reasonably good terms with her family through all this (her mother had helped her with birth control needs). She described her family as expressive, affectionate, stable, with no history of alcohol problems (except hers), and her present relationship with them as close.

At the end of her session, specific directives given encompassed: (a) the problem-interaction pattern (they were to continue with the previous suggestions given); and (b) the goal of exploring in detail her sexual attitudes, fantasies, and so on (she was to keep a sexual log, was given the monitoring form, and was asked to complete a two-page sexual attitude exploration exercise). Each of these tasks was mentioned, respectively, in Chapter 4 and Chapter 7. Besides contributing to further assessment of the desire problem, self-monitoring can often have a paradoxical effect in that clients make changes precisely because they are not asked to change. (deShazer, 1983).

Andrew gave an account of his youth and family that contrasted considerably with that of Allie. Growing up in an emotionally distant family, he recalled from his teen and young adult years strong feelings of loneliness and inferiority (except intellectual), lack of friends, no contact with girls or dating, and early and frequent masturbation (and occasionally sex with a prostitute). He was, however, his family's model child and their star. He volunteered that he thought he had a "sexual problem" stemming from his lifelong high level of desire. Further assessment revealed thought patterns and emotional reactions suggestive of an obsessive-compulsive use of sex to counter anxiety and doubts about personal adequacy.

To impact on both the couple's interaction pattern and the individual cognitive level, the intervention for Andrew was to think of ways he could be unpredictable, especially with Allie (deShazer, 1983). He was also instructed to make two lists, one of the ways she shows her love and the other of his positive qualities and achievements. As with Allie, he was not asked to change any behavior, but it was expected that some change might occur paradoxically.

EVOLVING ASSESSMENT AND TREATMENT

Factors uncovered about the self-system of each individual pointed to the power of the couple's pursuer-distancer pattern, but an important missing part of the picture was an explanation for Allie's loss of desire and interest in sex starting 2 years before; prior to that time she had enjoyed sex "tremendously." The initial hypothesis, based on learning theory, was that pain due to the endometriosis had triggered the negative associations to sex and produced sufficient anxiety for Allie to want to avoid it, and that she had taken this legacy to her relationship with Andrew.

The next couple session brought new developments. Because Allie's doctor had again talked of putting her into a drug-induced menopause, she had monitored her pain in the past few weeks and found that she had no pain or had not noticed it. As a result, she had told Andrew not to initiate sex because she wanted to work alone on what must be her own mental block. Seeing this as more of her avoidance of the problem, Andrew was angered and upset by her fiat. He complained that she had not completed assignments or did so only at the last minute. Allie defended her way of working on the problem as simply different from his.

At this point an integrated set of interventions was aimed at addressing the intensified anger and control issues between them and at further assessing for sexual aversion and the potential for using cognitive restructuring or systematic desensitization for Allie's desire dysfunction. I suggested that neither of them should have the prerogative of initiating sex in the coming week (which removed her option to do what she told Andrew he couldn't do). And I instructed Allie in how to work on a hierarchy to identify specific sex acts, her thoughts about them, and her anxiety level for each. While this self-monitoring assignment could provide diagnostic data, it might also enable her to reevaluate the actual degree of her sexual aversion, since this had happened when she monitored the pain.

REFOCUSING AND EVOLUTION OF A POWER INTERVENTION

Subsequent individual sessions led to ruling out the use of systematic desensitization. Refocusing centered on each partner's idealized projections that had started in courtship and were being maintained by their present unconscious expectations of each other with regard to sexuality. The sessions dealing with Allie's self-structure led to a new explanation for the onset of her sexual symptoms and to a key ingredient in a power intervention based on Ericksonian utilization and metaphor. Before proceeding further, I verified that Allie wanted to enjoy sex again for herself (since she had not offered this originally as a goal).

Allie described Andrew as stable, calm, honest, and satisfied with life—the opposite of Zack and her previous boyfriends. She and Andrew also shared similar values and interest in a metaphysical philosophy emphasizing the oneness of all of nature. She remarked, "When our eyes first met, our souls embraced." She said she loved him deeply, but the sexual passion she had in other relationships was not there, and she did not understand why. She saw him as a man she could commit to, who would love her for herself, not just for sex (she was very conflicted about her previous and early active sex life). When they had first met, they did not have sex for the first 2 months; to her this had meant he put his needs second and hers first.

From Andrew's session, however, it became apparent that he had projected an equally idealized image onto his partner. To him, she was a "sex-pot" (she had told him from the beginning about her sexual history), the answer to his dreams, someone perfectly matched to boost his self-esteem and validate his worth through a regular supply of affection and exciting sex. Clearly, their interlocking unconscious projections were operating collusively to maintain the sexual problem, create a stable but unsatisfactory relationship pattern, and arrest the emotional growth of each partner.

At this point interventions during individual sessions centered on exploring and interpreting the unconscious needs each associated with sex and their unverbalized expectations that marriage and the partner would meet these needs. Interwoven with this was an ongoing attention to circular relationship patterns, as well as to each partner's conscious cognitions about sex. Throughout this process the therapeutic relationship with both partners was characterized by trust, expressiveness, spontaneity, and humor.

Several cognitive interventions were used with Allie, but their utility was not in changing her thinking directly but in what they revealed about her way of perceiving and knowing. For example, for a task in which she was to refute negative thoughts about sex and substitute positive ones, her written responses often contained metaphors such as: "Changing my emotional pattern is like chipping away at a mountain, one piece of stone at a time." In a letter she was asked to write to her parents (but not mail), she signed with: "I love you both past the moon and the stars." And on several occasions, she repeated that when she met Andrew, their "souls embraced." As a result of Allie's new goal to enjoy sex for herself, the ban on her initiating sex was changed to her having the choice to initiate, but only if she wanted it for herself. She did initiate lovemaking once, having a very emotional, fulfilling experience, but on another occasion telling Andrew afterward it was "repulsive." She often expressed remorse that she had lost her virginity so early, saying that at times she felt dirty, like a whore, and that she had been too young to get into sex.

BREAKTHROUGH ASSESSMENT AND POWER INTERVENTION

Prior to this session, when reviewing case notes, I made a connection between Allie's history of alcohol use starting at 13, the onset of her sexual development and sexual activity at about the same age, and the sexual problem starting 2 years ago (coinciding with the point at which she gave up her last drug, marijuana). This connection provided a new hypothesis that complemented prior assessments: her symptoms had appeared at that time (while she was still with Zack) when she had to encounter her sexuality for the first time in a sober state. During her youth she had missed all opportunities to learn gradually about her sexuality and fully integrate it into her identity.

She had gone through these years appearing and thinking of herself as highly sexual and skilled at it, but it had all been under the cloud of alcohol. Now that the cloud was gone, she was like an adolescent just starting to confront the realities of sex and having a lot of growing up to do. Previously, on several occasions, she had pushed to find the meaning of her symptoms. And at this point I believed that a straightforward, cognitive frame for the explanation would not match Allie's way of experiencing and knowing. On the other hand, a metaphysical metaphor might. The process for incorporating the various elements of a power intervention was underway.

In beginning the session, I held off and verified again the dates and extent of her alcohol use. She also brought up an emotional experience in the past week when she had "sort of freaked out" from a mental image she got out of nowhere of "a woman inside of her who is scrawny, frail, weak; there's a lot of black water and she lives in a sort of brown scrungy bubble." She said she initially felt despair at this image but later knew it was a part of herself she had to get "friendly with."

Picking up on this image, I began to develop a metaphor that she had implied in previous expressions. We briefly reviewed the magic of meeting her husband, how it was a fairy tale romance, ending the unhappiness she had endured and fulfilling her dream of a true love and a family. In response to the question of which fairy tale character she could most identify with, she said the Good Witch in the *Wizard of Oz*. The intervention emerged. I told her that at last I thought I understood her problem and that it was so simple I had almost missed it. I told that when she was growing up and becoming a woman she had been under the spell of an evil potion (alcohol), and that the spell had been so powerful and lasted so long that it stunted her growth and development and prevented her from learning about her own sexuality and about herself. Through her own strength and magic she was able to break the spell. And, though magically she and Andrew had found each other, she now had to decide whether and how to go beyond the ending "they lived happily ever after" to the reality of discovering her sexuality and how it could fit into the world of marriage. Allie, misty-eyed, appeared entranced with this account and responded that it was true, that it made sense to her.

There were three more individual sessions, one for Allie and two for Andrew. The next week Andrew reported that Allie had been "more accepting" and "it was a good explanation for her." She had also said once during sex, "Let's make it better." Nonetheless, Andrew was still worried that their relationship was a charade, that she was not really aroused by him. The interventions during this and Andrew's last session were intentionally framed in a logical, analytical manner (laced with empathy, humor, Socratic dialogue, and confrontation) that matched his intellectual approach to life and his obvious interest in his own unconscious processes. We dealt with the irony of his idealized image of Allie (instead of a sex-pot, he got a shy, embarrassed 14-year-old) but also with the reality that he too was like a 14-year-old with her, essentially saying, "Love me, prove to me that I'm attractive and lovable." He was very receptive and thought he was beginning to see her and himself more realistically and as separate persons with their own histories and problems. In Allie's session, she reported that things were better: "The feeling of disgust is going away." In the past week each had initiated sex, which she enjoyed and called "real, real good." There was some discomfort once, but they changed positions, and it was "fine." She reported feelings of arousal that were "like coming alive again." When she asked if I had any other suggestions, I intentionally hedged and said I would put something in the mail if I thought of anything. She volunteered, "Just experience is what it's going to take," and I agreed. Andrew gave similar positive reports in his next session, including: "tremendous progress," "real good," sex being "fun and frequent," and Allie's initiating oral sex, which she had never permitted before. The remainder of the session dealt briefly with some of his personal goals and the fact that they should expect ups and downs in the sexual relationship. They were scheduled for a 3-month follow-up session.

At the conjoint follow-up session, both stated that their sexual relationship was "good" and "very enjoyable." They also happily reported that Allie was 3 months pregnant and that she had quit smoking. Although she had been having some "morning sickness," Allie enthusiastically reported: "Sex is great when you're pregnant." In a follow-up 5 months later, the couple still reported no sexual problems.

FINAL THOUGHTS

The reality of therapy does not readily lend itself to theoretical analyses nor to detailed reporting. Certainly, theory and techniques are critical to the process, but there is so much more than the literature acknowledges or edited videotapes present.

The therapist enters into the client's present and past and inner and outer worlds and selectively looks for the pieces of the puzzle that make up the complaint and perhaps hold a solution. In the case above, concepts from one theory allowed the placement of pieces in certain sections, which were left in place, while yet other concepts permitted attention to a new section or troublesome pieces. Intense focusing on these at times brought progress, but it also helped to put them aside and return to them later with a fresh vision. Both scanning the total, but incomplete, picture and studying certain pieces in depth for color, shade, and exact shape led eventually to their placement. Flexibility in being able to view the larger picture as well as appreciate detail was seen as a strength in this integrative approach. It was both a planful and a serendipitous process, logical yet intuitive at the same time, and filled with value judgments at every step. These are all elements that constitute the reality of an integrative therapy.

The metaphor strategy used with Allie proved to be a power intervention. Its design (see Table 8.1 above) called primarily for therapist activity: the metaphorical account. It matched Allie's metaphysical and emotional view of reality and thus did not emphasize rationality or require a task of her. It was congruent with the immediate problem definition that saw her sense of an impaired self as restricting her sexuality. It aimed to achieve the specific goal (stated as a need by Allie) of helping her find a meaning for her blocked sexual expression. It drew upon strategies with established effectiveness, namely, hypnotic utilization and metaphor. And, finally, the metaphor was aimed at a linkage point for the relationship and sexual problem: Allie's self, and could thus be expected to impact on interacting system factors.

Case Analysis 2

The case of Brent and Barbara (cited earlier as a vignette in Chapter 2) also illustrates the holistic nature of intimacy and sexual disturbances. The problems of this couple demanded an integrative theory base and a flexible treatment approach. A multiple focus early in the assessment process led to a power intervention that accomplished several goals and impacted on several different dimensions of their problems. The power intervention consisted of the therapist's activity of interpretation, explanation, confrontation, and a task for the couple. It derived not from any one theoretical explanation of their problem but from an interactional, systemic explanation. There had been two individual sessions with Brent and two couple sessions when the intervention was used.

Twenty-eight years old, married, and the father of a 2-year-old child, Brent entered therapy when faced with two simultaneous events that rocked his world. First, his wife Barbara discovered his ongoing affair that had started early in their 4-year marriage; and subsequently Brent learned that Barbara was also having an affair. Second, a member of his family of origin was facing criminal charges for incest, and this situation had triggered Brent's concern about some of his own sexual behaviors. These included several paraphilias—exhibitionism and making obscene telephone calls—as well as strong fantasies of control and rape and actual marital rape. He was also distressed by his compulsive masturbation and attendance at adult "peep shows." Brent acknowledged a lack of intimacy with both his affair partner and his wife and overall dissatisfaction with himself and with his marriage. Although his wife was orgasmic and he enjoyed this quality in her, they rarely had sex that included her sexual satisfaction.

The initial assessment period focused on Brent's psychological turmoil, confusion, and efforts to cope with the crumbling marital structure. Both of the events had led him to question his "normalcy." His initial goal for therapy was a broad one: "to get healthy and be a normal, responsible husband." But this goal was quite remote given the immediate crisis that he and Barbara were in. The initial treatment strategy called for (a) including his wife in the therapy in order to explore her intentions about the affairs and the marriage and (b) having Brent monitor his sexual behaviors via use of the sexual log technique.

Neither Brent nor Barbara was ready to break off contacts with their affair partners; so continuing deceit, interrogation, spying, and emotionality alternated with their tentative efforts to convey caring and understanding for each other. Their present relationship was highly unstable and clearly not conducive to Brent's fully devoting attention to his own sexual disorders. Yet it was not possible nor advisable to see these as problems separate from the marital crisis.

Initial couple sessions focused on assessment of their relationship structure and the function of the affairs in this; their present coping and decision making abilities within this crisis; and the individual/family-of-origin interface. The power intervention that emerged out of the integrative assessment centered on the therapist activity of interpretation, explanation, confrontation, and on a task for the partners.

The immediate challenge with the couple was to pull them from the mire of hopelessness, ambivalence, and powerlessness to enable them to cope more effectively with the current crisis. Filled with fears about separating, they were unable to face the fears, comfort each other, or recommit to the marriage. Instead they continued to seek solace in brief, clandestine contacts with their affair partners, which led to inevitable discovery, which further engulfed them in hopelessness and ambivalence. The vicious cycle was obvious.

Consider the pieces in the power intervention that was developed. Interpretation centered on unconscious processes involved in their mating. Explanation encompassed a straightforward effort to teach the couple about their needs, their relationship structure, and the role of the affairs. Confrontation stressed the immediacy of their problem in light of what they expected of therapy. And a task assignment aimed to add an action-oriented element for them to carry out.

The pieces fit together to address their present paralysis in the face of the crisis and its connection to the origin of the affairs, the emptiness in their marriage, and the nature of their self-structures and mutual projections, which were legacies from their families of origin, that guaranteed that neither would grow emotionally. But what were the assessment data that gave way to this multifaceted assessment and intervention?

Brent came from a successful middle-class family but could recall little attention from his parents; instead, he always felt alone and different and daydreamed a lot. He had two sisters, but he was left to his own devices and spent time with cousins from the "bad side of the family." He was molested by an uncle from age 13 to 16. He would also later recall that he too had had sexual contacts with his sisters during adolescence. Throughout high school he regarded himself as a weird nobody and a loser; an unhappy romantic attachment with a girl added to this self-concept. In college he unexpectedly found acceptance within a social group and girls who pursued him, although his first serious girlfriend turned out to be quite pathological.

At this point he met Barbara, who appeared different—stable, normal, and liked by the group; they seemed headed for success as a couple. Brent unconsciously drifted into a marriage to Barbara as it promised a new identity, one that might allow him to escape his own and his family's "craziness and degeneracy."

Barbara too brought her insecurities. Extremely enmeshed in her family of origin and somewhat infantilized by them, when she met Brent, she was living away from home for the first time. Prior to marriage she had told Brent of some type of childhood or adolescent trauma (not disclosed in therapy). In courtship, they became emotionally enmeshed as each seemed to meet deep unconscious needs for maintaining self and identity integrity. For Brent, Barbara was a good, rational person; he wanted to be with her and be good to her. The connection to her allowed him to believe in "love" as opposed to the strictly sexual relationships that he had pursued with other girls. These inevitably had proved to be bizarre and overwhelming and thus confirmed his own sense of defectiveness. For Barbara, Brent's intense pursuit of and emotional involvement with her brought security and validation of her femininity. She also experienced the relationship as another avenue of independence from her family. In spite of their unconscious idealized projections, the marriage in reality immediately gave way to a lack of intimacy, mutual emotional withdrawal, and the maintaining of a superficial image of "coupleness" and the accoutrements of marriage.

The intervention consisted of *interpretation* of their courtship dynamics: the relationship promised to heal wounds to self and complete their shaky identities, both of which were legacies from their families. Due to their extreme projections they had married symbols not real persons. Instead of facing up to each other's shortcomings and vulnerabilities early in the marriage, they preserved an empty marital structure while playing the parts required of a "successful couple." Their needs to share their real selves were rechanneled to contacts outside of their relationship. Brent's sexual escapades increased, including an affair, and Barbara too connected with another partner.

The *explanation* asked them to notice their relationship structure in the past and a similar structure now in which they still sought refuge from the pain of betrayal through continuing the extramarital contacts, which further fueled more pain and chaos in their relationship.

The *confrontation* suggested they could continue as they were—slogging in the emotional mire and continuing to struggle (doing more of the same) and yet sinking. Or they could use the explanation to understand how all this had happened. They were challenged to see whether this rational explanation might enable them to stop the mutual blaming, face up to the pain, and expect that trust would be a long time coming.

The *task* assigned was framed in general terms. Each was to focus on getting mentally healthy as an individual, to discover personal needs, and then eventually evaluate to see if the partner could meet some of these needs. To begin on this, they were given a cognitive task. In the coming week, they were to accept their own and their partner's imperfections and vulnerabilities and acknowledge to themselves that both had hurt the other and that this was part of their humanness. Each was to make the effort to change his or her own thinking along these lines without regard for the partner's effort. There was no specific suggestion about their contacts with the affair partners or about recommitting to each other.

Overall, this intervention aimed to tap unconscious, cognitive, and emotional dimensions of each person and to capitalize upon individual responsibility to act and make decisions—for their immediate and future well-being. The goal was to enable them to bring more rationality and stability to bear on the current situation and thus inhibit the continuing cycle of impulsive behaviors and prevent impulsive decision making. My ethical stance was one of respect for their pain and confusion and for the baffling complexity of their problem. A more directive or controlling therapist stance might have triggered resistance and even more impulsiveness as a means of coping with their dilemma.

In the following week they reported less tension and better communication between them. They gradually reduced the spying and interrogations. Barbara was successful in assertively refusing Brent's attempt to force sex. And Brent worked more faithfully on the monitoring of his sexual behaviors. In the next session, Brent worked well at cognitive restructuring and using rational analysis aimed at his unwanted sexual behaviors. He set individual goals of eliminating (a) all contact with his affair partner, (b) his attending "peep shows," and (c) forcing sex on Barbara. Barbara too expressed the goals of discontinuing all contact with her affair partner and communicating more openly with Brent. Therapy refocused at this point on Brent's sexual disorders. He achieved the above goals, drastically decreased his masturbation at home, and set a new goal of more intimate and mutually satisfying sex with Barbara.

In the following 2 months they experienced both good and bad times in the overall relationship. Each continued to make individual contributions to improve it, but trust, as might be expected, was not forthcoming. Therapy continued to focus on these issues. They terminated when insurance coverage expired, although further therapy was recommended. Follow-up 2 months later revealed both had recommitted to the marriage. They felt the marriage was still fragile and needed improvement. Brent reported that sex overall was less central in his life. His sexual relationship with Barbara at this time was more fun, though intercourse was less frequent than before. Over a period of 4 months, there had been five couple sessions, eight individual sessions for Brent, and one individual session for Barbara.

Conclusion

Refocusing is essential in IST. Obtaining various conceptual perspectives need not scatter the clinician's understanding or energies. Instead, it can ignite a creative process whereby we identify the interacting pieces of the problem, see them wholistically, and better grasp the nature of the tenacity of the system that contains the problem. The multifaceted assessment can lead to power interventions which are designed to impact on several dimensions of the problem. Their power resides in their effectiveness in serving as a catalyst to move the client in the direction of solutions.

A power intervention may take various forms. It may look like a singular technique, such as a behavioral/experiential sensual-sexual task. But, as suggested above, the clinician builds into such a task additional dimensions derived from the IST assessment. Or a metaphorical explanation, such as that used with Allie, may embody a holistic linkage between past and present, individual and couple issues, unconscious and conscious, and cognition, emotion, and behavior. Or as in the case of Brent and Barbara, a power intervention may consist of an integrated set of techniques that together address interlocking facets of the problem.

In summary, the elements to consider in designing an intervention are (a) determining whether it will center on therapist activity or client activity, (b) matching it to client qualities or views of reality, (c) connecting it to the immediate problem definition, (d) aiming it to achieve a specific therapeutic goal, (e) basing it on a therapeutic strategy with proven effectiveness, and (f) designing it for multiple impact on several or interacting system factors. This same composite of carefully integrated elements also plays a part in interventions in the last stage of therapy—maintaining progress and terminating.

References

deShazer. S. (1983). *Keys to solution in brief therapy*. New York: Norton.

Duncan, B. L., & Parks, M. B. (1988). Integrating individual and systems approaches. *Journal of Marital and Family Therapy, 1*(2), 151-161.

Greenberg, L. S., & Johnson, S. M. (1986). Emotionally focused couples therapy. In N. S. Jacobson & A. S. Gurman (Eds.), *Clinical handbook of marital therapy* (pp. 253-276). New York: Guilford Press.

Weeks, G. R., & L'Abate, L. (1982). *Paradoxical psychotherapy: Theory and practice with individuals, couples, and families*. New York: Brunner/Mazel.

Woody, J. D. (1989). The reality of an integrative sex therapy. *Journal of Sex & Marital Therapy, 1*(1), 62-73.

9

Maintaining Progress and Terminating

> Processes of forming, making, building go on even if we are not consciously aware of them at the time.
>
> ROLLO MAY, *The Courage to Create*

The therapy process is predictable in its unpredictability. Ideally, treatment moves the client toward achievement of articulated goals, and the assumption is that both client and therapist will agree on indicators of goal achievement. Often, however, gaps exist between this ideal and clinical reality. Client's goals may change, or the importance attributed them shifts. A client might be satisfied with less than full attainment of the goal as originally defined. Financial considerations may dictate the amount of energy and commitment given to therapy. And clients may terminate out of dissatisfaction with the treatment or the therapist.

This chapter aims to capitalize on what is needed and what is possible during the final stage of treatment. There is no attempt to cover the basics of termination nor this process as described by different models of therapy. Rather the intent is to suggest how integrated systems therapy (IST) can strengthen this latter part of the helping process through offering a range of strategies for the creative grist mill.

The Client's Reality and the Final Stage of Therapy

As therapy changes, the client's reality, where the problem actually plays out, also changes. Some of this change is planned, and some is not. We need to remain attuned to this factor and judge progress and what else is needed in accord with the client's reality.

The clinician is usually well prepared to handle change in the predicted and desired direction. For example, as a couple achieves improved communication about sexual matters, intimacy increases, but also different expectations of their sexual encounters or relationship may also emerge. This type of change may lead to new concerns that need attention. When the symptomatic partner overcomes a sexual dysfunction or disorder, the partner may begin to doubt his or her own sexual attractiveness or question whether the now functional partner will remain faithful or demand more sex, and so on. As clinicians, we know to expect these kinds of changes in the couple system. Further interventions can then aim to help them maintain progress through new adaptations required by a changing system.

More difficult to manage are changes in the client's reality that evolve without the therapist's full participation. External events occur and change things with regard to the problem. Someone in the family may become ill, the client may decide to move, or a baby arrives—and the original problem loses its salience. For example, in the case of Carla (cited in Chapter 4), she and her husband entered therapy because of her lack of desire and aversion to sex. But she was pregnant at the time, and after several sessions, she developed toxemia and was confined to bed by her doctor. This event changed many aspects of their life, and the sexual distress lost priority. After the baby arrived, Carla once more called about therapy, but did not follow through. Subsequently, she reported that she had begun to make some changes that had improved the sexual relationship for both her and her husband.

It is simply a fact of professional life that clients often determine independently that they have improved enough or that they no longer wish to work on the therapeutic goal. Under these circumstances, the challenge is to take a hard look at the client's new reality in the context of original goals. At that point, even if the therapist judges it to be premature termination, it is possible to utilize the client's perception so as to also help anticipate barriers to current gains achieved and find ways to consolidate progress.

The case of Brent and Barbara (discussed in Chapter 8) illustrates this latter situation. The first step toward their goals was achieved when they were able to become more rational and bring a degree of stability to the relationship. This was sufficient to allow each partner some energy to take responsibility for contributing to the chaos in the marital environment. Brent was highly motivated to focus on his unwanted sexual behaviors. This was a necessary step since these impacted so dramatically on his self esteem as well as on his relationship with Barbara. Brent set personal goals and made changes in his sexual behaviors. But his reality was still filled with ambivalence as to whether he and Barbara would stay together or be able to create a meaningful relationship. Changing his sexual behaviors was a goal couched in terms of bringing personal benefit to him, probably benefiting his current relationship with Barbara, as well as benefiting his future well being—regardless of the outcome of the present marriage. As a result of the crisis situations in his family of origin, Brent had already stopped the obscene phone calls, exhibiting, and cruising. This change was certainly a positive step, but Brent acknowledged that it was probably only temporary since he still had the urges to act in these ways.

As Brent made progress, therapy helped him to anticipate future road blocks and consolidate the changes in emotion, cognition, and behavior that would enable him to be a "normal" person sexually. Behavioral analysis had revealed that much of his sexual acting out was controlled by environmental cues. For example, his job as a manager allowed him a high degree of independence and time alone in his car—conditions that elicited the cycle of exhibitionism and masturbation in the car. Other variables were his fantasies, cognitions, and the reinforcement from sex that he typically obtained without any negative consequences. Therapy centered on changing all of these variables and enabling Brent to learn new adaptive cognitions and behaviors. His continuing progress was beginning to have a positive impact on him and his marital relationship. Further therapy was recommended for Brent and Barbara as individuals and for their still shaky relationship. But when insurance coverage expired, termination came in spite of this assessment.

A somewhat different termination situation arose in the case of Harry and Helen (cited in Chapters 6 and 7). Once Harry decided that he wanted to stop cross dressing in order to preserve his marriage, treatment consisted of individual sessions for Harry. It was based, however, on an integrative systemic understanding of his behavior that encompassed Harry's sense of self and identity, the current marital relationship structure, the interactional problem-sequence that contained the cross-dressing, and its cognitive-behavioral dimensions.

The diagnostic classification was an important first step in the assessment process. Gender disorder not otherwise specified was accurate in that Harry's cross-dressing was not for purposes of sexual arousal and masturbation, but appeared transient and stress-related.

He had started cross-dressing 2 years before when he had learned of this behavior in a college textbook. His employment history and job success had always been unstable and marginal. But his wife was a well-paid professional who provided the family a steady income. At the time he first started cross dressing, major stressors were present—his mother had died and he had lost yet another job.

Currently Harry had a new job in sales that demanded long work hours. He and Helen often argued about his uncertain income, his long hours, and the burden of income and family responsibilities that fell on her. Harry's pattern was to dress at home in the mornings after Helen and the children were gone. While dressed, he did the phone work that was required by his sales job and achieved this task with some degree of relaxation. He then did whatever household chores were necessary before changing clothes to go to work in the afternoon. Harry reported that he and Helen had a satisfactory sexual relationship, but their arguments troubled him.

The comprehensive assessment suggested the cross-dressing to be a means for Harry to cope with his lack of a sense of masculine adequacy in career, marriage, and family. The anxiety and fear of further failure that were triggered each morning as he began work was relieved by the dressing. He was reinforced by the calm it afforded him and by his productivity in the job. Nonetheless, this solution to one problem became the problem when Helen learned of it, as it further reduced Helen's respect for him, a development that further assaulted his self esteem. The vicious cycle was obvious.

The treatment was multifaceted. There were efforts to help the couple improve their communication and sense of being a team. Through cognitive-behavioral strategies and interrupting the problem-interactional sequence, Harry began to decrease the cross-dressing and then got rid of his feminine clothes. Once this occurred, however, Harry apparently felt that he had achieved his goal. A follow-up session was to have focused on consolidating his progress and the couple's relationship as a part of the plan of relapse prevention. But he did not keep the appointment. Upon follow-up a month later, Harry reported that things were going well and that the relationship with Helen was also "good." He said he was not missing the cross-dressing and that he was busy at work on a new sales promotion. So, once again, the differences between the therapist's plan to help the client maintain progress and the client's reality did not mesh.

Maintaining Progress

Typically, the clinician has plenty of ideas about what the client will face in implementing the changes made through therapy. But the client is the expert of what will actually help and what might hinder in the real world. Together, then, they can find strategies to enable the client to overcome the barriers after treatment has ended.

IST has much to offer in this stage of therapy. An integrative systems approach offers a broad base for accepting and working for whatever the client produces. For example, a couple or an individual might mention the tendency to get into a rut (in other words, an unproductive circular pattern). Or they might mention environmental or interpersonal cues that elicit ineffective responses or coping. Or there could be continuing self-doubts, family roles, or life events that could tax their present gains and cause a downward spiral. Especially the client's labels for such likelihoods would be critical to overcoming them. The possibilities are limitless, but IST allows evaluation of the client's concerns for the future in the light of different theoretical components. It is then possible to devise effective strategies to help the person to meet and master negative future situations.

Consider just a few of the broad strategies that are possible through IST. Norcross (1986) has noted three common factors that cut across the different models of therapy that account for positive outcomes. These are support, learning, and action; and IST encompasses all three. When it comes to consolidating client progress, we can view identified future barriers in light of these factors and devise strategies to meet the challenge. Table 9.1 below presents these factors.

TABLE 9.1 A Sequential Listing of Factors Common Across Therapies that Are Associated with Positive Outcomes

Support Factors	*Learning Factors*	*Action Factors*
Therapist warmth, respect, empathy, acceptance, genuineness	Insight	Encouragement of facing fears, taking risks, and mastery efforts
Positive relationship	Rationale	Reality testing
Reassurance	Cognitive learning	Modeling
Identification with therapist	Changing expectations for personal effectiveness	Practice
Structure	Self-acceptance	Working through
Trust		
Catharsis		
Release of tension		

Reprinted by permission from Norcross, J. C. (Ed.). (1986). *Handbook of eclectic psychotherapy*. New York: Brunner/Mazel, p. 445.

The case example of Ann and Adam (cited originally in Chapter 1) illustrates how IST involves the client meaningfully in maintaining progress and accommodates with strategies to match the task ahead.

Therapy for the couple's sexual distress was not provided because Adam wanted no part of this. Ann, however, continued individual therapy to help her cope with the continuing crisis due to Adam's ongoing affair. The power intervention that seemed most critical to Ann's progress was the therapeutic encounter. This encompassed many interventions but primarily empowered Ann to set her own pace in deciding about reconciliation, separation, or divorce. This strategy enabled her to learn effective coping for the painful and chaotic situation that she chose to stay in. The following were some of the many goals that Ann accomplished—gradually and only one step at a time: asking Adam to move, restructuring her social and work contact with him, exploring her sexuality, accepting responsibility for her sexuality, consulting an attorney, developing an independent social life, making new living arrangements for herself and her child, and defining her expectations for an intimate relationship.

As concrete progress came only one step at a time, Ann was readily able to identify future barriers that might trigger a setback at every step of the way. For example, even after the separation, she identified that Adam's criticisms might elicit unwanted emotions and behaviors from her. We worked to prevent her relapse by various strategies. Efforts aimed to consolidate her learning in the area of self-acceptance and defining her own expectations of personal worth instead of accepting Adam's definitions of her. Other interventions stressed action in the form of having her rehearse anticipated future interpersonal contacts with Adam and rationally analyze the reality of those situations.

Ann's case followed the ideal model for the therapeutic process. She made concrete progress on clearly delineated goals. She identified realistic barriers to her maintaining new behaviors and decisions. And she stayed in therapy through the final stage to work on ways to master future challenges.

IST offers many choices for stabilizing the client's gains. Only a few are noted here simply to suggest the breadth of the options.

In cognitive-behavioral therapy, the term "relapse prevention" encompasses strategies to strengthen the client to meet future hazards specific to the problem treated. These encompass a range of self-control techniques, such as learning skills to predict risky scenarios, label situations and external cues, identify emotional responses associated with unwanted behaviors, and develop and use adaptive coping statements and behaviors.

Other valuable strategies that can fit the termination process needed for some clients come from the MRI problem-interactional component. If the goal is to enhance client control and minimize resistance, the therapist may claim surprise by the extent of progress. Success may be attributed to a temporary condition or a "fluke." Furthermore, when the therapist worries that relapse may occur or tells the client to go slowly or expect problems, this is a way of strengthening the client to take control, meet the barriers head on, and prove the therapist wrong. This method aims to keep the therapist out of a new problem-interactional system. These may be effective methods for some clients.

Focus on other theoretical components such as the individual-family of origin interface and relationship structure give way to still different strategies. But concrete tasks can be designed to accomplish the goals of various therapy models. For example, the couple may need to discover and institute new routines in their lives in order to maintain progress made toward individuation, or to assure time for newly valued intimacy with a partner or to add variety to their sexual encounters.

Co-creating integrative interventions for maintaining client progress emerges from the therapeutic system. The therapist guides the process by considering the same elements that go into design of a power intervention: (a) determining the degree of activity of the therapist and the client, (b) matching the activity to the client's reality at the point of termination, (c) defining the immediate problem in the context of major barriers to maintaining progress, (d) devising intervention to achieve specific goals critical to insuring continued progress, (e) using effective therapeutic strategies from any of the conceptual components of IST, and (f) constructing the intervention to maximize impact on multiple or interacting system factors related to consolidating progress.

Attending to these elements can lead to creative, integrative methods that will give the client the best chance of succeeding when therapy is over.

Termination

The elements of successful termination are in some ways the same as those present in the course of all successful therapy. Two that merit specific comment are tempering the therapeutic alliance and giving and accepting credit.

TEMPERING THE THERAPEUTIC ALLIANCE

Although the therapeutic alliance is central in working with clients with sexual distress, clients should also be gradually weaned from this support system. This process can go smoothly in IST because of the various types of interventions used.

Early in treatment the relationship accords authentic respect and valuing to a client who may be mired in self denigration for perceived "abnormality" or "weirdness." The reassurance and support prepares the client to accept challenges, try new ideas, take charge, and make changes. Later on, however, the therapeutic strategy must tap into the client's own self-respect, self-acceptance, and ability to find sources of support in the real world. Thus the therapeutic alliance is a means to an end. Its effectiveness throughout treatment and at termination depends on fostering the client's growth toward independence and participation in mutually supportive real life relationships.

Because the intensity of the therapeutic relationship varies with the client, the clinician continually judges whether the client is on course. Typically, with couples therapy the alliance is less intense than with individuals. Long term therapy, too, increases the risk for the client to rely overmuch on the therapist.

The fact that therapy focuses on a client's sexual life also demands awareness of how this content can affect the therapeutic alliance. The challenge is to remain therapeutically dispassionate but also to build trust that permits the client to talk about the necessary intimate details of sex. This is a stance of ethical concern about the client's sex problem. We want the person to achieve a level of sexual functioning or integrity that will work well for them in life. But we do not become special pleaders for particular solutions or for our own personal standards of sexual health, and we do not unnecessarily intrude into their sexual lives. Clearly, a finely tuned clinical judgment and ethical stance are required to resolve the many value-laden situations that come up in therapy.

An example from the case of Ann illustrates the dispassionate stance that must be part of an effective therapeutic alliance. One of Ann's goals was to explore her own sexuality, since she had essentially bought in to Adam's criticisms of her as responsible for their problems and his affairs. Ann read about female sexuality and orgasm and did some self-exploration exercises (Heiman & LoPiccolo, 1988). She happily discovered that she experienced desire, arousal, and orgasm rather easily. But achieving this goal increased her awareness of her needs for affection, intimacy, and sexual expression that had never been met in the marriage. Her frustration grew as she realized that she continued to block fulfillment of these needs by her own choice not to divorce Adam yet. But during this period Ann became sexually involved with two men with whom she had developed friendships.

Although Ann found much needed support in the therapeutic relationship at this time, the therapist's role was not one of blindly cheering her on in these attempts to get her needs met. The aim was to help her evaluate her actions in terms of their overall benefits and risks to her well-being. Discovering one's sexuality carries with it the responsibility to make decisions about how it will fit into the person's total life situation. Ann was still married to a powerful man who had threatened to "pull out all stops" if they divorced, she could be risking her custody of the child, and she took no precautions in the relationships to protect herself from sexually transmitted disease, although this had been one of her criticisms of Adam in his affairs.

This element of the therapeutic relationship was focused on the future. The goal was to help the client become independently able to analyze her decisions and assume responsibility for their consequences. A part of successful termination is to downscale the therapeutic relationship and prepare the client for autonomy.

GIVING AND RECEIVING CREDIT

Crediting the client is simply another piece of termination that needs to take place throughout treatment. We may be somewhat stingy on this count out of concern of claiming premature success. But clients deserve credit even for continuing therapy and for enduring the process of pouring out the often painful details of their sex lives to a stranger. It is valuable to acknowledge their efforts all along, especially since termination is not always under the full control of the therapist. Nonetheless, credits to the client for progress should increase and become more planful in anticipation of completing treatment.

IST permits many opportunities for authentically giving the client credit for work and progress. Having used a variety of treatment strategies, the therapist will determine what to do about crediting the client in light of the exact conceptual note emphasized in the latter part of treatment. This segment may have relied primarily on one conceptual dimension or on a holistic, integrative way of working with the client. As with previous stages of treatment, flexibility and the therapist's creative process allow for strategies to suit the exact situation. The following discussion suggests examples of the integrative stance.

By the end of an effective course of therapy, clients genuinely feel appreciation and want to express it, and many will have done so throughout the process. It is the authentic therapeutic relationship that leads the client to feel free to express thanks. And it the therapist's secure belief that the relationship is on track that permits genuine acceptance of these sentiments. There is no need to discount them out of zeal to credit the client. The benefits of the therapeutic alliance are valid throughout the treatment process.

What about straightforward positive reinforcement to credit the client for progress? At termination we need to become very conscious of this strategy. We can acknowledge the client's specific gains and the exact behaviors used to achieve them and especially those that will need to continue to maintain progress. Moreover, IST allows us to connect this type of reinforcement to various other facets of the problem that therapy has touched on. For example, with a couple: "The sensate focus was a real breakthrough in solving the problem, and better still, now you enjoy it in real life, not as a task. It looks like you've changed the sex problem but also your overall approach to each other." This crediting comment aims to reinforce specific behaviors for the future but also links them to the larger couple relationship. The same possibility for integrative reinforcement strategies exists with techniques such as utilization, metaphor, rituals, and so on.

If the final segment of therapy has employed power interventions, these were likely composites of techniques from several theoretical models or a unified intervention designed to impact on several dimensions of the problem. Crediting the client can continue within the same framework of the power intervention that worked.

In the case of Allie and Andrew (discussed in Chapter 8), the metaphorical explanation of her sexual aversion was designed to match her experiential grasp of the world. She had given plenty of cues supporting the need to do things her way, to be in charge, to find her own solution. So final comments conveyed that she knew how best to continue learning about her own sexuality. Her situation did not call for concrete suggestions or helping her develop specific skills for meeting future barriers. This integrative intervention was thus aimed at accomplishing several goals of the termination process—increasing client autonomy, giving credit, validating her individuality, and decreasing therapist centrality.

Evaluating Therapy

The clinician is continually engaged in the process of evaluating therapy. As IST affords an increasingly rich understanding of the problem, new perspectives emerge for guiding the client toward achievement of goals. The overall responsibility to assess our work encompasses the ongoing evaluation, soliciting informal client feedback, and formal evaluation.

The ongoing evaluation is essentially automatic and inescapable. With each session, the therapeutic gestalt conveys whether therapy is accomplishing an initial or prioritized step to remedy the problem. It also reveals whether a specific technique accomplished its purposes. Sometimes the evaluative feedback is instantaneous. All of this permits continuous adjustment and correction so as to stay on track with a process to provide the help that the client wants and needs.

For example, in the case of Ned and Nancy (cited in Chapter 7), when Ned reacted negatively to the discussion of masturbation as an optional first stage in the "stop-start" behavioral/experiential assignment, this immediate feedback led to designing the strategy without this stage.

Knowing when to make subtle or major shifts or stay the course in the therapeutic strategy is never an easy decision. IST, however, allows for a holistic view of sexual distress, which should promote flexibility. Clearly, this book argues against conceptual rigidity. In a recent presentation dealing with systemic aspects of sexual dysfunction, the speaker cited a case in which sensate focus was assigned again and again to a couple even though they refused to do it or see its application to their problem. This stance seemed rigid in holding to Masters and Johnson's (1970) universal intervention as valid for all clients. A systemic perspective would suggest other ways of evaluating both the problem, the concept of resistance, and the nature of the therapeutic relationship.

Another aspect of evaluating therapy is to ask clients for specific feedback of what was and was not helpful. This definitely has a place in the final stage of treatment. It is all the more important with IST, since the client can provide clues as to whether the treatment experience felt like a planful, unified whole or as haphazard, scattered enterprise.

The request for client feedback must be authentic. It is easy to pick up on a request structured to elicit only positive comments. As an introduction, the therapist can honestly disclose some aspect of treatment that "bombed" to show that he or she can handle negative evaluations. It can be useful to discuss negative comments in order to judge whether uncomfortable client emotions such as anxiety or anger were part of the intended goal of the strategy. Clients' comments about specific homework tasks can reveal whether their design fit the individual client or consisted of an ineffective, cookbook format. IST emphasizes designing an intervention so that it uniquely matches the client and impacts on various dimensions of the problem. We need to know if it works.

Another time to press for specific client feedback is when clients terminate prematurely. This can reveal whether simply circumstances or therapeutic ineffectiveness were involved in the decision. Again, one can ask directly whether specific aspects of treatment were unhelpful. Needless to say, some clients may prefer not to disclose their dissatisfactions, but the clinician has the responsibility to seek full feedback for evaluating treatment.

Formal evaluation usually follows a prescribed format. It may consist of methods developed by individual practitioners or by agency procedure. It typically encompasses evaluative data obtained through telephone contacts, client questionnaires, or outcome measures. These are often used at the point of termination as well as at a prescribed follow-up point.

Relevant to IST, formal evaluation methods should be structured to assess the type of treatment actually provided. If the intent was to impact on several dimensions of the problem, what were the intended changes, and how can they be included in the evaluation? This means also that at least part of the format needs co be tailored to the individual client treatment plan and to the specific goals set to remedy the sexual distress. Data to obtain might include items relevant to specific and overall sexual functioning for the symptomatic partner(s) and the quality of the overall relationship (in terms of these areas addressed in therapy). Questions tapping client satisfaction can focus on both global and specific therapeutic strategies.

Formal outcome measures can be another piece of evaluation. If objective measures were used at the beginning of treatment, they can be administered at the conclusion of treatment and at further follow-up. Again the therapist would need to determine what would be valid for each client. For example, the MMPI, the Dyadic Adjustment Scale, the Sexual Interaction System Scale or others highlighted in Chapter 7 might be appropriate for a given client. The point is that with a multifaceted integrative treatment model, decisions about outcome measures must be made in the context of the actual therapy that was provided.

In clinical practice evaluation often has low priority. Many clinicians think that the time and planning it requires are better devoted to the immediate needs of current clients. Seeing both processes, past and current treatment efforts, as sides of a single coin may spur us on to increase the effectiveness of therapy by conscientiously evaluating it.

A Case Example of Termination

The case of Vera and Van suggests how some of the issues discussed in this chapter can play out when IST is used to treat sexual distress. There is no attempt to detail all of what went on in the earlier stages of treatment, but simply to convey enough of that content to capture the tenor of the termination stage.

Vera came to the first session alone, although Van would be included in treatment as needed. Married 10 years, the couple had a 5-year-old girl and a 3-year-old boy. Van was a military officer who had duty away from home for periods of a week or more several times a month. Vera was a full-time homemaker though she held a masters' degree.

She reported that sex had been okay until the children were born, but that afterwards, her interest declined. In the past year her feelings had changed to intense dislike not only for sex but also for affectionate hugging and kissing. Moreover, she did not think she had ever had an orgasm. Sexual aversion and inhibited orgasm were the diagnostic starting points.

The evolving assessment pointed to extreme stressors in the past surrounding the birth of the children, Vera's graduate work, separation from Van during the second birth while Vera completed her masters' degree, Van's ongoing absences from home, and Vera's difficulties in coping alone with the demands of young children. The couple's present relationship structure appeared cohesive and adaptable, as reflected in satisfactory scores on the Dyadic Adjustment Scale, except for the sexual dimension. Their current life circumstances insured a problem-interactional system that contained and exacerbated Vera's sexual dysfunctions. Due to Van's regular absences of 8 to 10 days, Vera felt obligated to have sex with him when he returned. And under these circumstances, she had not told him of the intensity of her feelings of repulsion for affectionate gestures and sex. But because they continued to have sex, Van still enjoyed it (even while knowing of her disinterest). His response increased Vera's disgust, but because he would leave again, she would not discuss it honestly, and the same sexual interaction would repeat again upon his return. The vicious cycle contained what they both thought was the only way they could conduct their sexual relationship, but it also contained and maintained the sexual distress. Vera carried considerable anger toward her mother, but this was not seen as central to the sexual dysfunctions.

An integrative approach was planned from the beginning. First noted was the intensity of her aversion to their present sexual encounters, the rigidity of the sexual problem interaction cycle, and possible resistance on Vera's part suggested initially by defensiveness and a lack of interest in psychological factors. The intervention would proceed via prioritized steps of interrupting the interaction cycle, and gradually promoting self-awareness in Vera through written assignments. Individual and couple interviews focused on the enmeshment between the partners exemplified by their never disagreeing about anything (except for Vera's low-level complaints about her lack of desire for sex). Specific interventions for the enmeshment aimed to interrupt their high degree of mutual predictability. Informal sex reeducation and Vera's low self-esteem associated with her mothering abilities were also part of these sessions.

Progress was steady. Vera was adept in carrying out written homework tasks (e.g., the sexual log, describing past pleasurable sexual encounters, creating a sexual fantasy, etc.). After three sessions for her (and two in which Van was involved), she began to experience intercourse as pleasurable and to initiate sex. She was interested in further exploring her own sexual responsiveness and potential for orgasm and readily completed further assignments. At this point, termination was brought up in a general way because of my plans to leave the area. We discussed the number of remaining sessions and the extent to which she had achieved her goals.

In the next session, Vera reported continued progress in her sexual relationship with Van. She was reading and doing exercises from Barbach's (1975) book on female orgasm. The original hint of resistance had never materialized, and trust was high. Because this appointment occurred near Christmas, she brought me a home-baked gift. It was an appropriate gesture of appreciation and acknowledgement of the approaching end of therapy.

I commended her work and initiative toward solving the problem and especially her thoroughness in the written tasks (the graduate student mentality showed through). She was into the masturbation exercises, but expressed surprise that the book mentioned that a woman masturbated for up to an hour. I made an "off-hand" comment that when she was masturbating that she might make an effort to continue at the point when she thought that she should stop, and that she might try the same thing when Van was pleasuring her (Kaplan, 1974).

This and other interventions at this point were attuned to possible future barriers to Vera's sexual fulfillment. In the next session with both Vera and Van, both again acknowledged improvement in their sexual relationship. The discussion focused on possible future barriers that might block their maintaining this progress. Vera said that she definitely wanted to achieve orgasm but expressed doubt that Van would be satisfied with anything less than her having it through intercourse. He reassured her that that was not so, but also told her that he too was learning new sexual attitudes and behaviors—at their own initiative, they had been trying oral sex. I credited both of them for being open to new learning. The stance was to continue to capitalize on the trust in the relationship and let Vera continue to take the initiative and proceed at her own pace. She requested another session.

The last session centered more on Vera's positive reports about her high arousal through oral sex. She was not sure she had experienced orgasm but couldn't "see how it could get much better." This comment suggested no further intrusion into her sexual life was merited, and letting it stand was a way of according Vera future responsibility for her own sexual fulfillment.

Further anticipating the future, Vera wondered about the difference between her current high levels of sexual arousal and "romantic feelings." She was not experiencing these as she had in their early relationship. This concern was reframed as possibly part of the way individuals and relationships change and grow to bring different kinds of benefits. The aim was to reinforce her current positive experiences in sex and her future goal to continue enjoying sex.

The termination process with Vera and Van maintained the integrative framework of treatment. Final interventions continued to capitalize upon the strength of the therapeutic alliance and their active, almost academic, learning styles. Concern was maintained for both their individuality as well as their marital and intimate relationship. This combination seemed central to helping them maintain the improvement in sexual intimacy.

Conclusion

As therapy proceeds, it is best to keep in mind that it will also end. It also does not hurt to imagine that the end could come at any time—not simply according to an ideal plan in the mind of the therapist. The therapeutic hour is only a small part of the client's life.

As with all the stages of therapy, flexibility is a reasonable guideline in designing strategies for terminating and helping the client to maintain progress. There are many available techniques for these goals. But selection should proceed from the therapist's awareness of the client's changing reality, the progress made in solving the problem, and the strategies that proved effective. The therapist needs to let go by letting the client take the initiative in planning for the future and identifying the kind of help needed for going forward. This type of stance embodies the necessity to bring this phase of the helping process to a close, as the client takes on responsibility to care for and help himself or herself.

References

Barbach, L. (1975). *For yourself: The fulfillment of female sexuality.* New York: Doubleday.

Heiman, J. R., & LoPiccolo, J. (1988). *Becoming orgasmic: A sexual growth program for women.* Englewood Cliffs: Prentice-Hall.

Kaplan, H. S. (1974). *The new sex therapy.* New York: Brunner/Mazel.

Norcross, J. C. (Ed.). (1986). *Handbook of eclectic psychotherapy.* New York: Brunner/Mazel.

10

Critical Issues and Challenges

> The world is rumbling and erupting in ever-widening circles around us. The tensions, conflicts and sufferings even in the outermost circle touch us all, reverberate in all of us. We cannot avoid these vibrations.
>
> ANNE MORROW LINDBERG, *Gift from the Sea*

As the sexual revolution coalesced during the 1960s and 1970s, professionals experienced a new optimism about treating and remedying clients' sexual problems. That optimism has given way to a more restrained professional stance—one that acknowledges the increasing complexity of sexual distress and the therapist's responsibility to provide effective, ethical, and legally safe interventions. Meeting this responsibility in the 1990s is not a simple task.

Therapists live in the midst of society's contradictory and convoluted messages and scripts about sex. They also have to make sense of these in the light of professional theoretical and empirical knowledge. In essence, clinicians have the task of guiding clients as they maneuver through the morass of sexual options to find meaningful, satisfying sexual expression. The risk is always present that the professional's own personal position vis à vis sexuality and society will inappropriately influence the treatment offered.

This chapter will focus on several areas that need attention if we are to offer quality professional services for sexual distress. First, clinicians must appreciate the actual diversity of sexual attitudes and values that are pervasive in society and that impact on clients' lives. Second, professionals can bolster objectivity through the use of a multitheoretical conceptual base that accounts for the complexity of sexual distress (this will be only briefly noted since it is essentially the main focus of this book). Third, clinicians must consciously attend to the ethical responsibilities of the therapeutic endeavor. These center on serving the client's welfare, acceptance of the client's right to make personal sexual decisions from a range of options within a pluralistic society, and monitoring both professional competency and integrity to work with sexual issues. Fourth, there are standards of expertise for clinicians who work in the area of sexuality.

Diversity of Sexual Attitudes and Values

When people today discuss sexual issues, divergent views and controversies abound. These reflect a new era in which the liberalized sexual attitudes and behaviors that emerged with the sexual revolution interact with a new awareness of societal sexual problems. People struggle to find personally meaningful solutions to their sexual concerns amidst polarized positions that might be labeled "sexually conservative or reactionary" and "sexually liberated." Both positions might be seen as extreme and simplistic in that each seems to call for a return to an earlier era that does not exist in the present. For example, in a graduate course on sexuality that I regularly teach, there are always a few students in the "traditional" camp who feel under attack from the sexual liberals. And at the same time, there are always a few "sexual liberals" who feel that the "reactionaries" are stripping away the positive achievements of the sexual revolution. The reality is that there is no going back to either one of these simplistic value bases.

Although the sexual revolution brought with it positive messages about the goodness of sexuality and optimism about achieving greater comfort with sex and increased sexual fulfillment, other societal messages emerged in subsequent decades that would impact on these goals. The feminist movement brought significant changes in societal attitudes and held forth the goal of equality between the sexes in all areas of life—not simply in regard to sexual expression and fulfillment. As the social consciousness changed to permit identification of sexism in many areas of life, a number of societal sexual problems came under scrutiny. These included the abuse and exploitation of women and children as a result of rape, child sexual abuse and assault, and sexual harassment.

Although early sex educators had acknowledged the poor sexual decision making that led to teen and unwanted pregnancies, the assumption had been that sex information, education, and access to contraceptives would eliminate these problems. The problem, however, of unwanted pregnancy continued. Moreover the 1980s also witnessed epidemics of sexually transmitted diseases, and, most significantly, the appearance of AIDS. These new areas of focus concerning sexuality have contributed to the polarization of societal attitudes and values. During this same period, attention became focused not only on treatment for victims of sexual exploitation and abuse, but also on treatment for perpetrators as well. It was this same societal atmosphere that led to scrutiny of other sexual problems that came to be labeled with the global construct of "sexual addiction."

The present societal atmosphere surrounding sexuality is no doubt confusing for many persons as they attempt to sort out their sexual values and beliefs and make sexual choices. Clearcut societal moral codes, once supported by various social structures, are no longer clearcut and no longer serve to guide personal beliefs and behaviors. Instead, people must struggle amidst divergent values to find a satisfying degree of sexual fulfillment. They cannot help but be aware that sexuality holds the potential for both highly positive as well as negative consequences.

Most people find that making sexual choices is not merely a rational process of weighing costs and benefits. For some persons, "committed" rather than "casual" sex represents a solution congruent with both their values and emotional needs. Others assert that the choice to pursue casual sex works as a personal solution for them. And still others may follow a trial-and-error route in hopes of finding sexual fulfillment. Persons from all these groups may seek therapy when they do not achieve an acceptable degree of sexual satisfaction.

Therapists see the gamut of sexual attitudes, behaviors, solutions, and pseudosolutions among their clients. For example, some partners may find it very easy to find sexual fulfillment in a monogamous relationship. Others may aspire to this track but inexplicably pursue extramarital sexual affairs. Still others may assert the demand for complete sexual freedom, seek a partner's acceptance of this modus operandi, or be willing to end the relationship to pursue it. Clients with little sexual desire often feel guilty and abnormal because society expects everyone to be interested in sex. Yet those who have a high interest in sex are often labeled "sexual addicts" by that same society. The assumption is that therapists should be able to field the range of sexuality with equanimity and professional aplomb. But is this kind of competence attainable?

A Multitheoretical Understanding of Sexual Distress

It is necessary to attempt to understand sexual distress in all of its complexity—as it plays out in the person's inner life, in relationships, and in the more public societal context. Ideally the understanding will encompass the subtle interactions of all of these dimensions. The integrative systems therapy (IST) approach presented in this book aims to tap into the holistic nature of sexuality and intimacy. This kind of conceptual base increases the chance that the therapist will approach the client's sexual distress with a professional understanding that increases objectivity. The multitheoretical framework forces the clinician to take several perspectives of the problem. Rigid adherence to a singular therapeutic modality can be motivated by the therapist's own personality and character structure. Without consideration of various conceptual explanations for sexual distress, the therapist's personal value and behavioral biases may never come under scrutiny and may unknowingly and inappropriately influence the type of treatment given.

IST offers the potential to consider the ways in which sexuality connects to the individual's inner life—the core of the self and the identity. The individual family-of-origin interface permits understanding about why sexual attitudes and behaviors may be so intractable for some clients. The ways in which sexual and emotional gratification are pursued may emanate from early nurturing experiences that result in powerful unconscious self and relationship structures. Although sexuality is clearly subject to rational management by the ego, this capacity varies greatly across individuals. Self, identity, and ego may be critical factors as to why cognitive-behavioral, or problem-interactional, or structural techniques work with some clients but not with others. We may be able to help some clients with a range of interventions, and we may not be able to help others regardless of the interventions.

At the same time that IST permits focus on the individual's inner life, it also acknowledges the powerful impact of the other end of the continuum—the way sociocultural structures play out in people's sexual lives. For example, societal-based gender themes become internalized in a rigid way by some clients but not by others. IST acknowledges the validity of carefully assessing the impact of power and hierarchy issues in intimate relationships, but it does not posit that these have a direct or linear influence on the sexual problems of all clients.

To achieve professional balance and objectivity in understanding sexual distress, the therapist needs a finely honed sensitivity to the range of factors that may uniquely contribute to the severity of the client's problem and capacity for and interest in change. The IST conceptual base contributes to this much needed sensitivity. But theoretical knowledge alone will not do the job. There are ethical and legal considerations that extend beyond one's knowledge base that bolster sound professional functioning.

Ethical and Legal Responsibilities

Ethical responsibilities must pervade the therapist's thinking as he or she works in the area of sexual distress. Sexuality remains a highly charged aspect of life for both clients and clinicians. Conscious effort is needed to meet the ethical obligations surrounding the intense focus on sexual material in treatment.

The Code of Ethics of the American Association of Sex Educators, Counselors, and Therapists (AASECT, 1992) clearly and specifically addresses the many potential ethical intricacies associated with treatment for sexual distress. This is a new document that incorporates both ethical and legal issues and offers guidelines relevant to the 1990s. "Sex therapy" or any treatment for sexual problems is viewed within the broad framework of "psychotherapy" as it is currently practiced as part of the mental health industry. Consequently the 1992 Code emphasizes different assumptions from those of the previous AASECT Code of Ethics (1980).

The earlier 1980 version of the Code was largely adapted from a code of ethics developed by the Reproductive Biology Research Foundation of St. Louis, now named the Masters and Johnson Institute. Reflecting the philosophy of sex therapy and sex research prevalent during the late 1970s, it aimed to protect both the newly emerging fields of sexology and sex therapy. It also aimed to set standards for clinical practice that would protect the welfare of clients. This was indeed a complex challenge. The 1980 Code established that ethical research on human sexual behavior could involve observation and measurement of subjects during sexual activity. At the same time, the 1980 Code more or less validated as ethical for sex therapy alone certain methods not typically accepted as part of psychotherapy. For example, "procedures involving nudity of either the client or the therapist or observation of client sexual activity" were defined as going beyond the "boundaries of established practice" and permissible "only when there is good evidence that they serve the best interests of the client" (AASECT, 1980, p. 7). Also explicitly permitted was the possibility of using surrogates as part of sex therapy, although the Code describes this as controversial and identifies numerous guidelines and warnings if this method is a part of sex therapy.

Masters and Johnson (1967, 1970) had struggled to legitimize the study of human sexuality in the face of opposition from the medical and scientific establishment. The 1980 AASECT Code reflected the intent to hold on to the gains that had been achieved. The assumption was that certain methods that might not appear on the surface to meet ethical standards were, in fact, justifiable for sexologists and sex therapists to carry out their professional functions. Although Masters and Johnson had abandoned the use of surrogate partners as a result of a malpractice claim (Schiller, 1989), the 1980 Code's specific discussion of this method and of nudity maintains the assumption of the uniqueness of sex therapy in contrast to general psychotherapy.

Today sexology has an established place in basic, social, and medical science, and sex research does take place. The mechanism for assuring ethical standards for research in these disciplines is the institutional board or committee that reviews all research with human subjects. The guidelines derive from many sources, not just those adopted by the field of sexology. But this structure does not assure that sex research is regarded as routine or readily approved or implemented. Such research is highly affected by the sociocultural/political context regardless of its meeting scientific and ethical standards. For example, approved and funded National Institutes of Health surveys that would encompass adult and teen sexual behavior were recently halted because of the influence of conservative political elements (American Psychological Association, 1991).

When it comes to therapy for sexual problems today, we must also look to the sociocultural context of the 1990s. This treatment function falls to physicians and the various mental health professionals, including the highly specialized sex therapists. The new AASECT Code of Ethics (1992) offers guidelines and standards for this current context. Several assumptions of this Code are discussed below. The full Code is reprinted in the Appendix for close examination and ongoing reference.

One assumption is that the professionals who treat sexual problems come from various disciplines. Thus when they provide education, counseling, and/or therapy for clients' sexual concerns, they are expected to honor not only the AASECT Code of ethics but also the ethical principles derived from their other disciplinary or professional identities.

Another assumption is that all counseling and therapy today fall under the broad umbrella of the mental health industry. This label emphasizes that therapy is often subject to constraints other than professional ethical obligations. Such constraints are broadly encapsulated in the term "public policy," which includes such facets as statutory regulation of professionals, consumer protection under law, and the bureaucratic structures under whose auspices therapy is rendered or paid for (i.e., agencies, hospitals, healthcare insurance or provider plans, etc.).

Given the first two assumptions discussed, another position of the 1992 AASECT Code is that "sex counseling" and "sex therapy," are not accorded any unique status that would justify unique methods. It offers no position on controversial methods that in the past were seen as possibly justifiable in clinical work by sex specialists. Professionals treating sexual problems must assume responsibility for the selection of all therapeutic methods.

The 1992 Code does, however, proscribe, as do other professional ethical codes, "dual relationships" with clients (AASECT, 1992, II, B; III, M). It also specifically forbids sexual behavior with a client and identifies behaviors that constitute sexual misconduct on the part of a professional (III, N).

A final important assumption is that in accord with the tenor of the 1990s, ethical guidelines can also reflect the legal and societal obligations of professionals that may impact on clinical practice. The 1992 Code acknowledges the client's rights as a consumer of services. Accordingly, it offers detailed guidance on maintaining confidentiality and advocacy of client privilege but also on the need to clarify with clients the limits of confidentiality. Finally, many of the guidelines aim to assist practitioners to protect themselves by meeting current standards of care as determined by public policy (e.g., keeping meaningful records, documenting treatment plans and their effectiveness, etc.).

Any code of ethics is of little use, however, unless the professional studies, learns, and internalizes it. It must become second nature so that it operates as the therapist's professional conscience. This assures that the guidelines will be applied intuitively to most ethical concerns in the belief that following them will generally produce the best decision. The rest of this discussion will explore several specific ethical issues with regard to treating sexual distress. These are serving the client's welfare, client self-determination, and the therapist's personal-professional identity.

SERVING THE CLIENT'S WELFARE

All professional codes of ethics refer to serving the "client's welfare," but translating this abstraction into actual clinical decision making is not a straightforward task.

Defining the Client and the Client's Welfare

First and foremost are the complexities surrounding the definition of who is the client. This is usually clear cut when an individual alone seeks treatment. Ethical problems can arise, however, if a spouse, partner, or other family member is brought in after treatment has begun with the individual.

In treating sexual distress, it is often appropriate to bring in others, but this decision demands careful evaluation of several issues. What is the explicit purpose for involving another person? Will the content of previous individual sessions be shared with the other person? Has the individual client assumed or asked for confidentiality for all or some of this content? Is there information that needs to be shared so as not to compromise the effectiveness of the therapist? The therapist needs to anticipate these issues and arrive at answers before enlarging or taking on a new client system.

Also inherent to defining the client is the need to understand what is meant by the abstraction, "the client's welfare." The implication is that therapists always know what will benefit the client. Presumably, they obtain this insight from various theoretical premises that posit assumptions about and definitions of human nature, behavior, pathology, and health. These premises then guide the therapeutic process for promoting client welfare with principles and guidelines for helping clients move in the direction of "health." A feminist therapist would likely define a client's welfare much differently than would a behavioral, a psychodynamic, or a family systems therapist.

Consider the following situation. A single young man starts individual therapy to deal with his difficulty in making a commitment to his partner. He discusses his pattern of having many casual female partners. He also participates in anonymous homosexual encounters in adult video shops. He subsequently asks to bring in his current live-in female partner for therapy to enable them to build a strong relationship. Clearly there are many elements within even this little vignette that give rise to questions about the therapist's ethical and possible legal obligations relative to defining who is the client and what is meant by the client's welfare.

Similar issues must be considered if the original client is a couple, but the therapist decides to also provide individual sessions. Ethical dilemmas are pretty much guaranteed if one does not anticipate and resolve questions of purpose, client goals, and confidentiality. The codes of ethics for professional counseling and therapy evolved from the tradition of helping the individual patient. As such, they are often inadequate for the new emphasis on working with couples and families. Therapists, essentially on their own, have had to anticipate or otherwise deal with ethical problems arising from these changes in practice. The new AASECT Code (1992) now offers guidance relevant to this aspect of current clinical work.

Other ethical concerns emerge in working with couples. For example, partners may not share the same view of the problem, the same commitment to the relationship or to therapy, or the same goals for treatment. Such circumstances challenge the therapist's objectivity. How far must one go in helping clients negotiate common goals? How much effort should go into instilling hope in and commitment to treatment? Do the therapist's personal values and needs produce greater empathy for and interest in the welfare of one partner over the other? These are questions that do and should come up for the therapist's consideration, and there are no clearcut answers. General guidelines in codes of ethics may not help with these issues. What is needed are critical analyses by the therapist of his or her own reactions; clarification and review of the clients' stated positions; and open discussion with partners on the dilemma surrounding goals, commitment, and so forth. This process should produce clarification of commitment or negotiated new goals and a decision on whether individual or couple therapy can proceed.

As suggested above, many ethical concerns can be resolved quickly in an almost intuitive manner by simply adhering to the guidelines of professional codes of ethics. But other situations are more complex and demand critical thinking. This means that the therapist will need to weigh several factors before reaching a decision to resolve the ethical question. Table 10.1 outlines five decision bases than can be used for resolving complex ethical concerns. These are theories of ethics, codes of ethics, professional theoretical premises, sociolegal considerations, and the therapist's own personal/professional identity (Woody, 1990).

Dual Relationships

Another ethical issue relative to the client's welfare is that of dual relationships. Professional codes of ethics proscribe a therapist's entering into a personal, social, sexual, or business relationship with clients. When clients reveal the most intimate details of their sexual lives, they do so with trust that the therapist will not abuse their vulnerability.

Research has consistently shown, however, that a certain percentage of therapists from all the mental health disciplines violate this trust, most often by entering social and sexual relationships with clients. Such relationships are in direct violation of the ethical obligation to serve the client's welfare. They arise when the therapist attempts to meet his or her own needs through the client. As a result, professional objectivity is lost, clients become confused, often blaming themselves for this situation, and their original problems worsen. A recent study has documented harm to clients not only from sexual relationships with their therapists but also from nonsexual relationships as well. These often set the stage for later sexual involvement (Borys & Pope, 1989).

Having a dual relationship with a client is the primary basis for complaints against therapists that are brought to ethics committees, to state licensing and certification boards, and to attorneys for malprac-

TABLE 10.1 Overview of the Decision Bases for Resolving Ethical Concerns in Clinical Practice

Theories of Ethics	*Professional Code of Ethics*	*Professional Theoretical Premises*
Offer logical methods for ethical decision making based on universal principles.	General rules, norms, and principles should become a second nature for the professional. Encompass therapist competence/integrity, confidentiality, and promoting client welfare, self-determination, dignity, etc. Many values stem from the tradition of individualism.	Different assumptions about and definitions of human nature, behavior, pathology, and health.
Intuitive thinking draws on contract theory: Honors natural duties stemming from the principle of justice and the special professional duty to promote client welfare, dignity, liberty, self-determination, privacy, etc.	Contain conflicting principles and obligations.	These determine meanings for promoting "client welfare."
Critical thinking draws on contract theory of social justice and on utilitarian theory: The greatest good for the greatest number of persons involved.	Abstractions require definition and interpretation.	Diverse concepts about right or effective therapist conduct relating to: competence integrity therapeutic relationship confidentiality power resistance symptoms role of strategy.
	Codes are evolving to interface with sociological interface.	Compare family systems, psychoanalytic, behavioral, structural, strategic, feminist, etc.

(Continued)

tice actions. In spite of the ethical and legal risks such relationships pose, many professionals remain oblivious to the ethical guideline proscribing such behavior. The reasons that some clinicians do not internalize this or other guidelines are probably quite diverse. In general, however, the problem stems from the therapist's inability to understand and monitor his or her own personal/professional identity. The immediate impairment may be linked to stressful life events, chemical or substance abuse, or to a more chronic personality characteristic, such as narcissism (Maeder, 1988). The persistence of this problem points to the need for substantive training in ethics in professional education programs, the importance of screening for persons

TABLE 10.1 (Continued)

Sociolegal Context	*Therapist's Personal/Professional Identity*
Sociocultural values and their evolution affect client and therapist values, societal priorities, and laws. Public policy guidelines derived from statutory law, state regulatory boards, and precedent cases create responsibilities for therapists. Organizational context, mission, roles, policies, etc. impact on the conduct of therapy.	A "person" is present in the helping relationship, does the intuitive or critical thinking, and ultimately makes choices based on beliefs integrated from the personal conscience, secular philosophy and/or religion, professional ethics, and theoretical concepts. Identifies and weighs information from all decision bases, including judging one's own knowledge, integrity, and personality needs. An ethical "character" plus professional values, knowledge, and skills make an integrated personal/professional identity.

Reprinted from Woody, J. D. (1990). Resolving ethical concerns in clinical practice: Toward a pragmatic model. *Journal of Marital and Family Therapy, 16*(2), p. 135.

unsuited for professional functioning, and the validity of ongoing supervision for clinicians.

CLIENT SELF-DETERMINATION

Professional codes of ethics point out the client's prerogative to be self-determining on critical life decisions. As this principle is often highly relevant in treating sexual distress, it can give rise to rather complex ethical questions.

Although therapists do not make decisions for clients, they do have the function of helping clients acquire information, facts, understandings, or new experiences that might bear on the decision. But clients vary in their openness to participate in such explorations. Typically, it is necessary to judge how much effort to use in engaging the reluctant client to try the therapeutic experience as an avenue to the decision making process. There could also be a question as to whether a therapist accepts a client's initial decision as a starting point for treatment. Consider the following vignette.

A 33-year-old single woman entered therapy with the goals of wanting to lose weight, dress in a more feminine manner, and overcome her shyness with men. She had been sexually abused as a young child. She had recently ended an 8-year lesbian relationship with a woman. She said that she had been coerced into becoming sexual with the woman. She also reported that she was not attracted to women and asserted an interest in a man with whom she worked.

A major question is how client self-determination fits into this client's stated goals for therapy, which seem to hinge on her wish to develop a heterosexual relationship. Should the therapist accept that she has the necessary understanding and insight for making this life decision or provide her with opportunity to review and evaluate the decision? Because there are likely to be conflicting ethical obligations in this situation, the issue bears critical analysis and thinking (as the process is outlined above in Table 10.1). From professional ethics, one could argue for a strict definition of client self-determination and for accepting her immediate goals. Therapy would then proceed to help her make behavioral and attitudinal changes and add new behaviors to her repertoire. But one could also argue for a broad definition of client welfare and for the need to assist her in exploring the basis for her decision. Therapy would then proceed to help her identify needs and their basis in her past and current developmental and relationship experiences.

Professional theoretical premises could also conflict on determining exactly what therapeutic activities would promote the welfare of the client. Consider the possibility of differing viewpoints coming from the following: concepts from human sexuality, behavioral theory, psychoanalytic theory, feminist theory, and so on. The sociolegal context might have some impact on the type of decision reached; for example, does the agency have a stated or implied policy on homosexuality? Finally, the therapist needs to consider his or her own personal/professional identity and level of knowledge and competence for dealing with the client's goals and for resolving this ethical question. For example, is there a personal issue that would lead the therapist to prefer to guide this client in either a heterosexual, lesbian, or bisexual direction? This kind of careful analysis of the various ethical dimensions of the question should produce a decision that the therapist can defend to self and others.

Similar ethical questions may arise as clients struggle with making decisions around such sexual issues as: how much masturbation is reasonable, whether to give up a paraphilia, whether to ask a spouse to adapt to a sexual fetish, whether to pursue casual, recreational sexual relationships, and whether to inform a partner of past or current unsafe sex practices. The list could go on. The bottom line is that therapy certainly can play a role in how clients reach decisions. But careful ethical analysis is needed to ensure that therapy does not sacrifice client self-determination in the process of promoting informed decision making.

A range of sexual choices exists for people in a pluralistic society. It is irrelevant to make advanced judgments in a vacuum about these choices. The therapeutic task is to help the individual client anticipate and evaluate how a potential choice works or does not work in his or her unique life situation. Helping the client to acquire the informational and experiential basis for making such decisions calls for a high degree of therapeutic competence and integrity. The therapist inevitably makes clinical and ethical judgments throughout the process.

THE THERAPIST'S PERSONAL/PROFESSIONAL IDENTITY

The character and personhood of the therapist are always present in clinical work. Some theories, especially psychodynamic ones, openly acknowledge this and require effort to stay aware of personal issues and their potential impact on treatment. Other theories, for example, strategic and cybernetic ones, assert the possibility of a value-free, neutral stance and essentially deny the importance of the therapist's personality and emphasize, instead, technical competence.

In reality the therapist is present both as person and expert. The structure of his or her character and moral vision were in place before professional education got underway. It is the interaction between personality and education that partially determines the kind of therapist a person becomes, for example, which theories one will favor, which types of problems or clients are preferred, etc. And in the area of sexuality, the ever-developing personal/professional identity determines how one internalizes knowledge of sexuality and translates this into therapeutic skills.

In the midst of therapy, when ethical questions arise, it is that same personal/professional identity that must examine whether the therapist's personal issues are exerting an inappropriate influence. This identity must possess sufficient objectivity to evaluate self and even one's own critical thinking abilities. This identity must trust that it has achieved sufficient professional integrity and competence to discover what serves the client's welfare. Without this integrated identity, the entire clinical judgment process is compromised.

The nature of sexual distress readily gives rise to personal feelings and reactions on the part of the clinician. The therapist needs to pay attention to these reactions and ask hard questions. Do I have enough knowledge of sexuality to help in this case? Do I continue to work on my own sexual history, attitudes, and problems so that these do not negatively affect the therapeutic process? Have I achieved a balanced view of human sexuality—as a positive force in life as well as a source of problems? Have I been able to internalize knowledge of human sexuality and professional values that allow a reasonable degree of objectivity for working with sexual problems?

These questions only begin to suggest the extensive ongoing personal/professional scrutiny demanded of therapists. Clinical work consists of an unpredictable mix of the personal and the professional, of intuition and rationality. Recognizing this is a first step to effective treatment. Wylie (1989) clearly acknowledges personal character, not simply technical skill, in defining the qualities of the ethical therapist as "honest, trustworthy, sensitive, knowledgeable, courageous, open-minded, modest, and rigorously self-reflective" (p. 33).

SPECIALIZED SEXUALITY EDUCATION, TRAINING, AND SUPERVISION

Various types of mental health professionals see clients with sexual concerns or sexual distress. How should we determine competency for treating these problems? While it may not be necessary for a professional to hold formal certification as a sex counselor or sex therapist, there is a need for standards. Competency to deal with sexual problems encompasses the areas of knowledge, attitudes, and skills (Kaplan, 1977).

Ideally, all professional education programs would recognize the centrality of human sexuality and offer study in this area. Since this is not the case, however, practicing mental health professionals often attempt to obtain this specialized training independently via postgraduate academic courses, seminars, professional conferences, specialized sexuality institutes, and ongoing supervision of clinical work with sexual problems. Two major components are central to this specialty; these are basic human sexuality and sex-related problems. The study of each component should include a knowledge base, values and attitude clarification, and professional skill development.

Basic Human Sexuality

The knowledge base must begin with an overview of the entire field of human sexuality. Training that begins and ends with simply exposure to a certain sexual problem is not adequate. For example, the only knowledge some professionals have obtained about sexuality is from seminars in a specific area such as incest or sexual addiction. These typically derive from a singular philosophical or theoretical position and often posit a singular treatment methodology. What is missing is basic knowledge of normal human sexuality. The participant may come out of such a training program with a rather narrow perspective of sexuality. This can limit the helper's ability to define long-range goals of sexual health for clients affected by the problem.

The comprehensive study of basic human sexuality should include the following topics: sexual and reproductive anatomy and physiology; developmental sexuality from a socio-psychological-biological perspective (from conception to old age); the range of sexual values, behaviors, and choices and the sociocultural facets of these; the human sexual response; dynamics of interpersonal and sexual relationships; dynamics of marital and family relationships relative to sexuality; overview of personal and societal sexual problems; and ethical issues for professionals working in the area of sexuality.

As the person acquires this knowledge base, there must also be opportunity to examine personal sexual attitudes, behaviors, and choices in preparation for working effectively and ethically with clients. The third facet, skills, are developed through practice opportunities and supervision. In the context of studying basic human sexuality, the student should acquire the skills to carry out the following professional functions: providing formal and informal sex education and re-education; fostering the client's exploration of sexual material; and promoting the client's clarification of values, decision making, and coping regarding such developmental sexual concerns as understanding one's sexual needs, resolving value conflicts, whether to engage in sexual activity, issues in managing one's sexuality and fertility, and potential benefits and difficulties stemming from a same-sex affectional preference.

Sex-Related Problems

The professional who wants to work with sex-related problems needs further study of the complex dynamics involved in sexual disorders and sexual dysfunctions. The study should distinguish between problems that have a primarily personal impact, such as sexual dysfunction, and those that have an obvious societal impact as well, such as sexual victimization. In-depth study is required since multiple factors contribute to the range of sexual complaints as well as to severe sexual problems such as dysfunctions, sexual victimization, paraphilias, and compulsive sexual patterns. For example, sexual dysfunction is now acknowledged to involve many factors other than simply society's sex-negative messages and sexual myths. Similarly a multifaceted understanding is needed for working with persons with unwanted paraphilias or with individuals and family members impacted by sexual victimization.

Again, the exploration of personal attitudes is critical to this area of study. The content of sex-related problems can trigger doubts and concerns about one's own sexual "normality" or memories of sexual trauma or secrets within one's own life or family history. Only through this type of evaluation of personal sexual history, attitudes, and current adjustment can we assess our competency to work with clients' sexual problems.

Many professionals will not be able or wish to work with all types of sexual problems. The choice to specialize would be appropriate if predicated on exposure to basic human sexuality as discussed above. This constitutes a rational basis for the decision to further specialize or not. Knowledge is constantly expanding with regard to treatment of all of the more serious sexual problems, and the therapist who chooses to specialize must take on the commitment to stay abreast of professional developments. This may necessitate joining specialized professional societies, obtaining training from specialized programs, and regular attendance at professional conferences dealing with the specialty. An example is the rapidly developing area of treatment for sex offenders. A colleague recently mentioned the ethical and liability factors in this type of work in that therapists routinely advise probation officers and the courts of the client's ability to remain in the community. He wisely said that he was going to discontinue his assigned work with sex offenders unless his employing agency would provide for the specialized training that he needed for effective and ethical practice.

Specialization within the field of sexuality requires a high degree of professional competency that would derive from the following: knowledge of various theories of human behavior and pathology, knowledge of various theoretical explanations of the etiology of sexual problems, knowledge of and skill in various models of psychotherapy, knowledge of the efficacy of therapy for sexual problems, competency to conduct outcome evaluation, and an ethically integrated personal/professional identity developed and maintained through supervised clinical practice.

Conclusion

As suggested above, considerable effort and commitment must go along with the interest in treating sexual distress. Knowledge and research on human sexuality and sexual problems continue to expand. And people's sexual lives become more complicated as they encounter the range of sexual attitudes, values, and problems that characterize modern pluralistic societies.

The professional too faces the same task of resolving sexual issues in his or her personal life and yet claims to be a helper to others. Ongoing study and self-scrutiny are necessary to keep therapists on track to meet their ethical responsibility to clients. There is always room to do a better job in general. And this is especially true with specific client groups who present special challenges to professional competencies. For example, relatively little attention has been given to treating sexual distress among gays and lesbians, single persons without partners, and older and minority persons. Theoretical, clinical, and research writings essentially ignore these groups. Yet we cannot assume that therapists automatically can adapt their skills to provide effective treatment for them. There is need for more specialized knowledge and clinical insights. But clinicians and researchers will likely need to get past personal/professional biases and values before they can contribute to this knowledge and develop professional skills for working effectively with underserved client groups.

References

American Association of Sex Educators, Counselors and Therapists. (1980). *Code of ethics*. Washington, DC: Author.

American Association of Sex Educators, Counselors and Therapists. (1992). *Code of ethics*. Chicago, IL: Author.

American Psychological Association. (1991). Suppressing sex study puts all science in jeopardy. *APA Monitor, 22*(10), 21.

Borys, D. S., & Pope, K. S. (1989). Dual relationships between therapist and client: A national study of psychologists, psychiatrists, and social workers. *Professional Psychology, 20*(5), 283-293.

Kaplan, H. S. (1977). Training of sex therapists. In W. H. Masters, V. E. Johnson, & R. C. Kolodny (Eds.) *Ethical issues in sex therapy and research* (pp. 182-189). Boston: Little, Brown.

Maeder, T. (1988). *Children of psychiatrists and other psychotherapists*. New York: Harper & Row.

Masters, W. H., & Johnson, V. E. (1970). *Human sexual inadequacy*. Boston: Little, Brown.

Schiller, P. (1989, May). Moderator's comment at the annual meeting of the American Association of Sex Educators, Counselors, and Therapists, Chicago, IL.

Woody, J. D. (1990). Resolving ethical concerns in clinical practice: Toward a pragmatic model. *Journal of Marital and Family Therapy, 16*(2), 133-150.

Wylie, M. S. (1989). Looking for the fence posts. *Family Therapy Networker, 13*, 22-33.

Appendix: Code of Ethics for the American Association of Sex Educators, Counselors, and Therapists

Recognizing its responsibilities to society and given its organizational objectives, AASECT has adopted the following Code of Ethics. The Code is: (1) a condition for membership; (2) applies to all AASECT members, regardless of their certification or member status; and (3) embraces any activity that directly or indirectly relates to professional identity or training. The Code does not replace or modify the requirements for or purposes of certification as a sex educator, counselor, therapist, or supervisor.

Public Policy: By public policy, AASECT has a duty to promote and enforce quality services from and proper conduct by its members. Professionalism is a product of society. Professional status is a privilege, not a right earned by holding a degree, certification, or membership. While professional ethics are not law, they are permissive and aspirational standards and guidelines for professional practice; and

---

AUTHOR'S NOTE: Prepared by the AASECT Code of Ethics Revision Committee: Robert Henley Woody, JD (Chair); Linda P. Alperstein, MSW; Dennis M. Dailey, DSW; Ralph H. Earle, PhD; Lyman G. Gilmore, EdD; Beverly Hotchner, PhD; Janis A. Lundquist, MA; and Mary Lee Tatum, MEd (deceased). Approved by the AASECT Board of Directors on April 1, 1992 and reprinted by permission.

AASECT accepts that a professional association has a public duty to advocate standards for the services offered by its membership, so as to ensure protection of and benefits to the consumer. Therefore AASECT promulgates ethical standards that must be honored by its members.

Objectives: The Code of Ethics is intended to advance the status of sex education, counseling, therapy, supervision, and research. The Code of Ethics should not be viewed solely as disciplinary in intent. The benefits are primarily for the consumer and society, and only secondarily for the practitioner and AASECT.

Self Regulation: Integrity, competence, confidentiality, responsibility, and other applicable standards are not always subject to finite definitions, descriptions, prescriptions, or proscriptions. Virtually every professional situation requires that the practitioner make judgments as to propriety. Through setting forth rules of ethical conduct for practice-related conditions, qualities, skills, and services, the Code of Ethics is intended to assist AASECT members with such judgments. Each member must exercise self regulation and satisfy governmental-regulatory and legal requirements.

Accountability to AASECT: While ethics do not have the same authority as law, membership in AASECT is predicated upon strict adherence to the Code of Ethics. That is, members of AASECT, in the conduct of all aspects of their life that relate to their professional work and identity, are expected to honor the Code of Ethics, *and* to act according to general principles of professional ethical practice that may not be directly dealt with in this Code of Ethics.

The Code of Ethics creates accountability for the member to AASECT. It should be underscored that the Code of Ethics is relevant to justifying membership in AASECT, and is not intended to serve as a standard of care for professional practice in legal proceedings.

Termination of Membership: Membership in AASECT may be terminated for cause. Sufficient cause for such termination of membership shall be a violation of the Bylaws, the Code of Ethics, or any resolution or other action by the AASECT Board of Directors. A prerequisite for initial membership and a requirement for continued membership in AASECT is that each potential member or member must: (1) satisfy all standards set forth in the AASECT Code of Ethics; (2) notify AASECT in writing of any previous, current, or pending legal (civil or criminal), ethical, or regulatory (licensing) complaint(s); (3) provide any documentation or information requested on behalf of the AASECT Board of Directors; and (4) inform AASECT in writing of the adjudicatory outcome. Such notification must be done within thirty (30) days of the members knowledge of the complaint; and any request from AASECT for information or documentation must be fulfilled within thirty (30) days. Termination shall be by two-thirds vote of the entire Board of Directors, in accordance with the policies and procedures established by the Board of Directors.

Disciplinary Action: Allegations of a member's failure to fulfill the Code of Ethics shall follow a systematic complaint process, with firm allegiance to due process, equal protection, and other rights. Instances in which grievances are filed with AASECT shall be investigated on the merits of each set of circumstances and shall be judged both on the Code of Ethics and on the basis of general principles of ethical conduct. Furthermore, since ethical dilemmas frequently arise when there is a conflict between two or more ethical precepts, it is necessary to judge each case on the basis of interpretation of this Code of Ethics in the context of the particular situation.

The Ethics Committee shall determine the appropriateness of continued or terminated membership in AASECT for any AASECT member who is: (1) found to have violated standards set forth in the Code of Ethics; (2) adjudged to have violated a civil law that is material and relevant to professional practice; (3) convicted of a criminal misdemeanor or felony; and/or (4) disciplined by a professional ethics committee or a state licensing board. The information available to and the deliberations of the Ethics Committee shall be deemed confidential by all AASECT sources. The Ethics Committee shall submit a recommendation, with supportive reasoning and selective documentation, to the AASECT Board of Directors; at the discretion of the Board, any or all other information and documentation available to the Ethics Committee shall be made available to the Board of Directors. Any action regarding continued or terminated membership, with concomitant conditions, made by the Board of Directors is final; no appeal right exists.

(1) When a report of a civil judgment material relevant to professional practice, a criminal conviction for a misdemeanor or felony, or an ethical or licensure disciplinary action is received by the Ethics Committee, the Ethics Committee shall notify the member that he/she may submit information in his/her defense in written form only to the Ethics Committee; and (2) following notification of the review and recommendation by the Ethics Committee, the member shall be entitled (at his/her own expense) to a copy of all materials in the case file, and may submit additional information in his/her defense in written form only to the Board of Directors. The member shall have no right to a personal appearance before or a transcript (or other recording) of deliberations by the Ethics Committee or the Board of Directors. The Decision about continuation or termination of membership, with any concomitant conditions, is final; no appeal right exists.

Principle One:
Competence and Integrity

The AASECT member shall accept responsibility for the consequences of his/her acts, by omission or commission, and make reasonable efforts to ensure that all professional services are appropriate and adequate for the consumer.

(A) The member shall bear a heavy social responsibility because society deems the services as representing specialized expertise and because the consumers using the services are vulnerable. The member shall, therefore, be committed to maintaining high standards of scholarship and practice and shall be accountable as an individual to the standards of the profession. At a minimum, the member shall perform any professional service in accord with the prevailing standards of performance in professional activities when measured against generally prevailing peer performance.

(B) The member shall have training in sex education, counseling, therapy, and/or supervision that is in accord with the standards promulgated by AASECT and the laws relevant to the jurisdiction in which the member practices.

(C) The member shall recognize his/her limits of competence, and shall communicate them at the earliest possible time and at any time thereafter to the consumer. When the member's level of competence does not afford optimal benefits to the consumer, the member shall, in a timely and efficient manner, recommend referral to better qualified sources.

(D) The member shall not knowingly permit any consumer to misunderstand the member's competency, and shall clarify credentials, training, affiliations, experiences, and skills in an honest and accurate manner.

(E) The member shall recognize the necessity and benefit of professional growth by participating in continuing education.

(F) The member shall not enter into association for professional practice with or assist, aid, or promote in any manner the practice of an unqualified or incompetent person, which shall include any person who, the member knows or has reason to believe, does not adhere to the standards of AASECT or is in violation of any law. This shall include, but is not limited to, making a referral to an unqualified or incompetent person. The member shall verify the competence and integrity of the person to whom a consumer is referred.

(G) The member shall not willfully make or file any false report, record, or information, or induce another person to make or file any false report, record, or information.

(H) The member shall not provide any remuneration, regardless of form, to any source for receiving the referral of a consumer for professional services, unless the source of the referral maintains continued involvement in the care of the consumer. Conversely, the member shall not receive any remuneration, regardless of form, from any source for providing the referral of a consumer for professional services, unless the member maintains continued involvement in the care of the consumer. Any such financial arrangement must be disclosed to and approved and acknowledged in writing by the consumer.

(I) The member who becomes emotionally, physically, or otherwise impaired or disabled to a degree that it impacts on the best interest of the consumer shall, in a timely and efficient manner, make a referral of the consumer to a qualified and appropriate professional source so as to avoid any undue abandonment of the consumer.

Principle Two: Moral, Ethical, and Legal Standards

The AASECT member shall accept that the quality of his/her professional services are dependent upon both personal morality and professional ethics, and on the ability to maintain legal standards.

(A) The member shall be aware of and monitor the fact that his/her personal needs may influence judgments and actions in the therapeutic relationship, and shall, regardless of experience or training, have a qualified review source, such as a supervisor, available to assist in safeguarding against unwise or inappropriate judgments and acts.

(B) The member shall not enter into any dual relationship, regardless of nature, that jeopardizes the well-being of the consumer.

(C) The member shall avoid any action that might violate or diminish the legal and civil rights of the consumer.

(D) The member shall not engage in or condone practices by any source that are inhumane or that result in illegal or unjustifiable action, as relevant to race, handicap, age, gender, sexual orientation, religion, or national origin.

(E) The member shall make only factual, honest, and clearly stated (not misleading) public announcements, statements, or communications, such as (but not limited to) for advertising or promotional purposes.

(F) The member shall not set forth an identification with AASECT, such as (but not limited to) membership or certification status, in an announcement, statement, or communication, whatever the form, that also includes a college or university degree, unless that degree is based on academic merit and is from an appropriately accredited higher education institution.

(G) The member shall act in accord with AASECT ethics, standards, and guidelines related to education, counseling, therapy, supervision, and research.

(H) The member shall act in accord with the standards and guidelines for the protection of consumers promulgated by other professional associations with which the member is affiliated and the laws of the jurisdiction(s) in which the member provides professional services.

(I) The member shall report any ethical, regulatory or legal complaint filed against the member, with this report being submitted in writing, within thirty (30) days of knowledge, to the Chair of the AASECT Ethics Committee.

Principle Three: Welfare of the Consumer

The AASECT member shall accept that the consumer is in a unique position of vulnerability in respect to services related to sex education, counseling, therapy, and supervision, and shall constantly be mindful of the responsibility for protection of the consumer's welfare, rights, and best interests and for the rigorous maintenance of the trust implicit in the educational, counseling, or therapeutic alliance.

(A) The member shall, from the onset of professional contact with a consumer or a potential consumer, clarify:
   (1) Professional training, experiences, and competencies;
   (2) The nature of the professional services available to the consumer (with an explanation of mutual roles and duties);
   (3) The limits of intervention effectiveness;
   (4) Personal values or professional preferences that reflect biases rather than being responsive to the needs and well-being of the consumer;
   (5) Any exceptions to confidentiality and privileged communications (e.g., duty to warn, mandatory reporting, etc.); and
   (6) Any financial issues, especially the payment obligations of the consumer.

(B) The member shall treat all information received about a consumer as confidential, even if some portions of the information appear trivial, irrelevant, or not to require confidentiality; even the existence of an educational, counseling, or therapeutic relationship with the consumer is confidential.

(C) The member shall advocate the consumer's privileged communication, as granted by the laws of the jurisdiction applicable to the consumer and/or the member; in the event that there is uncertainty about the effectiveness or validity of the consumer's consent to releasing information that is potentially confidential and/or privileged, the member shall obtain appropriate legal determination.

(D) The member shall divulge information received from a consumer or prospective consumer to the extent required only in the following circumstances:

(1) When the consumer provides a written and informed consent, which indicates:

(a) the type and nature of information to be released;

(b) knowledge of the purpose for which the information will be used;

(c) designation of the source that will receive the information;

(d) that the consent is given voluntarily and with competency; and

(e) the consumer's name and the date on which the consent is given.

(2) When there is clear and imminent danger of bodily harm or to the life or safety of the consumer or another person; disclosure shall be made in accord with the laws of the jurisdiction in which the member practices.

(3) When applicable law declares that such information may be released.

(E) The member shall obtain the consumer's written informed consent for using any identifiable information about the consumer for purposes of education, training, research, or publication.

(F) The member shall reveal a consumer's confidential information to a professional source with a limited right to know, such as (but not limited to) a supervisor or consultant in an appropriate manner; it is the member's responsibility to take reasonable steps to assure that the other professional source will properly treat the information in a confidential manner.

(G) The member shall keep meaningful records relevant to the professional services provided to and contacts (of any nature) with the consumer, and shall have a secure system for the preservation of records, with the minimal contents and duration of retention being in accord with the laws that are applicable to the jurisdiction in which the member practices; at a minimum:

(1) A full record shall be retained intact for no less than three (3) years after completion of the last date of professional services or contact;

(2) A full record or meaningful summary of the record shall be maintained for no less than twelve (12) additional years.

(H) The member shall have a formal (written) arrangement for the preservation of consumer records upon his/her ceasing of practice, death, or incapacity; this arrangement must be in accord with the laws of the jurisdiction in which the member practices.

(I) The member shall, when providing professional services in a group context or to a couple or family, make a reasonable effort to promote safeguarding of confidentiality on the part of each consumer in the group, couple, or family.

(J) The member shall orient the minor consumer to the limits of confidentiality pertaining to a parent's right to know, as defined by the laws of the jurisdiction in which the member practices.

(K) The member shall, regardless of the reasons for which the consumer sought professional services and regardless of the theory or technique being used by the member, predicate every sex counseling or therapy intervention upon diagnosis and a meaningful consumer(s) treatment plan, which shall be consistently documented in writing, justified academically, evaluated for effectiveness, monitored for strengths and weaknesses, and modified accordingly.

(L) The member shall, as needed to protect the best interest of the consumer, seek consultation and/or supervision, with special reference to the treatment plan and to the personal elements of the therapeutic relationship.

(M) The member shall not engage in any dual relationship, regardless of nature or circumstances, with a consumer or persons with a primary relationship with a consumer served by the member which could potentially be detrimental to or jeopardize the well-being of a consumer.

(N) The member shall not engage, attempt to engage, or offer to engage a consumer in sexual behavior whether the consumer consents to such behavior or not; sexual misconduct includes kissing, sexual intercourse, and/or the touching by either the member or the consumer of the other's breasts or genitals. For purposes of determining the existence of sexual misconduct, the counseling, or therapeutic relationship is deemed to continue in perpetuity.

(0) The member shall terminate professional services to the consumer when it is reasonably evident or should be evident that the consumer is not obtaining benefits sufficient to justify continued intervention; upon termination, the member shall make referral to another profes-

sional source and/or offer reasonable follow-up to further the best interests of the consumer.

Principle Four: Welfare of Students, Trainees, and Others

The AASECT member shall respect the rights and dignity of students, trainees, and others (such as employees), maintain high standards of scholarship, and preserve academic freedom and responsibility.

(A) The member shall, from the onset of professional contact with students, trainees, and others over whom the member has administrative, educational, or supervisory authority, clarify: the member's professional qualifications and competencies; the objectives, responsibilities and duties of all concerned; and any financial issues, especially any payment obligations.

(B) The member shall accord confidentiality to information of a personal or intimate nature obtained in his/her professional role; the provision of confidentiality does not, however, preclude fulfilling a professional responsibility or duty to consumers, educational or training institutions or programs, professional associations, or governmental-regulatory or legal sources.

(C) The member shall maintain high standards of scholarship and present information that is accurate and timely in all administrative, educational, and supervisory activities.

(D) The member shall keep meaningful and systematic records of all administrative, training, and supervisory activities.

(E) The member shall not coerce or require a student, trainee, or other to serve as subjects for research projects.

(F) The member shall not provide diagnosis, therapeutic counseling or therapy, or any other clinical service to students or trainees or those over whom the member has administrative, educational, or supervisory authority.

(G) The member shall not harass in any manner a student, trainee, or other whom the member has administrative, educational, or supervisory authority.

(H) The member shall not during the administrative, educational, or supervisory period, enter into any dual relationship, regardless of nature, that jeopardizes the well-being of the student, trainee, or other.

(I) The member shall not, during the administrative, educational, or supervisory period, engage, attempt to engage, or offer to engage the student, trainee, or other in sexual behavior.

(J) The member shall be cognizant that a dual relationship subsequent to the administrative, educational, or supervisory period may potentially jeopardize the well being of the student, trainee, or other.

Principle Five: Welfare of Research Subjects

The AASECT member shall conduct his/her investigations with respect for the dignity, rights, and welfare of the subjects. Research must be ethical and legal at its inception and not justified solely by its intended or achieved outcome.

(A) The member shall be involved only with sex research that is carried out by persons qualified to do such investigations or under the direct supervision of persons so qualified.

(B) The member shall be involved only with sex research that designates and identifies (in writing) to the potential subjects the names and professional qualifications of the person or persons with ethical, scientific, and legal responsibility for the conduct of the investigation.

(C) The member shall be involved only with sex research that provides adequate protection(s) to human subjects at risk; any research project must:

(1) Include the voluntary and informed consent of each subject; and

(2) Be in accord with applicable legal prescriptions or proscriptions.

(D) The member shall be involved only with sex research that protects the confidentiality of research data, including the identity of participants or others revealed during the investigation.

(E) The member shall be involved only with sex research which requires all investigators to be honest and accurate in their dealings with research subjects and all persons receiving information about the research.

(F) The member shall be involved only with sex research that offers to provide an explanation of the purpose of the investigation and of the individual and collective results to each person who serves as a research subject.

(G) The member shall be involved only with sex research that has been prefaced by the submission of a research proposal for peer review, with special reference to ethical and legal safeguards for the potential research subjects; this peer review may occur in different forms, such as an institutional review board for evaluation for ethical propriety, and must be in accord with all relevant laws.

Index

About the Author

Jane DiVita Woody, Ph.D., M.S.W., has 16 years of experience in training M.S.W. students in the theory and practice of counseling, marital and family therapy, and sexual counseling and sex therapy. Currently Professor of Social Work at the University of Nebraska at Omaha, she also coordinates the social work specialization in marriage and family therapy.

Working in part-time practice since 1978, she provides primarily individual, couple, and sex therapy. She is a Certified Sex Educator and Sex Therapist of the American Association of Sex Educator, Counselors, and Therapists and is a life member of that association. She is also a Clinical Member and Approved Supervisor of the American Association for Marital and Family Therapy.

She has conducted research and published extensively in several areas of psychotherapy. Most recently, she edited *Sexual Issues in Family Therapy* and published articles on aging and sexuality, integrative sex therapy, ethical concerns in clinical practice, and compliance in therapy. She is presently conducting research on a scale she has developed to measure sexual dysfunction and sexual interaction of couples.

Her background encompasses extensive education in the humanities, subsequent training in the social work profession, and specialized study in sexuality and marriage and family therapy. These varied experiences contribute to her sensitive but practical approach to the treatment of sexual and intimacy problems.